Geoffrey Grogan's introduction provides an enlightening study of the rich theological heritage found in the Book of Psalms. Building upon the best of modern academic research, the author never looses sight of his desire to enable Christians to discover afresh how the Psalter serves as a witness to Christ. Written with both clarity and conviction, this study offers many fresh insights, while throughout affirming passionately the great central truths of the Christian faith.

T. Desmond Alexander,
Director of Christian Training,
Union Theological College, Belfast

Geoffrey Grogan has given us a marvellous handbook to the Psalms. He does not tack on theological themes at the end but places them front and centre, at the heart of the book, forcing us to face the God of the psalms. He has digested a mass of Psalms research and yet releases it in the most palatable and useful doses. I profited immensely from his treatment of the literary design of the Psalter; he helps us see in the Psalms a consciously coherent work (in five books) rather than random bits of poetry. If I were teaching a course on the Psalms, this would be my textbook.

Ralph Davis
Reformed Theological Seminary, Jackson

Throughout the history of the Church, the Book of Psalms has provided an inexhaustible spiritual treasury for praise and prayer. Until recently most commentators and expositors have tended to explore the riches of individual psalms. However, the Book is more than a random collection of poetry, but one that has been skilfully and purposefully compiled. In this volume Dr. Grogan provides a knowledgeable introduction to the Book as a whole, and by adeptly drawing on material from modern studies he brings out the interconnection between the psalms in two main ways. First he examines themes that recur throughout the Book and provide it with a unity which derives from the various aspects of God's relationship with his people. Then he charts the process by which individual psalms were brought together to form the collections that eventually grew into the Book that we now have. Much light is thrown on particular psalms by understanding them in terms of their setting in the Book as a whole. Furthermore Dr. Grogan places the finished book into its total canonical context by examining how the New Testament interprets the psalms and how we may appropriate them today. This is a volume that is written with reverence, care and clarity, and is a significant addition to evangelical literature on the Psalms. It is to be commended to those who wish to have new vistas on a well-known and well-loved part of Scripture, and also to students who looking for an entry point into modern literature on Psalms.

John L Mackay
Free Church of Scotland College, Edinburgh


Geoffrey Grogan's name is sufficient to guarantee a quality work, a high doctrine of Scripture and impeccable scholarship. The latter is carried lightly, but with sharp discernment of what is biblically sound, what is practically useful, and what outruns available evidence. The twenty pages of references are a small gold mine in their own right. If Grogan writes with one eye on the specialist 'state of play', the other eye is firmly fixed on being biblically illuminating to any and every Bible lover. This very full introduction to the Book of Psalms makes one hope that the author has in mind a full scale commentary to follow.

Alec Motyer


Geoffrey Grogan brings out wonderfully the dynamic character of God's gracious engagement with his people, as represented in the Psalms, and his integration of the Psalter theologically with the rest of Scripture is profoundly helpful. He combines sound scholarship, illuminating insight, thoughtful reflection, and unashamed devotion with a faithful concern for highlighting the pastoral relevance of the Book of Psalms to the Christian's life in the real world. I commend this book warmly.

Eryl Rowlands,
International Christian College, Glasgow

# Prayer, Praise and Prophecy

## Geoffrey W. Grogan

Mentor

# Abbreviations

| | |
|---|---|
| AV | Authorised (King James) Version |
| BZAW | Beihefte zur Zeitschrift für die alttestamentliche Wissenschaft |
| JBL | Journal of Biblical Literature |
| JSOT | Journal for the Study of the Old Testament |
| JTS | Journal of Theological Studies |
| LXX | Septuagint |
| MT | Massoretic Text |
| NIV | New International Version |
| NRSV | New Revised Standard Version |
| TB | Tyndale Bulletin |
| TZ | Theologische Zeitschrift |
| VT | Vetus Testamentum |
| ZAW | Zeitschrift für die alttestamentliche Wissenschaft |

N.B.

1. In Biblical quotations, the New Revised Standard Version has been employed throughout the book except where otherwise stated.

2. In references to a particular psalm, this has normally been by number only (without the word 'psalm'), except at the beginning of a sentence or in a heading.

ISBN 185792 642 0

Published in 2001 by
Christian Focus Publications, Geanies House, Fearn,
Ross-shire, IV20 1TW, Great Britain

Cover design by Alister MacInnes

# Contents

# Preface

I have loved the Book of Psalms for a very long time. The first encounter I remember having with it was somewhat memorable, as, at about the age of 11, my class at school was required by one of the teachers to learn Psalm 1 as homework. I failed to do this and had my first painful experience of corporal punishment. How I would have felt if I had known that the Cistercian monks at Fountains Abbey in Yorkshire had to recite the whole Book of Psalms – in Latin – before being allowed to pass on from the novitiate, I hate to think! When I began serious Bible study after making a personal commitment to Christ at the age of twenty, it was one of the first books of the Old Testament to which I became strongly attracted. Over many years I have preached from it more than from any other book of the Bible and have taught it at the Glasgow Bible College (now incorporated in the International Christian College), the Scottish Baptist College and in several other settings. What it means to me as a Christian is beyond calculation.

It is exciting to be a student of the psalms at the present time, because there is currently an interest in it among Old Testament scholars that is probably without precedent. This is almost entirely due to a new emphasis on the book as a whole, with a desire to understand why its structure has been shaped in the way it has and to enquire as to the theological implications of this structure. Quite properly, there is concern that proper objective criteria should be established for this study, as it could easily degenerate into undisciplined speculation or even become a focus for the views of theological cranks. Much excellent work has been done, however, and I have tried to indicate some of the chief gains of this approach. No doubt more research needs to be done, but what has been discerned so far has great value.

I give thanks to God for the opportunity of engaging in this work. I also want to thank Dr Don Carson for a number of helpful suggestions for its improvement, and the Reverend Derek and

Mrs Joy Guest (my niece and her husband), who kindly read much of the work in manuscript to check particularly on matters of clarity and pastoral value. My wife, Eva, as ever, gave me a great deal of patient support. I have profited very much from the work of other writers, but want particularly to mention that gracious Christian gentleman, the Reverend Derek Kidner, sometime Warden of Tyndale House, Cambridge, whose commentaries on the Book of Psalms demonstrate so clearly that careful scholarship and warm devotion are not enemies but good friends, and that a theologically perceptive commentary may be written with both beauty of style and economy of language.

The Book of Psalms is an inexhaustible, inspired resource for the Christian church in every age, but its message is of special importance today. Some modern churches are facing reducing numbers and feel that they have their backs to the wall. The psalms of praise and thanksgiving will lift their eyes to the living God in all his greatness and grace and emphasize for them the glorious certainties of his plan and purpose for his people. Other churches are growing numerically, but some of these are in danger of triumphalism and tendencies towards a mild but disturbing form of Prosperity Theology. This makes it very important that they take the psalms of lament seriously, for intercession and pastoral care must always engage with the needs and sufferings of others, and worship should always be a preparation for living the Christian life in the real world and not simply a means of temporary escape from it.

# Theological Introduction:
# What is a theology of the psalms?

Please note the indefinite article in the sub-title of this volume!
If you miss it, you may easily confuse the author's aim and his
claim. He aims, of course, to write *The Theology of the Book of
Psalms*, but the result will certainly be *A Theology* ... This is
not only because of many limitations in the book's author, but
also because the material is far too great and wide-ranging to
be treated adequately in a comparatively small volume. Indeed
at times the author felt he was trying to get an ocean into a pint
pot.

There is however a third reason, and one that applies no
matter who the author or his subject are: the fact that the
subjective factor needs to be taken seriously. Modern thinkers
have increasingly recognized this factor in every attempt to find
truth, whether in philosophy (Kant, etc.), in history
(Collingwood, etc.), in science (Kuhn, Popper, etc.) or in
literature (Derrida, etc.). Recent literary theory, particularly the
form of it pioneered by Derrida and known as Deconstruction,
has often gone too far in this direction, but it at least warns us
not to assume we have achieved absolute objectivity. It is
important though for us to refuse to be deterred from the
enterprise. The matter is far too important for that.

The proponents of Deconstruction, at least in its extremer
forms, have raised a most radical issue. They argue that we
cannot find objective truth in any literature, no matter what its
nature or subject, for all our interpretation is conditioned by
our social and cultural background. If we accept this point of
view without qualification, there can be no theology of the
psalms which has any general validity. Our projected enterprise
is therefore doomed from the start.

Is it really true though that a meaning I find in a piece of
literature, although it may be meaning for me, is not necessarily

meaning for other people? As the pop group, Manic Street Preachers, put it: 'This is my truth; tell me yours.' Is there no such thing as Public Truth? Society has normally recognised – and insisted – that there is truth in written form that needs to govern both our thinking and our consequent actions. A judge in a law court can certainly insist that I find in the law the meaning he finds in it himself, and the Bible teaches me that I will have no excuse when I come before the judgement bar of the Almighty Creator and Judge of all.

Take the principles of Deconstruction to their logical conclusion and you destroy all meaningful human discourse or conversation. This would in fact spell the end of human civilisation as we know it, for without communication there can be no civilisation. In addition, such an outlook is self-contradictory and self-destructive. If I deny all possibility of objective truth, I will find myself having to deny my own denial, because even my denial is not objectively true. So then Christian believers need not fear that their belief in the objective character of Scripture faces a threat against which there is no answer.[1]

Certainly we can accept that *absolute* objectivity is unobtainable, but we need to be willing to be moulded by the Biblical text rather than to create a meaning for ourselves. We should seek to sit openly before it, willing to learn and to act on what we have learned, and to face unpalatable truths and their practical implications if necessary.

So then is a theology of the Book of Psalms really possible? There are some further weighty objections to be considered. Some of these relate to individual psalms and others to the Book as a whole.

### A theology of an individual psalm
The problem here is chiefly related to the devotional nature of the psalms. How can devotional material have any theological authority? In the Book of Psalms it is responsive, subjective and poetic. Surely this means it cannot be inspired and authoritative literature!

It has sometimes been assumed that the characteristic style of inspired literature is declamation, which is to be found notably in the prophetic books. B.B. Warfield's magisterial exposition of the doctrine of inspiration[2] is sometimes criticized as more appropriate to the prophetic books than to other types of Biblical literature. Legitimate comparisons may however be made between the prophets and the Mosaic Law (as divine requirement), the epistles (as divine truth applied to concrete situations), and historical and biographical narrative (as divine interpretation of events).[3] As devotional literature, however, the psalms seem at first sight to be more response to revelation than themselves revelation, for true Biblical devotion is always responsive.

Further reflection, however, reminds us that much of the Bible involves response to previous revelation. So, for instance, the prophets call the people back to the God of the Exodus and of Sinai or remind them of his love or his law which were made known in these events. Also the epistles rest on the great historical revelation given in Christ and recorded for us in the Gospels, and this in turn rests on the Old Testament revelation.

In fact, just about everything in the Bible builds on an earlier revelation, for God has not left anybody without some disclosure of himself. Would even the earliest special revelation given in Scripture have been meaningful without the prior disclosure of God's existence in the general revelation that is given in his creation? In this respect, the Book of Psalms is no different from other parts of the Bible.

Is the devotional nature of the psalms really a problem? Surely devotion, whether individual or corporate, should be promoted by thought and, in its turn, promote thought! How can we rightly worship God unless our worship has good theology in it? The great Christian devotional classics contain a great deal of theology. It is therefore a serious mistake, not absent from some modern pulpits and platforms, to polarize theology and devotion, usually to the debasement of the former. If this is done, there is a very real danger that much that passes for Christian devotion and worship will cease to be truly Christian because it will lose contact with its Biblical roots.

Have you noticed that every practical aspect of the Christian faith has a theology? There is a theology of preaching, of evangelism, of Christian witness, of Christian social concern, of prayer, and so on. If we believe that Holy Scripture is our final authority not only in matters of faith but also of practice, then this must be so.

What happens in personal devotion and in worship? In these activities, we direct our minds and hearts towards the God who made us and who has redeemed us, and so it is inevitable that our devotion and worship are shaped by the ideas we have of him. Good theology aims to make sure these ideas are Biblical. One of the most strongly theological passages in the New Testament is Ephesians 1:3-14, and yet it is essentially devotional, for Paul begins with worship, 'Blessed be the God and Father of our Lord Jesus Christ,' and at several points this great passage is punctuated by references to the praise of God. It is almost as if we are overhearing an apostle at worship, and what worship it is!

We can over-emphasize the subjective character of the psalms. Kraus, commenting on 115:1, has well said:

> Those who sing and pray are not proclaiming their spiritual experience, their personal or private destiny. Everything that they experience, suffer, and undergo becomes praise of Yahweh and proclamation of his name when they speak of their experience and suffering (Ps. 22:22).... The test of the objectivity of our theological work and its faithfulness to its subject matter is whether it really follows the witness of the text, the intention expressed in the language of praise and prayer.[4]

There is however another side to the matter. Much of the material in the psalms appears to be a response of an emotional kind. How would you like somebody to draw an authoritative theology from your own devotions?

When the psalmist says God has forsaken him, is he penning

objective truth? If not, how can we say this is the revealed Word of God? Are the emotions shown in the psalms in every case legitimate? What about the imprecatory psalms, in which the psalmists call on God to judge those who are seeking their harm? Are we to say these are proper godly feelings or not?

The Book of Psalms is quoted as the Word of God, and so as revelation from him, quite frequently in the New Testament. Did its writers use only certain types of psalm, perhaps those which focus in worship on great truths about God, or did they use the highly subjective material? Verses like 116:10 (quoted as 'I believed, and so I spoke,' in 2 Cor. 4:13) and the imprecatory 69:22,23 (quoted in Rom. 11:9,10) are certainly found in strongly emotional psalm contexts. How can the New Testament writers do this with any semblance of appropriateness?

These are important questions, but we are not yet ready to deal with them.[5] We can at least point out at this stage that there is always objective truth to which any particular psalm relates. For instance, in 89:49 the psalmist asks an agonised question about God's faithfulness to his covenant promise made to David.

> O LORD, where is your steadfast love of old,
>      which by your faithfulness you swore to David?[6]

Elsewhere the terms of the Davidic covenant are made plain and this actually occurs in earlier parts of this very psalm, where this covenant is quoted and extolled. Even though the psalmist asked this question, he allowed his statements of faith earlier in the psalm to remain. He did not cross them out and start all over again. So we can assume that the (unexpressed) answer to his question would be something like, 'Time will show that I have not forgotten.' The imprecatory psalms assume that Yahweh, the Lord, is a God of justice who vindicates those who are persecuted on account of their faithfulness to him. There is always objective truth in a psalm or in the theological background to it. This is an important consideration.

We should note too that there is quite a lot of material in the book that is propositional in form, material that makes affirmations about God and his ways. So, writing of the acrostic psalms, Seybold says: 'Their relevance to systematic doctrine and theory is indisputable. The individual proverbs are devised as pronouncements on a given theme. ...In the case of Ps. 119 it is possible to detect ... a claim to a comprehensive theology of the Word of God.'[7]

Can we go further than this? Kevin Vanhoozer has made the point that our emotional responses need to be brought under the authority of God's Word.[8] There is certainly truth in this, although we will need to give very careful thought to the matter when we come to consider the imprecatory psalms.

Another possible problem is raised by the poetic character of the psalms. C.S. Lewis says,

> Most emphatically the Psalms must be read as poems; as lyrics, with all the licences and all the formalities, the hyperboles, the emotional rather than logical connections, which are proper to lyric poetry.[9]

Poetry has an allusive quality, sometimes with studied ambiguity, and this feature is not absent from the psalms. Does this matter, though, if the allusions take us into truth or if the various senses conveyed are all true?[10] If the writer himself *intends* his thought to embrace two or more ideas within one word or phrase, then he is doing what poets must be allowed to do, for it is one means they employ in conveying truth as they see it. If this happens in the psalms, we find ourselves confronted by a literary corpus that, in theological terms, is immensely rich. Remember too that just as doctrine is better illustrated from parables than derived from them, so some kind of control may be exercised by the fact that this kind of psalmic material often illustrates truth plainly stated elsewhere.

Of course, there is other poetical literature in the Old

Testament beside the psalms. As Dumbrell says, 'Some of the most theologically significant literature in Israel appears early in poetic form (e.g. the Song of the Sea of Exodus 15).'[11] We should remember too that the declamations of the prophets were often in poetic form, and yet we do not normally have difficulty in thinking of these as divinely authoritative.

Seybold has shown that many of the psalms have a character like the writings of the prophets and that some of them show clear theological intent. Concerning the hymns of the Book of Psalms, he says that they seek

> to depict theological ideas objectively in 'descriptive praise', identifying them and giving them a precise definition. Since they generally deal with basic themes (creation, humanity, history, revelation), they are the medium of real theological work with a doxological character, a form of work which has become the pattern for all theological work (cf. Paul's letter to the Romans).[12]

He gives 8, 19, 33, 90, 104 and 136 as illustrations of his point.

If we do conclude that we can gain theology from a psalm, how do we discover the essential theological viewpoint and special theological interest of each of them? Seybold has given thought to this and he stresses the importance of the opening of each psalm as indicating the aim and intention of the writer. He says that the ending too is important because the writer would be aware of its continued power as it remained in the reader's mind.[13] Raabe encourages us to look for thematic key words and phrases, which are prolific in some psalms. These observations are really simply detailed applications of the principle that the revelation occurs in the psalm as a total literary unit.

Some psalms are of considerable theological importance, especially in the narrower sense of the word 'theology', for they present a very full doctrine of God. Many worship psalms extol either his acts or his attributes. Some present quite a full and balanced view of him and they do so in the context of praise.

Psalm 145 is a good example of this, for here he is described as great, majestic, gracious, merciful, good, faithful, just, near and holy, and it makes plentiful reference to his actions. So many of his names and descriptive titles are in the psalms. We can see also that he is a God who does not always explain himself or his ways. There are puzzles, but the overall context is one of worship and trust, prayer and love.

## A theology of the complete book

Does its multiple authorship rule out the possibility of a theology of the book as a whole? No, for a good case may be put forward for treating it as a theological unity. If we want to identify a theology in any literature, it must have points of unity which are central to it, and to be truly theological it must be concerned with God and his relations with his universe and with people. If the literature is written by many authors over a long period, there needs to be a unified view of God and some real historical continuity in the understanding of his nature and ways. As we shall see, this is certainly the case with the Psalter, and there is a further significant factor, for uniting everything in it is a common atmosphere of worship and prayer in which everything is brought into the presence of God.

This unified view of God common to the psalms is what was normative for the Old Testament writers as a whole. But, as Allan Harman says, 'We should not think, though, that the type of understanding of God revealed in the Psalms was universal in Israel. The fact that the prophets had to direct condemnatory speeches against the people shows a different picture.'[14] It is really a Baalised view of Yahweh, which some of the people had in defiance of his self-revelation, that is combated in 50, verses 12 and 13, where God says: 'If I were hungry I would not tell you. Do I eat the flesh of bulls?'

Can we go further still? Is it possible that the material has been brought together by one person or by a group with a common intent? Have editors been at work with a theological motive either at the final stage of collection and arrangement or at earlier points in the process of the book's growth?

Although, as we have seen above, Seybold is happy with the idea that individual psalms may be theologically significant, he maintains that the book in its final form, its totality, shows no real interest in bringing all the material together into a credal system.[15] He has assumed however that such a scheme depends on some kind of editorial imposition, but does it? What if theological unity already existed in the body of material itself so that the work of editors simply served to make it more explicit? It is the historic Christian conviction that behind all the authors of the Bible, including the psalmists, there is one inspiring Spirit of God. This conviction gives both an impetus to produce such a theology but also the apologetic necessity to show the theological oneness of the material. This we will certainly attempt to do.

In discussing whether there can be a theology of an individual psalm, we considered the objection that the material is devotional in content. Strange as it may seem, this problem is reduced when we think of the theology of the book as a whole. This is because much modern psalm research suggests that the purpose of its final editors was that its readers should prayerfully reflect on the ways of God with his people as a whole. If this is so, this is a theological purpose and it is appropriate to seek a unified theology in it. Not only so, but it suggests that theology should be pursued in a devotional spirit and with a worshipful purpose and not as an end in itself. This is something we can easily forget and it is important to be reminded of it.

Recent studies have emphasised the importance of the canonical order of the psalms.[16] It is increasingly recognised too that Psalm 1 was placed at the head of the book because of its emphasis on reflecting on God's word, not only in the Law but in the word of God expressed in the Psalter itself.[17] In this case, this would make clear that the book was intended to be understood theologically. Those who are interested in its canonical shape are pursuing a positive course of great theological and practical value, even though sometimes details of their studies may be open to question.[18]

Is the material truly unified? It would not be difficult to argue against its theological oneness and to quote passages which appear to contradict each other quite flatly. But even if the unification is not total we may still be able to speak of a theology. Some recent writers have seen polarity in the book, with two contrasting themes governing its content. Brueggemann, developing the thought of Paul Ricoeur, has promoted the idea of two theologies, not only here but in the Old Testament as a whole, theologies which act and interact with each other, producing full truth out of this interaction. There is a theology of orientation and one of disorientation or of protest or of suspicion, producing out of their clash a theology of reorientation.[19]

If he is right, this means that full truth is not normally to be found in one psalm but in a combination of psalms. Is this a rebirth of Hegelianism?[20] Not really, for its main inspiration seems not to have been philosophical but to be due to careful Old Testament study. Brueggemann's suggestion is in fact very fruitful, as we shall see later.

A further thought suggests itself. Suppose the Book of Psalms, and indeed the Old Testament as a whole, was not intended to be theologically complete? Suppose that, for real theological understanding of it, the whole Bible is needed? Certainly some psalms raise questions rather than give answers and in some cases these are not answered within the Psalter, nor even within the Old Testament as a whole, but only in Christ.[21] In this case, we could still speak of a theology, provided we added that this is preliminary or incomplete. Of course, we have also to remember that all theology must be incomplete as God has not revealed everything about himself to his people.

We have already referred to the agonised question which comes towards the close of 89. Is this in fact answered within the Old Testament? Yes, in the promises associated with the kingly child of Isaiah 9:6,7, in the words:

> He will reign on David's throne
> and over his kingdom,
> establishing and upholding it
> with justice and righteousness
> from that time on and for ever.
> The zeal of the LORD Almighty
> will accomplish this (NIV).

We may even find an answer, by implication, in the Book of Psalms itself when the king is also designated a priest 'for ever' (110:4).

## A microcosm of Old Testament Theology

What contribution may a theology of the Book of Psalms make to a theology of the Old Testament? A very considerable one. Both the Old Testament and the psalms were written over quite a number of centuries.

Martin Luther called this book, 'a Bible in miniature'. His germinal comment is particularly true theologically and especially in relation to the Old Testament. The great thematic variety of the Old Testament finds a measure of concentration here within the pages of one book. It is representative of various literary genres and various historical periods.

It has a great many thematic links with other parts of the Old Testament. The thematic variety of the psalms may be seen when creation psalms like 19, 104 and 136 are compared with Genesis 1 and 2, historical psalms like 105 and 106 with the narrative sections of the Pentateuch and with the historical books, problem psalms like 73, 77 and 89 with Job and Ecclesiastes, a marriage psalm like 45 with Song of Songs, wisdom psalms like 1 and 34 with Proverbs, and declamatory psalms like 95 with the prophets. Some echo many Old Testament passages, for example, in 135 there are echoes of Exodus 3:15; 18:11; Numbers 21:21ff; 33; Deuteronomy 32:26; Psalms 115:3, 36, 8-11 and Jeremiah 10:13, and there are important links between it and 136.[22]

It is noticeable that the Book of Psalms even includes the

wisdom theme and genre, which has often proved particularly difficult for Old Testament theologians to integrate with the remainder of the Old Testament. This makes the Book of Psalms unique both in the Old Testament and in the Bible as a whole.[23] The nearest to it is the Book of Proverbs, where, if we accept the material at its face value, there is some plurality of authorship although less genre variety.

This means that in some ways the Psalter may furnish a model for Old Testament Theology as a whole. Murphy says, 'Because these prayers are written over a period of some seven centuries they constitute a profile of biblical theology.'[24] Such an Old Testament Theology might be similar in some ways to a theology of this book, although of course there could be some differences in topics and also in arrangement.

Biblical Theology is of course interested in the chronological sequence of the theological content of Scripture, and many individual psalms do present problems of dating, some of them probably insuperable. Contemporary study of the structure of the Psalter as a whole however suggests that its arrangement has a chronological aspect. This suggests not only that the books of the Psalter with higher numbers were put together later, but that the whole corpus was intended to teach particular theological lessons when its psalms were read in numbered sequence. We will be looking at this idea in our final chapter.

There are numerous thematic contacts between the psalms and particular Old Testament books. For instance, the historical psalms have obvious points of contact with the historical books, especially those, like 105 and 106, which deal with the Exodus and Entry, frequent themes in these psalms. Psalms of the word of God and especially 119 with its many synonyms, remind us of the records of the Mosaic Law. Wisdom Psalms, such as 37 and 49, remind us of Proverbs while some of the laments, like 79 and 88, recall Lamentations or Job. As we will see later, there are psalms which are prophetic in type, while there are passages in the prophets not unlike psalms (e.g. Isa. 12, Jonah 2 and Hab. 3).[25] There are a number of links between the psalms and Jeremiah. These are quite strong for instance between 1 and Jeremiah 17:15-18. Haggai and Zechariah encouraged the people to build a new temple, where, of course, psalms were sung.

There may even be some rather different links, where one passage is a deliberate parody of another in order to make a point. Miles sees the Book of Jonah, in its second chapter, parodying the psalm of thanksgiving for rescue from the pit. The real difference between a psalm like 69 and this Jonah passage is due to the fact that in the psalm the water and drowning imagery are figurative while here they are literal. He says:

> The power of sea- imagery is only effective if it is in fact imagery and not direct description. If it is not to be merely bombastic, it cannot refer to real oceans and real water. In Jonah 2, it does.... Jonah's situation is not comparable to the situation of a man swallowed by a great monster. This *is* Jonah's situation.[26]

Some literary links within the Old Testament are particularly valuable to students of the psalms. Tournay says:

> If we wish to discover in the psalter a dominant theme over and above the great variety of literary genres or discern a possible liturgical setting, we must restore the psalms to their place in the religious life of the Jewish people. The books of Ezra, Nehemiah and Chronicles provide valuable information for us here even though they are too often neglected by commentators on the psalter.[27]

The Chronicler gives long psalm quotations, quoting 105:1-15; 96:1-13; 106:1, 47-49 in 1 Chronicles 16 and 132:8-10 in 2 Chronicles 6:41-42.

### d. A microcosm of Biblical Theology

Biblical Theology is, perhaps, the strangest subject in the theological curriculum. A survey of its literature over recent decades would show very clearly that even its practitioners are not agreed as to what it is. The whole question of the possibility of Biblical Theology has exercised many minds in recent years, although a substantial number of scholars remains convinced that such an enterprise is appropriate.[28]

Basic to all theology is the doctrine of God and the material for this in the Book of Psalms, as we have seen already, is extremely extensive. There is much here, as, of course, in the remainder of the Old Testament, to give body to such brief but important New Testament statements as 'God is light' and 'God is love' (1 John 1:5: 4:8, 16). So much of this material is taken for granted in the New Testament. This can really be the only explanation for the comparative paucity of explicit Doctrine of God teaching in the New Testament.

We will argue later that the Book of Psalms as a whole is rather like Psalm 73 or like the books of Job and of Ecclesiastes in that it tells the story of a search, in which at certain stages there is bewilderment and all looks dark but which eventually issues in enlightenment from a divine source. In the case of the Psalter, this is a search by a whole religious community in which the individual searches of some of its members are taken up and which has its background also in the blessings and problems of the nation itself. This does not mean that the whole thing is humanly motivated. After all, if we take the New Testament doctrine of grace seriously, a human being's search which ends in true faith in Christ has beneath it the deep gracious initiative of God, and such searches presented in the Old Testament canon are evidence that the operations of divine grace have points common to both Testaments.

The conclusion of the Book of Job is that we can live with questions if we have a great and constantly renewed view of God. All of us have questions, so that the book has an abiding message for us. The conclusion of Ecclesiastes is that reverence for God and obedience to his commands should be the controlling motives of life. This conclusion presents the same challenge to present-day readers The conclusion to the Book of

Psalms certainly appears to be that after all the trials and tribulations of the life of faith there will come to those who continue to believe an unclouded vision and the purest praise of God. Is this not what the Bible as a whole is saying to us? If so, it is as appropriate that it ends with the Book of the Revelation as that the Book of Psalms ends with Psalm 150.

# A. Its General Features

# Chapter 1

# The history of its study

## Prior to the nineteenth century

For many centuries, study of the psalms was carried on independently by scholars in the Jewish synagogue and the Christian church, both of whom regarded the Book of Psalms as inspired and authoritative Scripture.

The psalms were widely quoted by early Christian writers, who interpreted them in terms of Christ. The epistle known as *1 Clement*, probably the earliest Christian writing we possess apart from the New Testament books themselves, quotes frequently and at some length from the psalms and gives them Christian interpretation much after the fashion of the Epistle to the Hebrews. In fact the writer of *1 Clement* knew that epistle, and it is evident that he was influenced by its handling of the psalms.

Because of their concern to win the Jews for Christ, there was some awareness among Christians as to the outlook of the Jews. Justin Martyr wrote a *Dialogue with Trypho,* a Jew, in the middle of the second century, and in it he frequently quoted the psalms and sought to show their application to Jesus. From a late second and early third century Christian writer, Hippolytus, we learn that the rabbis recognised the fivefold division of the Psalter and considered it to be based on the five books of Moses, and there is direct testimony to this also from at least one Jewish work that is probably a little earlier than Hippolytus.

Unfortunately, few patristic writers had much Hebrew, and, so far as we can be sure, only Origen, Epiphanius and Jerome could be considered accomplished Hebraists. Others therefore quoted the psalms either in Greek or Latin and their comments were based on the way they were translated in the versions to which they had access. The patristic writers treated the author attributions in the headings very seriously, and they placed particularly strong emphasis on Davidic authorship.

We learn from Origen that he knew of two Hebrew manuscripts of Psalms 1 and 2, and he was interested in the fact that one of these treated them as a single psalm whereas the other divided them. His great scholarship is shown in many linguistic and exegetical comments, but as an Alexandrian with a Platonic background, he also ventured into the realms of allegorical interpretation.

Two major schools of interpretation emerged. The Alexandrian school, of which Origen himself was head for many years, practised allegorisation, following in this the way practised by the Alexandrian Jewish community, and especially by Philo, its greatest writer. The School of Antioch had scholarly interests and set its literal methods of interpretation over against this allegorism. Theodore of Mopsuestia, perhaps the Antioch school's most important scholar, was alone among the fathers in casting doubt on the reliability of the psalm headings. This was because he believed every psalm to have been written by David.

Athanasius wrote a delightful letter to Marcellinus about the interpretation of the psalms, telling him of the understanding of them which had been passed on to him by 'a certain studious old man'. In this letter, he interprets them Messianically and devotionally.[1] This was true also of Chrysostom, Jerome (the translator of the Vulgate), Ambrose, Augustine and other preachers and writers. This type of interpretation ruled in the church right up to and beyond the Reformation period.

The Jews had a number of eminent Biblical and Rabbinic scholars in the Middle Ages, and some of the greatest of these, such as Rashi and Ibn Ezra, both of whom belonged to the eleventh and twelfth centuries, and Kimhi, a century or so later, wrote commentaries on the Book of Psalms. These three men were interested in the historical background to the psalms. They focus on the literal sense and often discuss the exact meaning of particular words in the text. They were also interested in the psalm headings and clearly regarded them as authoritative aids to psalm interpretation. There was some interest too in the eschatological application of the psalms, although some, including Rashi, were wary of this because of the danger of playing into the hands of Christian interpreters who saw Jesus Christ in them. So, for instance, Rashi argues that Psalm 2, which is applied to Christ in the New Testament, is better understood to be about David than about the Messiah.

Incidentally, the rabbis and the early Christian commentators both anticipated somewhat the recent emphasis on structure in the Psalter. They were interested in connections between adjacent psalms and they discerned that there were catchword links between them, especially at the end of one psalm and the start of the next.

Two series of lectures on the psalms by Luther are extant. His handling of them is many-sided, for he applies them both homiletically and polemically and also makes useful comments on their language and its meaning. John Calvin was not only a great theologian but also a superb Biblical exegete who wrote a large commentary on the psalms. His comments on their interpretation are notable for their balance, for he avoided unjustifiable dogmatism about the significance of particular psalms and refused to see hidden meanings in them. He tended to think more in terms of typology than of precise prediction in seeking an interpretation of a psalm in terms of Christ. This enabled him both to do justice to the Old Testament setting of each psalm, so far as that could be ascertained, and at the same time to see it as part of the Old Testament's witness to Christ.

The use of the psalms in Christian praise was of interest to the Reformers. Protestants loved to sing the praises of Christ. Luther adapted a number of psalms for congregational singing, often with elements of Christian interpretation interwoven with the words of the psalms, while Zwingli and Calvin promoted the singing of the psalms put into a metrical form.

The work of Robert Lowth was of considerable importance

in the study of the psalms, as his was the first systematic treatment of the poetic device known as parallelism or sense-rhythm. He discusses it in his *Lectures on the Sacred Poetry of the Hebrews,* written in 1753. Some mediaeval Jewish commentators, notably Ibn Ezra, had some awareness of parallelism, but most Jewish and Christian scholars ignored it until Lowth brought the matter to scholarly attention.

## The nineteenth century and much of the twentieth

The Enlightenment was a time when everything was subjected to the test of reason and it affected psalm study profoundly. No longer did those who lectured on Scripture in the universities feel bound by either the church or the synagogue in the way they interpreted the psalms.

The nineteenth century was a period when there was much interest in history and in origins. Scholars like Olshausen, Cheyne and Duhm denied all the 'Davidic' psalms to David, and believed the psalm headings did not contain authentic traditions but were late additions of virtually no value. They gave late dates, at least exilic or post-exilic, often Maccabean or even later, to most of the psalms. They denied that there was any truly predictive element in them, so that the idea of a psalmic testimony to Christ was set aside.

There were, however, notable exceptions, representing a more conservative type of Biblical scholarship. Chief among them were E. W. Hengstenberg, J. A. Alexander and Franz Delitzsch. Delitzsch, for example, regarded the psalm headings as generally reliable and took a positive outlook towards the tradition of authorship expressed in them. He placed emphasis on the Davidic covenant and Messianism. He was very interested in the structure of the Psalter, and discerned the presence of themes, words and phrases that linked psalms in sequence.

Nineteenth-century Old Testament scholarship, whether liberal or conservative, tended to be dominated by historical questions. During the course of the century, however, there was increasing interest in social sciences such as anthropology and sociology, and these began to influence other disciplines, including Biblical scholarship.

Early in the twentieth century, Hermann Gunkel developed form criticism. It is obvious that the Psalter contains different types of psalm, and many earlier students of them had tried to classify them, but Gunkel's approach was quite distinctive, for it was anthropologically based. After him came Sigmund Mowinckel, who placed much emphasis on the cultic ceremonies, and particularly an autumn festival of Yahweh's re-enthronement, as the background to many of the psalms.

His views were very influential, although not all scholars accepted his theory of the autumn festival. Weiser accepted the existence of such a festival but he conceived of it as an annual ceremony renewing the Sinai covenant rather than as a re-enthronement ceremony and he connected the bulk of the psalms with it. Kraus argued for a Royal-Zion festival focused on the Davidic covenant, 'an annual festival of king and temple, a festival which dramatized the fundamental presuppositions of worship in Jerusalem, namely the choice of David and of Zion, and was connected with the opening ceremonial of the chief annual pilgrimage festival',[2] which he identified as the Feast of Tabernacles.

Beginning in 1929, many important discoveries were made at Ras Shamra in Northern Syria which revealed the literature of the North Canaanite Ugaritic civilisation. From this literature much has been learned about the religious beliefs and rituals of these people. They were influenced religiously by Mesopotamia. S. H. Hooke and scholars associated with him in the somewhat extreme 'Myth and Ritual School', along with some Scandinavians who accepted Mowinckel's general theory, were interested in the connection between mythology and particular dramatic rituals performed at festival times, including even ritual marriages between a divine being and his female consort, with the king acting the part of God. They found this kind of connection not only in Babylon but also at Ugarit, and assumed it would be present also in Hebrew religion.

The Ras Shamra finds were also illuminating because of the poetic forms used in the literature. The Ugaritic and Hebrew languages are close relatives, and these discoveries have cast light on some linguistic obscurities in the psalms as well as elsewhere in the Old Testament. The poetry of the Ugaritic texts is of special interest for students of the psalms, because the kind of parallelism found in the psalms is also present in these texts. Mitchell Dahood is one writer who has specialised in developing insights on the psalms from the Ugaritic literature, although some of his views have not found general acceptance.[3] More moderate application is given in Craigie's commentary.[4]

Gerstenberger gave psalm study a somewhat new slant in promoting the idea that many of the Lament psalms had connections with family rather than national rituals.[5] Writing of this theory, John Eaton says, 'There are affinities with modern social case-work, where an expert assists in communication and articulation of needs and in the rehabilitation of an individual in society.'[6]

Attempts to write a comprehensive theology of the psalms have been few. Special mention should be made of the theology produced by H-J. Kraus. This is influenced by his own form-critical studies and his theory of a Royal-Zion festival, but it has a great deal of useful theological comment which does not depend on this.

**More recent developments**
In 1969, J. van der Ploeg said that psalm study was in a period of groping and uncertainty. In fact, however, steps were already being taken to move the study in a new and fruitful direction. The work of Claus Westermann is of real significance in this. In a book which first appeared in 1961, but was reprinted in his larger and influential 1981 volume, he criticised the work of Mowinckel and others influenced by him. He wrote:

> This whole tendency to explain as many as possible or even all of the Psalms either by the 'ideology' of a specific (and only just

discovered) festival, by a cultic schema, or by the connection of a basic myth with a specific ritual (Hooke) seems to me, in spite of all the effort that has been expended on it ... to have produced meagre results for the understanding of the individual psalms.[7]

In an essay published in 1962 and also included in the 1981 book, he argued that there was once a Psalter which began with 1 and ended with 119. He then said:

this framework bears witness to an important stage in the 'traditioning' process, in which the Psalter, as a *collection*, no longer had a cultic function primarily, but rather circulated in a tradition devoted to the law. The Psalms have now become the word of God which is read, studied and meditated upon.[8]

After further interesting comments on psalm arrangement, he then said:

In the foregoing summary ... our intention has been simply to reintroduce the question, which up to this point has been so unjustifiably ignored, concerning the original relationship of the Psalms when they were gathered together into collections.[9]

Westermann's work marks a point of transition from the cult-dominated studies pursued earlier in the century to the more recent studies undertaken under the influence of literary theory and canonical criticism, although some scholars have continued to produce theories about the cultic significance of the psalms. The most important recent development has been the renewed interest in the structure of the Book of Psalms, so that attention has moved from individual psalms to the book as a whole, except insofar as particular psalms have their place within the book's structure.

This movement of interest also owes much to the work of B. S. Childs. Childs developed canonical criticism, placing much emphasis on the presence of particular Bible books in the Christian canon. Their acceptance as canonical and authoritative within a particular religious tradition should constantly be borne in mind in their study. Childs is much less interested in many of the traditional concerns, such as literary origins and the history of tradition.

His emphasis on the importance of Biblical books in their final, which is their canonical, form as the basic units of interpretation, raised an interesting question about the Book of Psalms. Should this be considered an exception, consisting of one hundred and fifty literary units rather than one, or should it be regarded as a greater unit binding the individual psalms together and having special features and even an integrated message through its arrangement?

The work of G. H. Wilson, a pupil of Childs, proved to be extremely suggestive and led to a spate of literature on the topic which shows no sign of abating.[10] Wilson was interested in the fivefold structure of the book, and he pointed to evidence that it had been organised with special emphasis on the kingship theme, and that one purpose of the present arrangement is to turn attention away from confidence in the Davidic kingship to recognition of the supreme kingship of Yahweh.

Focus on the overall structure of the Psalter also stimulated interest in particular collections within it, and in this respect the work of M. Goulder has been important, for he has made these the subject of several special studies. He began this work before the publication of Wilson's research,[11] and considers himself something of a pioneer in the contextual study of particular psalms. In his book, *The Psalms of the Sons of Korah*,[12] he says:

> I have tried a different approach, by treating more seriously the context given to the psalms in the Psalter; that is, the collections in which they are gathered, the order in which they stand, and the technical notes ... in the text. These matters are, of course, noted in all standard works, and a few authors, like John Peters and Gunther Wanke, have treated them as important, but I think that mine is the first attempt to offer a comprehensive theory of the psalms in which these contextual matters are determinative.

Also there have been quite a number of studies of single psalms or small psalm groups in relation to their structural significance.[13]

Largely, but not entirely, in the interest of determining the structure of the Psalter, there have been a number of studies of special themes.[14] Even studies of particular genres are now beginning to feed into this new interest.[15]

It is important that every major interpretation of a Bible book should be subjected to informed criticism. Norman Whybray has questioned the theory that the final redaction of the Psalter was undertaken with the intention of making it a coherent work of instruction. He considers that too much has been made of too little evidence and that the case for it falls short of proof, although he does think the positioning of 73 at the heart of the Psalter may be significant. He agrees however that the book may have been actually used as a consecutive book of instruction in piety but that this does not necessarily reflect editorial intent.[16]

In closing, we note the recent important work of David Mitchell.[17] He argues for an eschatological programme in the Book of Psalms, maintaining that in its present form it has a distinctly Messianic thrust. This fits well with the work of the group of Old Testament scholars who produced *The Lord's Anointed*,[18] which seeks to rehabilitate a Messianic understanding of the Old Testament. Many of the articles in this symposium focus on the Messianic message of whole books of the Old Testament, which, of course, is Mitchell's concern particularly with the Psalter. For too long the idea that the Old Testament is strongly Messianic has been downplayed, so that these recent developments are greatly to be welcomed.

# Chapter 2

# The diversity of its authors

## The references in the superscriptions
Can we identify the authors of the psalms? Our answer depends partly on the value and interpretation of the titles, for there are references to persons by name there and these certainly give the impression of being indications of authorship.[1] These have been part of the Biblical text at least since the translation of the Septuagint.[2]

Seventy three of them are superscribed, 'a psalm of David', twelve are linked with Asaph, eleven with the sons of Korah, three with Jeduthun (39, 62, 77), two with Solomon (72 and 127), and one each with Moses (90), Heman (88) and Ethan (89). The remainder are untitled and are known as 'orphan' psalms, although fourteen more are ascribed to David in the Septuagint.

Authorship issues are not, in many cases, crucial for a theology of the psalms, although, as we will see later, at least some application to David of many of those in Books 1 and 2 is important if God's faithfulness to the Davidic covenant is a major motif in the ultimate arrangement of the book. Is the expression 'of David'[3] in many psalm headings really an authorship claim?

Writing about this phrase, Longman says, 'Hebrew prepositions are slippery things without a context',[4] and this is true. We should note though that the heading of 18 does more than relate the psalm to David's life; it makes him its author, when it says:

A psalm of David, the servant of the LORD, who addressed the words of this song to the LORD on the day when the LORD delivered him from the hand of all his enemies, and from the hand of Saul.

The words that bring Book 2 to its conclusion, 'the prayers of David son of Jesse are ended' (72:20), strongly suggest that the editors, including the final editor, viewed them as actual utterances of David.

## Psalms of David

Earlier critics, for what to many scholars do not now seem adequate reasons, considered the development of individual piety, such as that to be found in many psalms, to be late, and, for this and other reasons, were sceptical about Davidic authorship. It was widely held that no psalms were by him. Then Mowinckel (1962) argued that the re-enthronement festival was pre-exilic and that many psalms were associated with it, so that scholars who followed his outlook tended to regard many in the 'Davidic' group as pre-exilic. Although the re-enthronement festival view is much less widely held now, recent writers still tend to treat at least the possibility of a pre-exilic date for many of the psalms seriously.[5]

Not only so, but the authorship claims in the titles are treated more seriously than formerly and some are even reckoned to be genuinely Davidic.[6] This means that there is real value in seeking to show that a psalm's contents are consistent with its superscription. It is worth remembering that we have evidence outside the psalms that David had a place of special importance in the development of sung praise. He is presented in the historical narrative as 'Israel's singer of songs' (2 Sam. 23:1, NIV).[7] His roles in music and psalmody are featured in the Books of Samuel (1 Sam. 16:23; 2 Sam. 1:17-27, etc.), and in Chronicles he is the founder of the temple choirs and the psalmodic tradition (1 Chron. 15,16).[8]

The Psalter is often popularly called 'the Psalms of David'. Although in its plural form not a Biblical phrase, this may be justified, not only because nearly half the psalms are headed, 'a psalm of David', but also because the sons of Korah, Asaph and other Levitical authors of so many of the others are all referred to in Chronicles as entrusted by David himself with work associated with the praise at the temple. If men like Timothy and Titus acted as 'apostolic legates', doing their work under the apostle Paul's authority, so the work of these Levites was virtually an extension of that of David. Only three psalms are in fact ascribed to anybody else, 90, 72 and 127, those attributed to Moses and Solomon.

The Davidic nature of the Book of Psalms is at its most intense in Book 1. Every psalm in that book is ascribed to David with four exceptions, and these can all be explained. Psalm 10 was probably the second half of 9 originally and 33 is a very obvious companion to 32, which *is* ascribed to David. Psalm 2 is attributed to him in Acts 4:25, 26. This leaves just 1, which was probably written late in the day as a general introduction to the Psalter.

Thirteen of the headings to the Davidic psalms make reference to episodes in David's life, while another one (30) is inscribed, 'for the dedication of the temple.' Eight of these are to be found in Book 2, nearly half the total number of Davidic psalms that are present in that book. Are these references fictitious, are they intelligent guesswork, or are they authentic? All these views have been held. Some have thought them due to guesswork, while others that the compilers have creatively linked these particular psalms with specific events in David's life, thus making them still more concrete and relating them to the tradition that he was the virtual founder of psalmody. Seybold says:

> the biographical references can easily be identified with passages in the two Books of Samuel ... Furthermore, they appear to be specifically intended to call attention to the Biblical passage, either to remind the reader of a familiar situation or to encourage him to read the complete biography found there.[9]

Why should this be done? It is now widely held that the compilers of the book had a teaching motive in making such links, with David serving as a role model for the godly life.

This has been advocated by Childs, who says, 'the move toward universalizing a psalm was achieved by relating it to the history of a David as a representative man.'[10] In these psalms he is presented as living a life in fellowship with God through changing circumstances and varied emotional experiences. The reader, identifying with him, is encouraged to bring everything into God's presence. This means, of course, that the book was not simply a hymn book but Scripture to be used for devotional reading. Murphy says:

> Situating psalms in the life of a human being, rather than in the liturgy – decultizing them, as it were, creates a wider hermeneutical context, at least for the Davidic psalms.[11]

Allen too thinks that, as in Chronicles, David is presented here as a role model, not so much now in terms of his kingly function, but in terms of his piety.[12]

This concept of David as a role model may go hand in hand either with acceptance or rejection of the authenticity of the psalm headings. It is true, of course, that we can learn spiritual lessons from edifying fiction,[13] but such lessons have considerable extra power if the events recorded are actually true. Now the Books of Samuel have an amazing frankness about the character of David, a frankness which witnesses to their truth. There are scholars too who maintain both the reliability and the canonical authority of the psalm headings. This is the view of Kidner.[14] He deals with objections and concludes that there is no valid reason to doubt the truth of the headings.[15]

The historic Protestant stance on the Old Testament canon is that we should accept the books held to be authoritative by the Palestinian Jews in our Lord's day, for these in fact constituted his own Bible. Without doubt these superscriptions were regarded as part of the Old Testament in New Testament times, and there are New Testament passages which take them very seriously.[16] The witness of Mark 12:35-37[17] is particularly important. Here, after answering many different interlocutors,

Jesus argues for a high view of the Messiah in such a way that his argument depends on the Davidic authorship of the psalm, and it is infinitely strengthened by his assertion of the psalm's inspiration by the Holy Spirit. This is most unlikely to be simply an *ad hominem* argument when the issue was so important and the occasion so significant.

## Mosaic and Solomonic psalms

As we have seen, there are other superscriptions, and so those who collected and arranged the psalms must have considered they came from different historical periods.[18] One (90) is even attributed to a writer as early as Moses in its heading.

> It has been pointed out by commentators of various shades of opinion that the psalm has distant echoes of early Genesis, in the Creation and the Fall, and in the apparent allusion to the longevity of the antediluvians;... also that it has affinities to the language of the Song and the Blessing of Moses (Dt. 32 and 33), and a wistfulness of mood which is very appropriate to the circumstances of a doomed generation in the wilderness. Even the individualism of the psalm has its counterpart in Deuteronomy... (3:23ff.).[19]

We might also note the reference to a return to dust immediately after statements about God's creative work,[20] the references to death and to the human lifespan (vv. 5-10)[21] and the author's impassioned plea for his people (vv. 13-17).[22]

The two Solomonic psalms also seem appropriate, for the first (72) is an anticipation of or a prayer for a royal ruler, while the second (127) begins as a meditation on the work of building, and Solomon presided over the building of the temple and other buildings.[23]

The Old Testament views Moses as the prophet of God *par excellence* (Deut. 34:10-12) and Solomon as having God-given wisdom (1 Kings 3:5-12), so that poems by each of them are not out of place in a canonical collection.

## Levitical Psalms

It is not surprising to find psalms attributed to Levites, for their special work was concerned first with the tabernacle, then with the temple, and David put them in charge of the temple worship (1 Chron. 6:31-46; 15:16-22).

> David also commanded the chiefs of the Levites to appoint their kindred as the singers to play on musical instruments, on harps and lyres and cymbals, to raise loud sounds of joy. So the Levites appointed Heman son of Joel; and of his kindred Asaph son of Berechiah; and of the sons of Merari, their kindred, Ethan son of Kushaiah (1 Chron. 15:16, 17).

2 Chronicles 5:12 refers to 'all the levitical singers, Asaph, Heman and Jeduthun, their sons and kindred', which suggests that Jeduthun is an alternative name for Ethan. Korah is referred to in the list of Levites (1 Chron. 6:22). The reference to 'their sons and kindred' suggests that the musical responsibilities of these men were intended to be passed on to their families. This would account for the fact that two of the psalms of Asaph (74 and 79) clearly refer to the destruction of Jerusalem and its temple by the Babylonians. These psalms were presumably composed by descendants of Asaph or members of the choir established by him. It means that the dates of the Levitical psalms must be settled, if at all, on evidence other than the names of those to whom they are ascribed in the headings.

## The work of redactors

The headings to the psalms contain other information beside ascriptions of authorship and references to events in David's life, but these need not concern us here. They are dealt with in all the major commentaries. It is clear enough that the headings as a whole were not added by the authors of the psalms but by others.

Who were these editors and when did they do their work? The translators of the Septuagint were not clear as to the meaning of many of the terms in the headings, for they left them untranslated. This suggests that many of them were fairly old by their time. The fact that some psalms of David occur after 72:20 – ('the prayers of David son of Jesse are ended') – strongly suggests that the work was done at different periods of history. Perhaps these notes were added as each group of psalms was put together into a definite collection on the basis either of oral or written tradition concerning them. Some may have had such notes associated with them shortly after their composition. Clearly we are in the realm of conjecture here.

We will look later at the way the fivefold structure of the Book of Psalms developed. In its complete form and read consecutively it conveys a particular message, which suggests the work of a single redactor, although more than one is not impossible. We will use the singular in later chapters of this book, not because the matter is settled, but simply for ease of reference.

Do individual psalms show evidence of a redactor's work? Some have maintained that sections of lament and praise in one psalm originally belonged to separate psalms, while others contest this, asserting such psalms to be true to spiritual experience, which may move between lament and praise in the life of one individual, even in a short time-frame. The latter view is growing in acceptance.

The close of 72 makes it clear that editorial work has been done on the Book of Psalms, but in most cases suggestions as to its presence at particular points need to be regarded as tentative and should be treated with caution. If a piece of literature has come down to us as a complete whole, we should respect its integrity and only dismember it as a last resort and with a willingness to keep open the possibility that we are wrong. When this literature is the Word of God, this makes our obligation to take this attitude all the greater.

# Chapter 3

## The variety of its forms

The Book of Psalms is similar to the Old Testament as a whole in exhibiting unity despite great diversity. For instance, Biblical truth comes to us in many different forms and styles. One result of this is that it has an aesthetic appeal.

This feature should affect our approach to Biblical interpretation, for different literary forms must be taken seriously if we are to understand any literature. We do not approach a novel or a play, a scientific or historical work, a note from a friend or a business letter in the same kind of way or with identical presuppositions. We must therefore seek to identify and understand the various literary forms or genres in the Old Testament and especially in the psalms.

Unfortunately, Biblical scholars have not yet come to agreed definitions of the terms, 'form' and 'genre'. Some treat them as synonyms, while others use 'form' for smaller units, such as legal codes or laments or sermons, reserving 'genre' for larger units such as histories, gospels or epistles. It is unnecessary for us to take up this matter in detail here, and we will use the terms as synonyms, employing them of particular types of psalm. The Book of Psalms embraces many of the genres to be found in the Old Testament, although we need to remember that there can be important variations within one genre, so that genre analysis and identification have to be done carefully.

### The thematic variety of the Psalms and their links with the rest of the Old Testament

We will consider first of all the variety of theme to be found in the Psalter, because although form and matter are distinguishable, the two are bound to influence each other, so that differences of theme may be expected to affect form. At the same time we will see how the psalms are linked thematically with other parts of the Old Testament, for there is obvious similarity of theme between particular psalms and particular passages elsewhere. As a consequence, the Book of Psalms can be looked upon, more than any other, as demonstrating the unity of the Old Testament.

Creation psalms, like 8 and 104, may be compared with Genesis 1 and 2. In fact 8 seems to be a meditation on the very language of the opening chapter of the Bible. There are also other psalms, like 19 and 136, in which creation is an important theme but which deal with other matters also, and many others, like 115 and 146, where God is referred to as the Maker of heaven and earth.

Historical psalms like 78, 105 and 106, which are strongly reflective, may be compared with the narrative sections of the Pentateuch and with the historical books. They reflect the strong interest so much of the Old Testament shows in the past as the sphere alike of God's action for his people and of the people's reaction to him. The writers of these psalms were convinced, as were the Old Testament historians, that God spoke to his people in and through the events of their history.

Closely linked to history is biography. There are plenty of psalms of an autobiographical type, in which the author tells how God has dealt with him. There are examples of this in 73 and in 34:4-6 and 40:1-3. It is perhaps a surprise to find that there is no book of the Old Testament which majors in autobiography (even the Book of Job is written in the third person), although there are autobiographical sections in Nehemiah and in some of the prophetic books.

For some years there has been a new scholarly interest in the Wisdom literature. The Book of Proverbs presents reflection on life, its meaning and the way the godly should live, and there is much like this too in the psalms (e.g. in 37 and much of 33 and 34). In fact the whole book commences with a psalm setting out in broad terms the two ways and destinies. Of course, the way of the godly is not always a smooth one and they often encounter problems. So it should not surprise us that some psalms, especially those in Book 3 like 73, 77 and 89,[1] wrestle with these difficulties, seeking an answer or at least sufficient assurance to enable God's people to continue to walk in his ways. These may be compared with Job and parts of Ecclesiastes and Jeremiah.

Psalm 45 is unique within the Psalter as an ode composed with a royal marriage in view. As such it may be compared with the series of love poems which constitute the Song of Songs, and which give it its unique place among the Old Testament books.

Then there are declamatory psalms, like 50 and 95, in which the psalmist assumes the role of a preacher, and which may therefore be compared with the books of the prophets. The wording of some psalms, such as 36, 45 and 49, may even suggest an awareness of inspiration, somewhat like that of the prophets.[2] So, for instance, 49:1, 2 reads:

Hear this, all you peoples;
    give ear, all inhabitants of the world,
both low and high,
    rich and poor together.

In a passage like 132:11, 12, there is reference to a past prophecy.[3] Do psalms with similarities to prophetic oracles reflect the presence of a court or temple prophet or a teaching priest who brings a prophetic word into the situation? Some think so, because, for instance, 2 quotes a divine decree and 20 appears to anticipate a divine answer. It is an interesting possibility, but we cannot be sure.[4]

Tournay holds that after the demise of prophecy,

the Levitical singers took upon themselves the mission of making up for the silence of the divine word by multiplying in their lyrical and liturgical works theophanic and oracular passages. To do this, they revived the themes, motifs and expressions of the ancient prophets in order to celebrate in the worship of the Second Temple the name and glory of YHWH, God of the covenant and of the messianic promises.[5]

If, however, as Chronicles indicates,[6] these Levites could be described as prophesying, psalms written by them would have the same status as God's word as was true of the books of the canonical prophets.

The Law too is here. The longest psalm (119) is a meditation on the place of the Law in the life of the godly. It is clear in the whole atmosphere of the psalm that its author had a deep love for God's Law. Psalm 19 too shows the place of the Law in God's revelation, while in 15 there is reflection on laws already given.

Much of the book consists of prayer and praise. Many of the prayers take the form of laments, in which the author faces all manner of problems and sorrows and brings them to the Lord in prayer. This lament material has important parallels in other parts of the Old Testament, especially in Job, Lamentations and the Confessions of Jeremiah.[7] There are great praise passages in the prophets (e.g. in Is. 12) and praise psalms in some of the historical books, such as the almost verbatim quotation of 18 in 2 Samuel 22.

There is also comment on Scripture, very clearly in psalms such as 89 and 136[8] and apparently also in 8[9] and 77,[10] among others. The reader who is sensitive to links between passages will discern many others, although it is not always clear whether or not there is literary dependence involved. To take two examples from Genesis, the life and character of Joseph exemplify the principles set forth in 1, as a study particularly of Genesis 39:2-5 and 49:22 will show, and God is both Shield and Reward for Abraham in Genesis 15:1, which may be compared with 3, where the psalmist indicates that God is both, the Shield explicitly and the Reward by implication:

You, O Lord, are a shield around me,
    my glory, and the one who lifts up my head. ...

> Deliverance belongs to the LORD;
> may your blessing be on your people! (3:3,8)

Some psalms remind us of many other parts of the Old Testament. Psalm 135 is a striking example of this for in it there are echoes of many other passages.[11] There are also important links between it and Psalm 136.

What then are the distinctive features of psalms when they have so many points of contact with other parts of the Old Testament? The chief difference is that the majority of the psalms have some form of address to God, either in prayer or in praise. Even those which are exceptions to this come in the wider context of the whole Book of Psalms, a book employed in worship.

There are, of course, other differences which are worth pondering. For example, the historical psalms are reflections on a history already well known to the readers, and the pedagogical element is usually more prominent than it is in the historical books. The psalms of the Law are meditations on it, rather than simply statements of it.

What a rich volume the Book of Psalms is!

## The form-critical approach to the book

Over the years there have been many attempts to classify the psalms, and no doubt many Christians who make no claims to Biblical scholarship have their own ways of grouping them. It is evident to any reader that some psalms are about creation, some reflect on history, others are prayers uttered by people in trouble, and so on. It was not, however, until the early part of the twentieth century that this became a major concern of scholars, and this was due largely to the work of one man.

Gunkel, the pioneer of form criticism, was particularly interested in the psalms, and was concerned that the study of them had been somewhat overshadowed by that of the prophets. He was fascinated by their rich variety, but also because of a concern he had to reconstruct the communities which shaped them.[12] He also had real interest in classifying them, and he made comparisons with other ancient literature unearthed by the archaeologists. His work had major importance for genre study, and every serious student of the psalms since his day has had to engage with his thought. Some books of Old Testament critical study give the impression of being rather coldly analytical, but Gunkel made a real attempt to identify with the psalm authors in their concerns.

He distinguished five main psalm types (*Gattungen*), plus others of less importance. The five main ones were hymns, in which the religious community expressed its praise of Yahweh, communal and individual laments, individual thanksgivings and royal psalms.

Others have modified his views over the years. Many different schemes have been produced, based largely on differing concepts of the cultural provenance of the psalms. Sometimes the background from which they emerged was regarded as the Israelite cult generally, at other times it was argued that the psalmist could be found facing and rebutting charges in a court of law, calling on God for vindication, while another view is that sometimes at least they were related to some domestic ritual.

The most influential work was done by Mowinckel. He was a pupil of Gunkel and learned form criticism from him, but he also studied under the Danish anthropologist Grønbech, who identified religion as the most important feature of ancient societies. He believed that the religions of the ancient Near East, especially that of Babylon, exercised a strong influence on Israel's religious institutions and on the religious ideas associated with them, and that this influence may be discerned in many psalms. He thought Gunkel did not place enough emphasis on Israel's cult, and he came to believe that as many as one third of the psalms were associated with the special annual festival of Yahweh's re-enthronement for which he had argued. Many scholars of this school[13] laid much emphasis on the special functions of the king in connection with this festival. Old Testament scholars became deeply divided over their attitude to the views of Mowinckel and those associated with him.

This type of thinking often erects a high hypothetical edifice on a very small Biblical foundation, and therefore many scholars today reject the theories of Mowinckel and those who developed theories based on his ideas.[14] How much hard evidence is there for his views and those of Hooke and others? The evidence of the psalms is at best indirect and at worst little more than conjecture. The most that can be said is that some of them are capable of being read in terms of this kind of background, but without necessity.

So, for instance, when David brought the ark up to Jerusalem he wore an ephod, normally a priestly garment (2 Sam. 6:14). He also offered sacrifices (2 Sam. 6:13-19), although this type of expression is flexible enough to mean that he offered them through a priest. In any case, we should remember that this was a very special event, occurring once only in Israel's history. Its special nature may have dictated special dress and functions for the king. We can hardly infer from this a regular sacral function for the king in Israel's religion and that this was similar to what took place in Babylon and Ugarit; there are too many unproved assumptions.[15]

Roland de Vaux, discussing the religious functions of the king, rightly says that

> the instances where the king's personal action is beyond question are all very special or exceptional: the transference of the Ark, the dedication of an altar or sanctuary, the great annual festivals.[16]

It is notable that there is nothing in the Pentateuch to indicate special ritual functions for the king.

Form criticism came to have a dominance in psalm study which many now regard as excessive. Brueggemann quotes Gerstenberger as saying, 'Most form critics so far have been overly fascinated by the communal or national aspects of Israel's faith ..... A better starting-point is individual prayers and their settings.'[17] Brueggemann also says: 'It would appear that Psalm scholarship is now tending to move toward a recovery of personal piety in the Psalms, a matter largely screened out by the dominant hypothesis of Mowinckel.'[18]

Broyles too says, 'Some caution needs to be expressed regarding a cultic approach to the Psalms. In some instances, the search for the institutional setting has blurred the principal object of study: the locus of meaning has become the situation of the psalm rather than the psalm itself. The texts became simply a means by which one could discern social rites and institutions.' He goes on to say: 'It would be a mistake to infer from the designation *Sitz im Leben* that the real 'life' of literature is not contained in the literature itself but in the social situation which it reflects.'[19]

As in so many other subjects, classification is useful but must not ride roughshod over genuine differences. Dahood, pointing out that there are several different genres within 36, wrote: 'The coexistence of three literary types within a poem of thirteen verses points up the limitations of the form-critical approach to the Psalter.'[20]

Westermann said that each psalm should be viewed as distinctive and that the most general background to the psalms as a whole is the way Yahweh intervened historically to deliver his people, both nationally and individually. He opted for a simple and very broad twofold classification of most of the psalms. He says:

> The literary categories of psalms of lament and psalms of praise are not only two distinct categories among others, but they are the literary forms which characterise the Psalter as a whole, related as they are as polar opposites.[21]

His treatment of the psalms of lament led to an increased interest in them which has lasted to the present day. He was interested also in the way psalms are grouped in different parts of the book, thus anticipating the contemporary interest in the structure of the Psalter.

However, a threefold analysis has much to commend it. As Tournay points out, *La Bible oecumenique* distinguishes three main groups, which may be broadly summarised as psalms of praise, of prayer and of instruction.[22] This is a good simple analysis. It also has special interest because it relates fairly closely to the three main stages in the development of the Book of Psalms, for many psalms emerged from individual experience, then were employed in corporate worship and finally provided material for reflection.[23]

The literary genres of particular psalms are still of interest to Old Testament scholars, but this aspect of the subject has come to be somewhat overshadowed by the recent attention given to the shape and shaping of the Psalter as a whole. If there is any convergence of the genre and structural interests, it is chiefly in relation to the wisdom psalms.

Old Testament theologians have often had problems in integrating the Wisdom literature with the rest of the Old Testament in an overall theological understanding. In relation to the psalms it has not even been possible to agree on criteria for their identification. R. N. Whybray says:

> This is partly due to their diversity of form: unlike the psalms in Gunkel's other categories .... they do not conform to any stylistic pattern or regular thematic sequence.[24]

As we will see, students of the structure of the Psalter are also interested in these, although it matters comparatively little to them that they be comprehensively identified.

## A practical approach

It is wise to remember the reservations of scholars like Westermann and Dahood noted above, while not rejecting altogether the attempt to identify the general form (or forms) of a particular psalm. We can learn something from the comparison of a particular psalm with others of a particular genre, but each psalm needs also to be treated as a distinct literary unit. Just as there is danger in adopting stereotypes for particular races and nationalities, so we may come to quite wrong conclusions about particular psalms if we simply regard them as permutations of standard literary types.

In practical terms, it is better to come to a psalm in its individuality first, for after all it existed prior to any attempts to classify it, and only after that to consider what else we may learn from a form analysis of it.

# Chapter 4

## The characteristics of its poetry

Most of us value the Old Testament chiefly for its spiritual message, and this is right. We should not forget, however, that much of it is regarded, even by experts with little concern with its message, as great literature.

Who can fail to be gripped by the simple majesty of Genesis 1, with its amazing economy of language, or resist the pull of the Joseph narrative as it moves from Judah's moving plea in Genesis 44 into chapter 45, where Joseph reveals himself to his brothers? What outstanding biography there is in the Books of Samuel, where David is presented with his godly virtues and his sinful lapses made equally clear and plain! What a dramatic account of the fall of Nineveh is given in Nahum 2! The prophet's song in Isaiah 5 has great power as he begins so gently,[1] then moves into a condemnation in which the hearers are invited to concur in their own doom. Was there ever such a moving literary presentation of the sufferings and bewilderment of a man of God as we find in the Book of Job?

There is a great deal of poetry in the Old Testament and the Book of Psalms is poetry throughout. Now poetical language takes many different forms and we need to examine the form taken by the poetry of the psalms.

Is there metre in Hebrew poetry and therefore in the psalms? There have been attempts to characterize it, but with little success.[2] The most distinctive formal feature of psalmic poetry, and of Old Testament poetry generally, is known as parallelism or sense-rhythm. Interestingly, this has also been found also in the Canaanite poetry of Ugarit and the Akkadian poetry of Mesopotamia. Hebrew, Akkadian and Canaanite are all Semitic languages, so this appears to have been a common feature of part at least of the Semitic language group.

What is parallelism? It is a poetic feature related to the actual meaning of the material in which it is found. So then it uses sense-rhythm rather than sound-rhythm. In it the thought of a second line has a special sense-relationship to the thought of a first, and this is sometimes continued also in a further line or lines. The major pioneer in the whole study of Hebrew poetry was Robert Lowth in the late eighteenth century.

**It is varied**

Much, although not all, of Lowth's work has stood the test of time. He showed that the relationship between the lines is not always the same. He made a threefold classification: synonymous parallelism, in which the lines are similar in meaning;[3] antithetical, in which they provide a contrast;[4] and synthetic, in which the second and any subsequent lines supplement or complement the first.[5] It is important to become sensitive to this feature of Hebrew poetry, for it is very pervasive in the Book of Psalms.

Synonymous parallelism is extremely frequent. We need therefore to be careful not to place too much emphasis on the element of variety within successive lines which have a measure of similarity, as we may be seeing as diverse what the psalmist, in synonymous parallelism, intends to be understood as closely related. For instance, in 103:7, the writer says:

He made known his ways to Moses,
　his acts to the people of Israel.

Here it is possible that he is drawing some distinction between the acts of God, which Israel simply saw, and the ways of God, their deeper significance, discerned by Moses. On the other hand, his change of language may be little more than stylistic. Considering the general context is often helpful, and, on the face of it, it seems unlikely that here the psalmist is concerned to make this kind of distinction in a psalm which is essentially an outpouring of praise to Israel's great Redeemer-God.

Antithetical parallelism is normally quite simple to identify. The Bible as a whole tends to use a good deal of the language of polarity. Life and death, light and darkness, truth and error, are familiar Biblical categories, and the Psalter is no exception to this. The clear distinction between the righteous and the wicked which is made in 1 finds eventual expression in the antithetical parallelism of verse 6:

> For the LORD watches over the way of the righteous,
>   but the way of the wicked will perish.

Some writers doubt the value of Lowth's third classification because it is too miscellaneous to be of much value and its differences from true parallelism are as important as its similarities. The formal similarities are probably due to a kind of habit or cast of mind induced in the poet by the extent to which he handles the true parallelism of comparison and contrast. Longman regards it as a bogus category, and he says:

> It is likely that synthetic lines are not parallel at all. The label has been used by some scholars as a 'catch-all' for those lines which are neither synonymous nor antithetical.[6]

Some psalmic language may be quite intentionally ambiguous. Rabbe, writing of this, says:

> My contention is that sometimes, maybe more often than we think, a word, phrase, or sentence could be understood in two (or more) ways because both were intended.[7]

## It is vivid

Poetic language abounds in metaphors and these give it much of its imaginative power. Seybold counsels attention to psalm metaphors, remarking that

> metaphor, which places one word alongside another and so releases a new understanding of the first, is a figure of speech particularly suited to the spontaneous expression of new experience.[8]

He gives Psalm 23:1 as an example, for in asserting that the Lord is his Shepherd the psalmist uses a figure familiar to his readers and which therefore conveys more, and does so more vividly, than any abstract statement about God.

In 61:2-4 God's provision of a place of safety is vividly presented, first of all as a rock, then a tower, then a tent and finally as the protecting wings of a bird. In 103:11-13, where the psalmist writes of the greatness of God's forgiving love, he gives first of all a cosmic illustration, followed by a geographical one and then he takes one from family life. This repetition, plus the intimacy of the final illustration from the attitude of a father to his children, makes what he says extremely memorable.

Contrasting images are also very telling, as when in 1 the righteous and the wicked are described in the images of a tree and chaff.

Because the Book of Psalms is part of a larger body of literature, the whole Old Testament, its language is enriched for the reader as it is nuanced by significant occurrences of its words and phrases elsewhere. For instance, there is great value in tracing the analogy of the rock (61:2) when this is used of God in passages like Genesis 49:24; Deuteronomy 32:4, 15, 18, 30, 31; Psalm 18:2, 31, 46 and, of course, there is a Christian interpretation of it in 1 Corinthians 10:1-5.

It is a general feature of the Old Testament that its writers tend to favour concrete rather than abstract forms of expression. Of course, in every language there are words which start life in the realm of the concrete, the visible and the tangible, before developing secondary meanings that are more abstract or that relate to the inner life. This is so to a particularly high degree in the Old Testament, and so it is not surprising that it contains such a lot of poetry.

Can we be sure whether material is literal or figurative? What about 18:4-5? Here the psalmist says:

> The cords of death encompassed me;
>     the torrents of perdition assailed me;

the cords of Sheol entangled me;
the snares of death confronted me.

Was he literally in imminent danger of death or is he simply saying that his distress is like that of a man about to die from drowning or in a hunter's snare?[9] We are sometimes helped, as we are here, by a change in imagery, because multiple imagery conveying the same basic thought certainly suggests metaphor.

There is much evidence too of word-play. For instance, Seybold, writing about 93:3, shows how assonance and onomatopoeia are employed here in three successive lines to imitate the thunderous beating of waves on a shore, but all in vain as God's throne and house and laws are all immovable.[10] How assured and therefore reassuring are the statements of the psalm's final verse:

Your decrees are very sure;
holiness befits your house,
O LORD, forevermore.

The figurative language in which poetry abounds should not be misused by interpretive extremism. We should not draw out the implications of a figure beyond what the writer does.[11] This is important for literature generally, but especially when we are dealing with the authoritative word of God. We could be making Scripture teach our own ideas rather than submitting obediently to its teaching.

## It is valuable

Poetic language is valuable for it is often more memorable than prose, and this is particularly true of the sense-rhythm of the Old Testament, for the very similarity of the synonymous lines or the marked contrast of those that are antithetical actually helps the memory. Some of the psalms are probably more deeply embedded in the memories of Christians than any other language in the Old Testament.

Another very valuable feature of parallelism lies in the fact that it is much more easily translated than poetry which depends for its rhythms on sound rather than sense, and it is so appropriate, because, although we may think much of the Bible's expression very beautiful, we value it chiefly for its meaning. The Christian believer will need little convincing of the providence of God in this matter.

The sense-rhythm of the psalms is also of value for the way it makes us think about the meaning. Several writers, for instance Clines,[12] have argued that, in synonymous parallelism, the second line of a couplet is often more precise and specific than the first. This does not mean that line A can be dispensed with, for line B drives us back to read it again so that we may get the whole thought. Of course, this increasing precision is not invariable, but it is a feature to look out for. Clines makes an additional important point:

> Because the relationship of the two lines within the couplet is not predetermined, the reader is more fully engaged in the process of interpretation, a more active participant in the construction of meaning, than when a text presents itself in more straightforward linear fashion.[13]

He also points out that the meaning of a couplet does not reside either in line A or in line B, nor even in the two simply added together, but in the two interpreted in the light of each other. He says:

> A has its meaning within the couplet only in the light, or sense, of B, and B in the light, or sense, of A. In the case of Isaiah 40:3, for instance, the couplet does not mean B, even if B is more precise than A. It means prepare Yahweh's way *in the sense of* making straight a highway, and it means (ii) make straight the highway *as an act of* preparing a way for Yahweh, and it means both of these things concurrently.[14]

This is, he reminds us, like Marshall McLuhan's distinction between hot and cool media, where cool presents an incomplete pattern of stimuli which requires a greater level of engagement on the part of the reader. We might compare TV and radio here. Hebrew poetry is more like radio! So, Clines says:

> the reader is constantly involved in the delicate and tantalising question of the relation of the parts and the product of their interrelationship. That relation ... is a dynamic one which cannot be mechanically delineated, but which often yields itself only to patient exegetical probing, each couplet in its own right.[15]

We should remember that the aesthetic features of a psalm are the servants of its meaning. There is nothing wrong in being captivated by the beauty of some psalms, for instance 103 and 104, the loveliness of each usually surviving even in translation, but we should also be concerned to understand their meaning. We need to move through the beauty to the truth, for this is essential divine truth for living. The words of God are a warning to us all:

> To them you are like a singer of love songs, one who has a beautiful voice and plays well on an instrument; they hear what you say, but they will not do it (Ezek. 33:32).

# B. Its Great Themes

# Chapter 5

## The God of the psalms

Every general theological work needs to begin with the doctrine of God. Why? Because what we believe about God affects what we believe about all else. In fact, some Christian philosophers have argued that we have not really understood anything in the universe until we have seen its relationship to God, for he is the unchanging eternal Fact and the Creator of all that exists, so that relationship to him must be the most basic relationship of all. Certainly, the doctrine of God (which theologians sometimes call 'theology proper') is the base from which all theology arises and to which it all returns. For all of us, our beliefs as well as our actions ought to have God as their focus.

For Christians, of course, what we believe about Christ is of central importance, but even this rests ultimately on the doctrine of God, because we believe the awesome fact that he, the Man Christ Jesus, is in fact God. To use a musical analogy, if Christology is the dominant, then theology proper is the tonic of Christian theology.

Some books begin with definitions, but not the Bible. It simply asserts that in the beginning God created the heavens and the earth. It assumes the reader has at least a rudimentary idea of what 'God' means and also that he or she believes in his existence. These are the assumptions of the Book of Psalms too. In Romans 1:18-32, Paul writes of God's revelation in the created universe. He also writes of the sinful suppression of that revelation and of the fact that people have not honoured God as they should and so have become subject to his wrath. It is clear though that they still have an awareness of God. This is an encouragement to Christians who seek to witness for God in Christ today.

Who was the God of the psalmists? A God of revelation.

They did not speculate about his nature and character, but knew him through his Self-revelation.

The pure revelation of God was under threat from the paganism with which Israel was surrounded and which often came into its own life, chiefly, as we see in the Books of Kings, when championed by apostate monarchs. This was itself countered, however, by revelation from God. Psalm 50, for instance, deals with the paganizing idea that God needed to be fed with sacrificial flesh and blood. This utterly unworthy concept is countered with the words:

> If I were hungry, I would not tell you,
>     for the world and all that is in it is mine.
> Do I eat the flesh of bulls,
>     or drink the blood of goats? (50:12, 13)

The doctrine of God in the psalms is so very rich and full. Here is the true and living God, vibrant with life, full of blessing for his people if only they will trust and obey him, but much to be feared by the rebellious sinner. None of this is denied in the New Testament, for what it teaches about God builds firmly on the already rich foundation of the Old Testament teaching about God, which is still deeply relevant for us today.

## The only God there is

Have you tried to serve two or more masters or worked in a business where the command structure was never made clear, before moving to another where everything was much more straightforward? If so, you may appreciate to some small extent what a relief and blessing it must be to move out of polytheistic paganism into belief in and obedience to one God, especially where that God is utterly unchanging and totally reliable, as was and is the God of Israel.

The prayers and praises of Israel were directed to One alone, variously called Elohim, Yahweh and Adonai, translated respectively as God, LORD and Lord in the main tradition of English versions. The name of Yahweh and of him alone is exalted (148:13) and an Asaphite psalm ends:

> Let them know that you alone,
>    whose name is the LORD,
>    are the Most High over all the earth (83:18).

Asaph was a Levite, and the Levites had a God-given vocation that centred in worship.

Elohim, the general word for God in the Old Testament, dominates Book 2, where it tends to be preferred to Yahweh, which, to an even greater extent, dominates Book 1. Does this variation have any deep significance? This is doubtful. Kidner is probably right when he calls it, 'a difference of customary religious language' between the different compilers of the psalms.[1] What precisely does Elohim mean?

It is the plural of El, also found in the psalms, although much less frequently. El is the general word for a deity in the Semitic language group, although it also designated a particular god in the Canaanite religion investigated by archaeologists at Ugarit in northern Canaan. Even there it is perhaps significant that it is the king of the gods who bears that name.[2]

Because plural in form, Elohim can be used as a true plural to refer to 'the gods' of paganism, and it occurs with this sense occasionally in the psalms, for instance, in 86:8 ('there is none like you among the gods, O Lord'), 96:5 and 138:1. What does it mean in 82:1 and 6?

> God has taken his place in the divine council;
>    in the midst of the gods he holds judgement ...
> I say, 'You are gods,
>    children of the Most High, all of you.'

Here it has been understood either of human judges, because they exercise what is properly a divine function under God himself, or else of angelic beings, so described because of their spiritual nature.[3] It is of course its distinctive use, its 'God' use, that interests us here.

God in the Old Testament is Yahweh, LORD, and the meaning of this name is expounded in Exodus 3:13-15. It occurs in the psalms well over six hundred times, nearly twice as often as Elohim. This should not surprise us, as it is a distinctive, personal name, and there is so much vibrant personal religion in the psalms. Moreover God revealed either the name itself or its meaning in the historical context of the Exodus, the supreme redemptive event of the Old Testament,[4] and so it retained connotations of redemption and associated ideas like grace and compassion and saving power.

In Psalm 9:10, the psalmist says:

> Those who know your name will put their trust in you,
> for you, O LORD, have not forsaken those who seek you.

What does this imply? That God's name is revelatory of himself and of his character and promises, so supplying a firm basis for personal faith. The numerous references to Yahweh in the psalms may all presuppose that this name reveals him, so that we are intended to recall this when we encounter it.[5] In much the same way, for the Christian, the name 'Jesus' gathers up within itself all that the New Testament tells us about his Person and work. So, for Old Testament believers and Christians alike, although for us even more fully, there is an immensely full, revelatory foundation for our trust in him.

So then 'Elohim' reminds us of his awesome majesty,[6] 'Yahweh' of his gracious concern and activity, so that the two together show that we should treat him with great awe and reverence and yet respond to his love with devotion. F. W. Faber struck the balance well when he wrote:

> Oh how I fear Thee, living God,
> With deepest, tenderest fears,
> And worship Thee with trembling hope
> And penitential tears!

> Yet I may love Thee too, O Lord,
> Almighty as Thou art,
> For Thou hast stooped to ask of me
> The love of my poor heart.

Adonai simply indicates lordship, and is less frequent than Yahweh in the Book of Psalms. Major English versions use small capitals for Yahweh and lower case with initial capital for Adonai, as in 35:22:

You have seen, O LORD; do not be silent!
O Lord, do not be far from me!

There are other designations of him.[7] Important among these are 'God of Israel' and 'LORD of hosts'. The first is to be expected and is fairly frequent. We may easily forget the link of the name 'Israel' with the historical Jacob, but the psalms remind us of this link when God is called 'the God of Jacob' (e.g. in 20:1; 46:7; 81:1). This phrase also highlights, as does 'the God of Abraham, Isaac and Jacob', his personal nature as One who graciously brings other persons into relationship with himself. The combination of 'God of Jacob' and 'LORD of hosts' in 46:7, 11 suggests that he combines compassion for his weak and failing people with almighty strength exerted on their behalf. We might compare Malachi 3:6, where, after God calls himself the LORD of hosts, he says:

For I the LORD do not change;
therefore you, O children of Jacob, have not perished.

There however it is their sinfulness, not their frailty, which is chiefly in view.

The phrase 'God Most High', or simply 'the Most High', is fairly frequent in the psalms (e.g. in 46:4 and 57:2), and recalls that in Genesis 14 Melchizedek, described as 'priest of God Most High', was king of Salem, which is mentioned in parallel with Zion in 76:2. There may have been a continuing tradition in Jerusalem of the use of this particular name for the true God.

The psalmists recognised of course that powers of evil exist, but not that they threatened Yahweh's sovereignty. Sometimes pagan deities are treated as if they are real but should acknowledge his supremacy, as, for example, in the words of 97:7, 'all gods bow down before him'. At other times they are treated as if they do not exist at all, for the sheer impotence of the idols in 115 certainly suggests the non-existence of the gods they represent.

Psalm 96:4,5 combines both thoughts when it says 'he is to be revered before all gods', and then, 'for all the gods of the peoples are idols.'[8] Of course something without objective reality may still play a big part in people's minds, leading them completely astray, and so worship of false deities, even non-existent deities who are foolishly believed to exist, needs to be attacked, in our day just as much as in the time of the psalmists.

Then there are the names Rahab and Leviathan. These designate mythological creatures that appear in Babylonian and Ugaritic texts, although there under the names Tiamat and Lothan. They are examples of dead mythology, in which words originating in a mythological context are given a changed application. They assume familiarity with the mythology, but not belief in it, for those who used it in the Old Testament were all Israelite monotheists. They do however bear witness to belief in the existence of a realm of evil external to humanity.[9] The God of Israel is totally sovereign over all such and demonstrates his power in crushing them (74:14, 'you crushed the heads of Leviathan').[10] These passages are really saying that nothing, no matter how strong and fearsome it may be thought to be, can withstand God's mighty power. The New Testament applies this great truth to the total overthrow of Satan and his kingdom, all the more amazing because it was accomplished by a Man hanging on a cross.[11]

The term 'Rahab' in particular is sometimes applied to a monstrous human foe, to Egypt (87:4), the very symbol of oppression and antagonism to the true God and his people. In Isaiah 30:6,7, the prophet pictures the emissaries of Judah taking the dangerous journey southward through the Negeb to obtain help from Egypt, ferocious Rahab, but whom God calls, 'Dragon do-nothing' (Moffatt's translation).[12]

However such beings are to be understood, they cannot threaten Yahweh or his power. In the Book of the Revelation, too, Satan is pictured as a great dragon or serpent (Rev. 12, 13, 20:2,3). There too it is clear that he is no ultimate threat to the purposes and power of the God who is almighty. Christians should never underestimate Satan, but they need above all complete confidence in the comprehensiveness of Christ's victory over him.

## Revealing himself in verbal images

Israel was forbidden to make tangible images of God (Exod. 20:4). Yet much that could be seen and touched revealed him to his people, for there was an important sacramental dimension to their experience of him. There was however no disclosure of a physical form, as Moses reminds the people in Deuteronomy 4:15-20.[13] Isaiah 40-48 contains very strong passages of polemic against idolatry in which idolaters are subjected to scorn and ridicule, and 115 sounds the same note. Most effectively, the psalmist makes two simple but far-reaching assertions: 'Our God is in heaven; he does whatever he pleases' (v. 3), before moving into his polemic. The New Testament apostles too refer to 'these worthless things' and contrast them with 'the living God who made the heaven and the sea and all that is in them' (Acts 14:15; cf. 1 Thess. 1:9).

In some parts of the Old Testament, God manifests himself in a theophany that takes human form.[14] There is no reference in the psalms to this particular kind of revelation, although theophanies in which he uses the natural elements are mentioned quite a number of times.[15]

What we do find, however, is a considerable amount of picture language when the psalmists write about God. Mason says:

It is remarkable that a people who were forbidden (officially, at least) to make any visual image of God (Exod. 20:4; cf. Deut. 5:8) yet produced this array of literary images. The Old Testament talk about God abounds in simile and metaphor. Not all the pictures were unique to Israel. Some of them ... were the common stock of the people among whom Israel lived in the Ancient Near East ... Yet the use she made of these images and the rich and multi-coloured tapestry she produced from them in her scriptures are unique and have become part of the devotional heritage of three major world religions.[16]

Mason deals with a number of these images, those of God as Redeemer, Craftsman, Father, Human, King, Judge, Shepherd, Warrior, Lover and Feminine. There are others too, for we may identify, for instance, God as Farmer (65:9-13), Viniculturist (80:8-16), Teacher and Guide (25:8-10), Bird (61:4), Healer (6:2), Home (90:1), Rock, Stronghold and Shield (18:2), as well as more abstract terms such as Light and Salvation (27:1). This language shows how many-sided was the Old Testament believer's experience of God, and this too is the inheritance of the Christian. Some of this language continues into the New Testament.

Of course, our understanding of these images needs to be subject to some discipline. We are not justified in extending their use to anything such words may suggest to us. For instance, the bird image is related to the protection young ones receive under the wings of the mother.[17] It would be quite inappropriate for us to infer from it that God inhabits a higher sphere than human beings even if we can discover that idea elsewhere. It has been well said that a most important function of a theologian is to balance Biblical metaphors, and we need to do this here. Mason is really recognising this principle when he says, 'we need many pictures, each filling out a little the imperfections and incompleteness of others.'[18] So he says that Lover would be sentimental without Judge and Father domesticated without King. Yahweh is both Warrior and Shepherd. It is good to have such a plenitude of verbal images.[19]

It is all the images taken together, plus other passages which present truth about God in more literal forms,[20] that provide us with this Bible book's doctrine of God. In this way so much that is familiar may remind us of him.

## Revealing himself in constant activity

The God of the psalmists is an active God, constantly at work for his people, just as he is in the rest of the Bible. He is their Creator, Redeemer, Deliverer, their Father and Shepherd. This is one of the chief points being made in 115, where the God who does whatever pleases him is so starkly contrasted with the totally inactive idols.[21]

The psalms show people making prayer requests. To pray such petitions is to believe in a God who is essentially active and therefore able to respond. Certainly there are psalms which complain of God's inactivity,[22] but even here the presupposition is that this is unusual and that he normally works for his people. Statements such as 'God is good' or 'God is great', in which one of his attributes is selected, do occur, but normally the psalmist goes on to write of the acts of God, either generally or with reference to specific deeds, because it is in his actions that these attributes may be seen by his people.[23]

## Revealing himself as consistent in character

Character is important in any authority figure, and its importance increases as the person's authority increases. Enough examples of this have appeared in twentieth century history to make illustrations superfluous.

This is true most of all in the case of Almighty God. His character is so many-sided in the Old Testament and in the psalms that it is not easy to give a systematic account of it. We may perhaps discuss whether one of his moral attributes is the dominant one and perhaps should even be reckoned the fount of all the others, but this is the province of the systematic theologian and is a doubtful enterprise in an exercise in biblical theology such as this present volume.

There are frequent references to his character or to some aspect of it. In 99, for instance, his holiness is the focus of worship, and it has connotations both of greatness and of justice,[24] for the author says:

> Let them praise your great and awesome name.
>     Holy is he!
> Mighty King, lover of justice,
>     you have established equity;
> you have executed justice
>     and righteousness in Jacob.
> Extol the LORD our God:
>     worship at his footstool.
>     Holy is he! (vv. 3-5)

Holiness implies separateness, and the God of the Old Testament and of the psalms is separate from his creatures by the simple fact that he is their Creator. Not only so but he is separate from every sinful creature in his righteousness and his commitment to justice.[25] So all nations are called to tremble before him (v.1).

From his holy throne he dispenses justice and punishes the wicked (11:4-7), and his wrath is to be feared (2:10-12). This kind of teaching comes very frequently in the psalms. Yet he is also a gracious God, for, being good and upright, he instructs sinners in his way, giving guidance to the humble, and all his ways are loving and faithful to covenant-keepers (25:8-10). His steadfast or unfailing love, that love which is committed to act in accordance with his covenant promises, is often celebrated in the psalms.[26] His wisdom is shown in the works of his hands (104:24; 136:5). Most of these great truths could be documented many times over, not only from the psalms, but also from other parts of the Bible.

Can we say, however, that the psalms show God to be consistent? The psalmists certainly assert this quite frequently. He is faithful and true;[27] his word is to be trusted when that of others is at best unreliable and at worst deliberately deceitful and malign; he has always been true to his character.[28] All this is stated over and over again.

But there is another side to the story. Many lament psalms might better be called psalms of complaint, for in them the psalmist complains to God that he has not been active for his people, that he is apparently not listening to their prayer, or even that he seems to be forgetting his word of promise. So, for instance, in 13:1,2 he says:

How long, O Lord? Will you forget me forever?
　How long will you hide your face from me?
How long must I bear pain in my soul,
　and have sorrow in my heart all day long?
How long shall my enemy be exalted over me?

and in 77:7, 8 he asks:

Will the Lord spurn forever,
　and never again be favorable?
Has his steadfast love ceased forever?
　Are his promises at an end for all time?

What are we to make of this? The positive statements about God can, of course, be paralleled quite fully elsewhere in the Old Testament and they form part of the general Old Testament doctrine of God as the source of order who can be trusted implicitly. This is, however, also true of the more negative material, much of which can be paralleled in Job,[29] and the Confessions of Jeremiah.[30]

We may conclude that the positive statements are not simply extrapolated from the experience of the psalmists, but that they are much more firmly grounded than that. This is what God has declared about himself and it is to be believed because it is God who has said it. There may be times in the experience of the psalmists when they are tempted to wonder if such affirmations are true, but it is noticeable that it is always God the psalmists come to with these problems of theodicy, so that at rock bottom their faith in his veracity has not been shaken. To be puzzled and to give up belief are not the same thing.

Christians too may be puzzled by the ways of God, but he has given us such affirmations of his holiness, grace and wisdom in the cross and resurrection of Jesus that faith is constantly renewed as it contemplates these wonderful facts in a spirit of trustful worship.

# Chapter 6

## God creates his people

In the psalms, as in the whole Bible, the sole Creator is the true God who is Yahweh, God of Israel. This fact is many-sided in its implications, suggesting authority, initiative, purpose, power and, on the part of all his creatures, dependence.

### The Creator of the world

The theme enters a number of praise psalms. Seybold identifies about twenty psalms as alluding to creation, but sees this as an explicit theme in a somewhat smaller number. He places 33, 74, 89, 95, 104, 135, 136, 147, 148 in this latter group.[1]

There is never the slightest suggestion of the gods of the nations being involved in the creative work, nor even a trace of the Zoroastrian dualism of the Persians. A psalm which refers to Yahweh as the Maker of heaven and earth (115:15), sets up a stark contrast. On one side is the true God, whose power enables him to carry out every purpose of his mind, while on the other are the idols, the works of human hands which have received in the process bodily parts that are totally non-functional and impotent. Blind, deaf, dumb, with no sense of smell, paralysed in both hands and feet and so totally inert – all these are conditions which impose limits, often very severely, on human beings. Thankfully, humans rarely experience more than one or two of them. How powerless therefore are the idols in which all these impotencies find their combination!

Yahweh has designed the world to reveal his glory in it. Psalm 19 does not emphasise so much the actual creation of the heavens, although it implies this in saying that God pitched a tent there for the sun. Rather it stresses their function in revealing his glory. In Genesis 1 the sun and moon and the other heavenly bodies, so important as deities in the astral worship of Babylon, are dramatically cut down to size, for they are simply lamps to give light on the earth. In 19, too, there may be a subtle attack on the sun-worship practised in Babylon and Egypt, because the sun, most glorious of the heavenly bodies, is given a place in subordination to the Creator. The visible universe speaks to all humankind of God's glory.

Paul quotes 19:4:

> Their voice has gone out to all the earth,
>     and their words to the end of the world,

and applies it to the wide dissemination of the gospel in apostolic days (Rom. 10:18). He was able to do this because he believed the God of creation and the God of redemption to be one God, as also, incidentally, the God of the Old Testament and of the New. It is important too for the modern Christian to recognise this. We worship him supremely in Christ, but also as the God of Israel and the great Creator.

The God of creation is also the God of providence, for he cares for all he has brought into being, and in the service of his providential purposes he uses elements of the universe he has made. This too should evoke heartfelt praise. Psalm 104 follows its description of Yahweh's creative work by telling of his good provision of food and shelter for both people and animals, and their total dependence on him. It is the providential work of God which is the focus too of 147. As in Isaiah 40, God the LORD determines the numbers of the stars and calls them each by name. He governs the elements and uses them to provide food both for animals and human beings. It is clear here that his care extends to human life and covers all else, from the stars to the ravens. How great is his goodness!

Creation is not, however, only about power, but also about order. Genesis 1 shows us the great power of the Creator, but also discloses his beautiful mind. In this respect it differs markedly from most accounts of the world's origins to be found in other religions. Everything is given the place designed for it in the Creator's mind. This in itself brought to Old Testament believers and brings to us too the assurance that God's purposes must succeed ultimately, in the interests not only of righteousness but of order. Psalm 104 has been aptly described as 'Genesis 1 set to music', and there can be little doubt that its author knew that chapter. The sublimity of this psalm is a fit counterpart to that chapter. It uses the boldest anthropomorphisms in depicting the universe as providing garments and vehicles for its Creator when the psalmist says:

> You are clothed with honor and majesty,
>     wrapped in light as with a garment.
> You stretch out the heavens like a tent,
>     you set the beams of your chambers on the waters,
> you make the clouds your chariot,
>     you ride on the wings of the wind (vv. 1-3).

Then his creative work is described, with special stress on the firmness of the earth and on his complete control of the elements. It may seem at times as if some of these, especially the waters of the sea, will threaten that firm order, but they cannot. They have to go to the place God has assigned to them (vv.5-9).[2] The psalmist then describes the ongoing providence of the Creator in the provision of food and shelter for both people and animals, and their total dependence on him. Here again we see God's concern to use his created universe for the good of his creatures. Psalm 136 also certainly seems to show knowledge of Genesis 1.

Psalm 8, too, reflects the thought of that great chapter. Here the Creator not only set everything in its place but also put the animal creation under human control, so that human beings were to function as instruments of his ordering of the world. This means that the church of Christ must have an ecological concern. Hebrews 2:5-10 shows that its writer was aware of the disordering effects of sin, which has upset something of that order, for 'at present we do not see everything subject to him' (v.8 NIV) but there is present fulfilment in the once crucified, now glorified Christ (vv.9, 10). This psalm presents us with a high doctrine of humanity, for the psalmist asks, with a touch of wonder:

> What is man that you are mindful of him,
>     the son of man that you care for him?
> You made him a little lower than the heavenly beings
>     and crowned him with glory and honour (8:4, 5 NIV).[3]

and all this was made more amazing by his consideration of the heavens and the heavenly bodies in all their greatness.

Of course, the ultimate threat to divine order is always rebellion. Several creation psalms recognise that the world is not now perfect, thus perhaps taking account of the advent of sin as recorded in Genesis 3, although without using that chapter's actual language. Psalm 104:35 calls for sinners to be consumed from the earth and for the wicked to be no more, and 95 calls for worship of the Creator but also warns against rebelliousness. The latter psalm has an important place in Hebrews 3 and 4, the first of several warning passages in that great epistle.[4]

Psalm 8 contains a striking metaphor. Following the Septuagint, which is quoted in Matthew 21:16, the NIV translates:

> From the lips of children and infants
>     you have ordained praise
> because of your enemies,
>     to silence the foe and the avenger.

The Hebrew of the Massoretic text, however has 'founded a bulwark' instead of 'ordained praise'. Perhaps we may see here again an apparent threat from disorder, (somewhat like that posed by the sea in 104), overcome by divine means, this time, however, not by exerting great strength but, in a beautiful paradox, by the cries to him that arise from the lips of little ones.[5] Here then is one of many Old Testament anticipations of that complete reversal of human ideas of power which culminated in the sufferings and death of God's Son impaled on the crucifixion tree. Perhaps it means too that Jesus recognised in the carping criticisms of the religious leaders the utterances of those who, even though unaware of this, were in fact foes of God (Matt. 21:14-16). How terrible to live and even more to die as an enemy of God!

Psalm 136 is very distinctive. It was almost certainly sung antiphonally, for it has a refrain, 'his steadfast love endures for ever', concluding each of its verses. It has something of a chiastic structure, for it starts with thanksgiving to God for his goodness and greatness, moves on to extol him for his great wonders, beginning with the creation and telling of his wonders for Israel from Egypt to Canaan, with the last four verses briefly recapitulating these items in reverse order. It is familiar to many Christians through John Milton's hymn, which begins:

Let us with a gladsome mind
praise the Lord for he is kind;
For his mercies shall endure,
ever faithful, ever sure.

Psalm 139 says nothing about the creation of the universe or of the human race, for the focus of the whole psalm is on God's dealings with the writer himself. It does however make reference to the beginnings of individual life in a passage often quoted in the abortion debate:

For it was you who formed my inward parts;
    you knit me together in my mother's womb.
I praise you, for I am fearfully and wonderfully made.
    Wonderful are your works;
that I know very well.
    My frame was not hidden from you,
when I was being made in secret,
    intricately woven in the depths of the earth.

Your eyes beheld my unformed substance.
In your book were written
    all the days that were formed for me,
    when none of them as yet existed. (139:13-16)

In his wonderment at the creative work of God before human birth the writer graphically compares the womb with the depths of the earth. Here is no mere operation of an impersonal natural law but the personal activity and all-seeing eye of the psalmist's Creator. If he cares for the sparrows (Matt. 10:29-31), should we be surprised at his concern for the unborn child?

It is no surprise that the group of praise psalms which brings the Book of Psalms to its close should make a number of references to God as Creator. There is a touching paradox in 146:5, 6, where the Maker of heaven and earth is at the same time the God of Jacob, with concern, as the following verses indicate, for all who are in need and unable to help themselves. Here is almighty power allied to the tenderest compassion, a combination so often seen in the ministry of Jesus. In 148 the Christian almost feels as if he is in Revelation 4 and 5, for here the whole universe is engaged in praising God its great Creator. Here are the heavenly angels and here the earth with all its teeming and varied life, including human beings of every class and age. The glory of this great God far exceeds all he has created.

## The Creator of his people, with whom he has entered into covenant

The theme of God as Creator takes a somewhat unexpected turn when it is brought to bear on his relationship with his people. There is often an intertwining of the two thoughts of God as Creator of the universe, establishing its order and guaranteeing its stability, and God as the Creator and Protector of his people. No wedge can be driven between the God of creation and the God of redemption, as if these are two quite different and even antagonistic beings, as in the teaching of Marcion, the second century Gnostic. Creation and redemption both proceed from him who is Israel's God and ours.[6]

When the psalmists say that God created his people, they are not simply following the logic of his creation of the whole world. Rather his creation of his people implies both election and covenant. He chose them and he entered into a special relationship with them. Sometimes it is not easy to tell whether it is his general or this special creatorship which is in view. For instance, in 95:5-7, the psalmist says:

> The sea is his, for he made it,
> > and the dry land, which his hands have formed.
> O come, let us worship and bow down,
> > let us kneel before the LORD, our Maker!
> For he is our God,
> > and we are the people of his pasture,
> > and the sheep of his hand.

It is, however, more likely that this is the special rather than the general because of the way verses 6 and 7 are linked together by the causal conjunction 'for'.[7]

God's benevolence extends to his redemptive purposes as well as to his general providence. After extolling Yahweh as the God of creation who controls the physical universe, 136 continues to use physical terms in describing God's dealings with Israel, for he divided the Red Sea, brought the people through the desert, gave them the land of Canaan (three physical realms) and provided food for all. The God of creation employs what he has made in the service of his redemptive dealings with his people. Both redemption and creation should be constant themes of Christian praise.

The great Creator of all chose Israel to be his own people. In 147, the themes of God as the universe's Creator and as the one who chose and cares for Israel are completely interwoven. In verses 2 and 3, for instance, he says:

The LORD builds up Jerusalem;
>    he gathers the outcasts of Israel.
He heals the broken-hearted,
>    and binds up their wounds.

He then goes on immediately to say, in verse 4:

He determines the number of the stars;
>    he gives to all of them their names.

At the close of this psalm, the author declares that only Israel has received God's word from him.

In 33, after writing of the making of the heavens and the earth by God's word (vv.4-9), the author goes on to say that he chose Israel for his inheritance (v.12), so that election is here almost a function of creation. Indeed the selection of a verb of creation or one of choice would seem to make little difference to the thought, for the one implies the other.

In Romans 9, Paul shows that the Old Testament bears witness to an election within an election. He could well have found material for his argument in the psalms, for in them election within the people of Israel is mentioned several times. Some of these are not particularly significant for our theme, for the choice of Moses (106:23) and Aaron (105:26) are obviously for particular forms of service within the nation. The choice of Jacob, however, is more significant as he was the nation's father (105:6, 43). In fact God's choice of him rather than Esau appears as part of Paul's argument in Romans 9:10-13.

Tournay[8] mentions that, following Weiser, M.Mannati proposed covenant as the central theme of the Book of Psalms. More than thirty years earlier, W. Eichrodt had identified covenant as the overarching theme in Old Testament theology, and we may perhaps see here his continuing influence although by 1960s this was beginning to wane and to be replaced by that of G. von Rad.

Strangely, after mentioning that *berit* ('covenant') appears only nineteen times in the Psalter but that the idea is suggested by the very frequent *hesed* ('covenant love' or 'steadfast love' or 'unfailing love'), which appears more than one hundred and twenty times, Tournay goes on to say, 'This is not, however, a truly specific and central feature of the Psalter.'[9] This may seem somewhat debatable. He probably means it is not always easy to tell whether the psalmist is writing about God's character in general or whether the language has specific covenant reference.

Yahweh's covenant with the patriarchs and with Israel through them 'for a thousand generations' is fundamental to the historical 105 (vv.8-11). Its companion 106 also extols him for remembering his covenant (v.45), which could be either the Abrahamic or the Mosaic. The importance particularly of the Davidic covenant can hardly be overlooked, especially if we see the actual arrangement of the Book of Psalms as reflecting in Book 3 the discouragement which came when the dynasty appeared to have gone into eclipse at the Exile, followed by the rebuilding of faith and hope in Books 4 and 5.[10]

The placing of 89 and 132 could well be significant in this regard. Psalm 89 comes at the close of Book 3. After extolling the divine covenant with David at considerable length, the psalmist expresses his concern at the way God seems to have acted to undermine it. He utters the wistful cry, 'Lord, where is your steadfast love of old, which by your faithfulness you swore to David' (v.49)? Psalm 132 in Book 5, on the other hand, seems to look forward to the advent of a new Davidic monarch. The psalmist says: 'There I will make a horn to grow up for David; and I have prepared a lamp for my anointed one' (v.17). We see here how the Messianic hope, fulfilled in Jesus, built on the promises of God to David. So for the Christian, the Old and New Testaments together show the great faithfulness of the God with whom he is in new covenant through Christ.

Within Israel itself, God had chosen David, Judah and Jerusalem. We have already noted the element of divine discrimination within the seed of Abraham, so that Jacob is

chosen and Esau rejected. However, discrimination within the
nation itself appears in 78:67-70, where the psalmist says:

> He rejected the tent of Joseph,
>     he did not choose the tribe of Ephraim,
> but he chose the tribe of Judah,
>     Mount Zion, which he loves.
> He built his sanctuary like the high heavens,
>     like the earth, which he has founded forever.
> He chose his servant David.

Here God passed over Ephraim, the largest tribe, and chose
Judah, and then, within Judah, extended his choice to Mount
Zion and to David. Here is a concentration which reminds us of
the themes of the Books of Chronicles, where Judah, Jerusalem
and the worship carried on at the temple there, and David and
the Davidic dynasty, are leading motifs. This linking of God's
choice of Zion and of David is found also in 132. The election
of David is found also in 18:43; 21:6 and 89:27, 29.

The intertwining of the idea of God as Creator of the world
and also of his people and their institutions, already noted, may
be seen in 24. Here the writer begins by referring to the stability
of the created world, before writing of Zion's hill and temple.
The implication appears to be that the same divine firmness is
to be found there too. In verse 1, God's possession of the earth,
the world, grounded in its foundation by him, is asserted before
the psalmist goes on to write of the hill of the Lord.

In 65, God's creation and care of his creation are both in
view, and the psalmist says of God:

> By your strength you established the mountains;
>     you are girded with might.
> You silence the roaring of the seas,
>     the roaring of their waves,
>         the tumult of the nations (vv. 6, 7).

Here the threat of the natural elements becomes a symbol of threatening nations, and it is emphasised that God controls both.

This kind of psalm, and a number of other Zion psalms, remind us of Isaiah's day, when God protected his city from the Assyrians (Isa. 36, 37) and when the prophet encouraged King Hezekiah to trust God for that protection. Things were different however in Jeremiah's day, for then the people of Judah were told that God had doomed their city and its temple because of their constant rebellion against him (Jer. 7). Did this negate the promises of God? After all the city was both the location of the holy temple and the capital city of the Davidic dynasty.

The psalmists recognised that there are times when it seems as if divinely established covenant landmarks are under threat, and in fact when they appear to have been utterly destroyed. What do the psalms, as documents of faith, have to say in such a situation, when even what God has established, for instance the city of Jerusalem crowned with its holy temple or the dynasty of David which was underwritten by his covenant promises, appears to have come to its end? That such a situation calls for repentance on the part of the people is evident, but is there also a place for faith? What can re-establish faith when it has received a serious knock? This is not just an Old Testament but a perennial question. The psalmists return to the God of creation, the God who gave our environment its fundamental structure and security.

Those who gave the Book of Psalms its final structure showed great spiritual wisdom in placing 90 where it is. As we have seen, its predecessor, bringing Book 3 to its close, shows a deep concern about the apparent downfall of the Davidic dynasty, based as it was on the divine word of promise. So here is now placed a psalm which, through its ascription to Moses, reminds the reader that the purposes of God for his people preceded his dealings with David by hundreds of years. It is a psalm in which God the Creator (90:2) is shown to be from everlasting to everlasting, perhaps reminding the reader that in 89:5-13 it is implied that the Davidic covenant is really as secure as the heavens and the earth. It may have gone into eclipse (perhaps it is implied), but despite the present bewilderment of the psalmist God's commitment to it must become evident ultimately.

So it did, in Christ, for in the New Testament he is the ultimate Son of David (Acts 2:29-33; 13: 32-37; Rom. 1:3), even if, as another psalm shows, he was much more than this (110; cf. Mark 12: 35-37). So we can wholeheartedly praise God for his great faithfulness to his word of promise.

# Chapter 7

## God rules his people

Sovereignty is fundamental to the very idea of deity and is probably the first thought that comes to the minds of most people in connection with the word, 'God'. So, for them, 'God' means the one with supreme rule and authority. John Calvin's *Institutes of the Christian Religion* is acknowledged by many Protestants to be the greatest-ever work of systematic theology, and its controlling idea is the sovereignty of God.

All authority within the universe is delegated by God, and Jesus recognised this when he said to Pilate, 'You would have no power over me unless it had been given you from above' (John 19:11). Paul too acknowledged this principle in Romans 13:1, where he says, 'there is no authority except from God, and those authorities that exist have been instituted by God.' This is true in the Old Testament too, and is particularly marked in the Book of Daniel. It is also true of the psalms. Other authorities, like kings and judges, come into view from time to time, but it is clear they are all subordinate to God.

### God as king
Should we then have started our survey of the great themes of the psalms with the divine kingship? Certainly Mays would expect us to do so and, in fact, to make this the organising principle for the whole of this book. In a beautifully written volume, *The Lord Reigns,* he argues that God's kingship is the major motif in the Psalms.[1] He says that the sovereignty of God is an active one:

> All the topics and functions of Psalmic language fit into this collateral pattern of active sovereignty. The *people* of God, the *place* God chooses to pre-empt in the world, the *Messiah* as earthly

regent, and the *law* of God are the principal topics. The *prayer*s are pleas and *thanksgivings* of God's servants to their sovereign, the *hymns* are praise of God's sovereignty, and the *instructional psalms* teach how to live in the reign of God.

He also says, 'The integrity of psalmic speech in all its forms, praise, prayer, and instruction, *depends* on the proclamation, "The LORD reigns".'[2]

All this follows, not simply from some abstract notion of deity, but from the way truth about God is presented both in the Bible in general and the psalms in particular. Doubtless a good case can be made out for Mays' thesis, although good reasons too can be given for the order of themes chosen for the present book. The emphasis Mays places appears to be an application to the Book of Psalms of John Bright's recognition of the Kingdom of God as the leading theological motif of the Old Testament.

Other writers come close to the same position. So, for example, Creach, whose book focuses on God as the Refuge of his people, says:

It seems relatively clear that to speak of Yahweh as refuge was a way ancient Israel described the auspices of Yahweh's rule as king. This is seen most clearly in texts that describe God's protection of the poor and passages outside the Psalter that indict Israel for 'seeking refuge' in kings or political forces other than Yahweh.[3]

He views the idea of God as Refuge as a kind of subset of the theme of God as King.

In the previous chapter we mentioned that Weiser held covenant to be the dominant theme of the psalms, following Eichrodt's identification of covenant as the leading theme of the whole Old Testament. Kingship and covenant both view God as active for his people. Perhaps then we should simply say that this activity and the people's response to it provide the overall theme, although of course this is the activity of one who is sovereign over all. God's supreme kingly and covenant activity was, of course, in the work of Christ, the Servant King, whose sacrificial death brings Christians into the new covenant (Luke 21:18, 20, 24-30). So these themes are important for us too.

Certainly Yahweh's kingship emerges very early in the Book of Psalms as Biblically arranged. Psalm 2 is sometimes regarded, with 1, as introductory to the book, and this psalm is about kingship, not just that of the kings of the earth (2:2-3), nor of the Israelite king (2:7), but even more fundamentally, the kingship of God, referred to as 'He who sits in the heavens' (2:4).

In Book 4 several psalms (93, 95-99) feature Yahweh enthroned as supreme, and these are anticipated, earlier in the Psalter, by 47. Several of these open with the words, 'The LORD is King.'[4] Mowinckel wanted to translate this brief but powerful affirmation as 'Yahweh has become king', linking it to ideas of enthronement renewal. Certainly such a rendering is possible, but the more commonly employed translation is far more likely.[5]

If Book 4 was given its eventual position in the Book of Psalms during or just after the Exile, as it may have been, we can see why it is preceded by 89, which brings Book 3 to its conclusion. This psalm complains that God seems to have forgotten his covenant with David, the promise of a lasting dynasty. Certainly many Jews must have felt like this psalmist during the long years of exile and when king Jehoiachin was incarcerated in Babylon.[6] The psalms of divine kingship give the assurance that God, the supreme King, is still on the throne. The more discerning of the early readers, reading these psalms in the light of 2, may have picked up from this the hope that the dynasty would be restored. If so, this part of the Psalter would be a major factor in keeping the Messianic hope alive during and after the Exile.

Westermann links the enthronement psalms with those which anticipate the praise of Yahweh, God of Israel, by all the nations, and he says the former are based on the descriptive psalms of

praise.[7] He says: 'The significance of these enthronement Psalms
lies in that a motif which was prophetic in origin, the
eschatological exclamation of kingship, was absorbed into the
descriptive praise of the Psalms.... It is praise of the Lord of
history – in anticipation'.[8] Faith is no leap in the dark, but feeds
on what God has revealed about himself. This is true too of
hope, which is really a form of faith, faith projecting itself into
the future and basing itself on God's sovereign control of events,
those to come as well as those in the past and the present.
Christians inherit this confidence, as the Book of the Revelation
so clearly shows.

Another group where Yahweh's kingship features
prominently is the so-called Zion group: 46, 48, 76, 84, 87,
122. The people regarded Zion not simply as their capital,
especially associated with David because of his capture of it, or
even simply as the place where they worshipped their God, but
also as the place of his dwelling. When he is said to be enthroned,
however, this is usually in heaven: 'The LORD is in his holy
temple; the LORD's throne is in heaven' (11:4). In 24:7, 9 though
the psalmist thinks in more earthly terms when he says, 'Lift up
your heads, O gates! And be lifted up, O ancient doors! that the
King of glory may come in.'

There is a link here with the fact that he is Yahweh of hosts,
the God of battles, who has taken this city as a victorious King.
If he dwells there in Jerusalem as the King who has conquered
his foes, this implies his enthronement there. Perhaps the people
thought of Zion as the place where heaven and earth came
nearest to each other, perhaps even that they touch each other
there, so that the heavenly throne and the throne in Zion may in
fact be one throne. For Christians, heaven and earth come closest
in Jesus (John 1:1,14, 51), himself the divine King.

In the psalms God's kingship is usually related to human
beings rather than to the natural elements. Psalm 29:10 should
probably be translated not as, 'the LORD sits enthroned over the
flood' (NRSV and NIV), but rather as, 'the LORD sat enthroned at
the [historical] Flood'.[9] It is from his throne that God dispenses

justice and executes his wrath against sin.

We might expect some important reference to Yahweh's kingship in the Egyptian Hallel (113-118), which celebrates the redemption from Egypt, and which was sung at Passover. The first (113) lays special stress on his kingship, declaring that he sits incomparably not simply in the heavens but even above them. From that exalted throne he looks on all creation and comes to the rescue of the oppressed and needy, as he did of course at the Exodus.

## Humanity as king

Psalm 8 is unique among the psalms and in the whole Old Testament in taking up the theme of human dominion over the animal creation, which is taught in Genesis 1:26-28 and which is an implication of the fact that we are made in the image of God, after his likeness. The psalm begins and ends with the extolling of God's majestic name. Most of the psalm meditates on Genesis 1. What is the status of human beings in the hierarchy of creation? It is a high one, for they rule the animal kingdom, and are 'a little lower' than God or the heavenly beings.[10]

The writer to the Hebrews applies the passage Christologically in chapter 2, asserting that what Genesis says is not now true of human beings but that it is of Christ, who was crowned with glory and honour (presumably through his exaltation and so in terms of kingship) because of the suffering of death. In him what, through the Fall, was not much more than an ideal came to full realisation on earth, and is to find fulfilment also in the 'many sons' he has redeemed.[11]

Here then is a psalm theme which is much more important than its solitary location in the Book of Psalms might suggest.

## Israel's monarch as king

There is now considerable difference of opinion as to how many psalms may be regarded as royal. Several factors need to be taken into account. Mowinckel, linking many psalms with an annual enthronement festival featuring the king, declared about a third of the psalms to be royal, but the recognition of a substantial number of royal psalms does not depend on his controversial theories.

If we restrict the number to those actually using the word 'king', these are 2, 20, 21, 45, 61, 63, 72 and 89. Psalms 110 and 144 too are obviously about a king. There are also references to God's anointed in 84 and 132.

What though if we treat seriously the Davidic ascription at the head of almost half the psalms? These show that in the minds of the editors they are psalms of the king, and can be so viewed when we are seeking to understand their function in the total pattern of the Book of Psalms. As this is a theology of the whole book, and not simply of a specific psalm, we will take the last option, but will give special weight to those showing clear signs of kingly application.

**a. The king has been established by God, the supreme king**

Psalm 2 sets the theme. The kingship is under attack. Other kings, clearly viewed as properly subordinate to him, are rebelling against the king who reigns at Zion, but their rebellion is bound to fail, for God, the supreme King, 'enthroned in heaven' (NIV), scoffs at their futile revolt. He says, 'I have set my king on Zion, my holy hill.' Here then the heavenly King underwrites the rule of the earthly one. The author of 110 also says to the king, 'The LORD sends out from Zion your mighty sceptre. Rule in the midst of your foes' (v.2). This can give Christians much confidence as they witness in the world, for their King's supremacy is ultimately unchallengeable.

The Davidic dynasty was established by divine covenant. 2 Samuel 7:11-16 is the basic passage, where God says to David:

The LORD declares to you that the LORD will make you a house. ... I will raise up your offspring after you, who shall come forth from your body, and I will establish his kingdom ... I will not take my steadfast love from him, as I took it from Saul, whom I put away from before you. Your house and your kingdom shall be made sure forever before me; your throne shall be established for ever.

A covenant is a solemn business and never more so than when it is established by divine decree. Psalms 89 and 132, which both quote it, take it very seriously. It is true that in 89:49 the psalmist says, 'Lord, where is your steadfast love of old, which by your faithfulness you swore to David?' Here though the psalmist is simply stating his perplexity at the fact that the covenant promises do not seem to be working out in his day. He is certainly not abandoning the whole idea that a solemn covenant exists, for he did not destroy or rewrite the earlier part of his psalm, in which God's faithfulness to his covenant is extolled at some length.

In two psalms the king is called God's son (2:7; 89:26, 27). Parallels may be sought in the ancient Near East, but we should follow Kraus, and be cautious in applying them.[12] Psalm 2:7 is quoted several times in the New Testament with reference to Jesus (Acts 13:33; Heb. 1:5; 5:5). Its phraseology is part of the word from heaven spoken at his baptism: 'You are my Son, the Beloved; with you I am well pleased' (Mark 1:11). The term features also in the record of Satan's tempting of Jesus which followed his baptism (Matt. 4:3, 6). It is therefore of real Christological importance.

Psalm 89:27 calls him God's firstborn, 'the highest of the kings of the earth', which inevitably reminds us of Colossians 1:18 where primogeniture and supremacy are intimately linked in the words, 'He is the beginning, the firstborn from the dead, so that he might come to have first place in everything.' The firstborn in a Jewish family had special rights and prerogatives.

## b. There was a kingly ideal
The king was a constitutional monarch, but with a constitution imposed not from below, as in some democracies, but by God himself. Deuteronomy 17:14-20 gives this divine constitution. He must be an Israelite, faithful to Yahweh, humbly concerned

to abide by his law, cherishing his liberation of the people from Egypt, not relying on military might ('horses'), and of simple lifestyle, with no concern to accumulate wives or wealth. This was a high ideal.

Eaton writes at length on 'the Ideal of the King's Office in the Psalms', and he lists no less than twenty-seven qualities of the ideal king as found in various psalms.[13] We cannot pursue this in detail here, but the reader is encouraged to study this section of Eaton's book.

The psalmists often wore their hearts on their sleeves. The kingly psalms are not exceptions to this. Every psalm is an engagement with God, even those making accusations against him. No matter what his problem, the psalmist always brings it to him. Here then is a life in which the reference of every aspect of life to God is habitual. This certainly has its lessons for the Christian reader today.

Not only should a king's personal life be godly, but his character should show in his public conduct of affairs. The Bible knows nothing of that dichotomy between private and public morals which is now so often taken for granted. It is uncertain whether 72 consists mostly of assertions or prayers,[14] but in any case it presents a most attractive ideal of kingship. Here is no harsh rule, motivated by pride and glory and materialism, but a concern for the afflicted, the weak and the needy, leading the monarch in his justice to crush their oppressors. As king, David was supreme judge in the land. Psalm 58 contains criticism of other judges[15] and therefore shows clearly his own profound concern for justice. Psalm 101 also combines personal and political rectitude, for its writer has power to deal with evildoers not only in his own house but in the city and the land.

Psalm 131 shows David's desire to remain humble and to avoid presumption, particularly remarkable in a monarch in the context of the ancient Near East. Like a weaned child that has learned to do without the breast, he will accept that he cannot have all he wants. Its final verse addresses the people, for the king is to lead them in godliness. He says, 'O Israel, hope in the

LORD, from this time on and forevermore.'

Although David never deviated from Yahweh to worship other gods,[16] he was certainly not perfect, and many of the psalms of penitence, including 51, the deepest of all, are headed, 'a psalm of David'. So even a king of such a quality as David shows us that there was no perfection until the coming of Christ, 'the Man born to be King'.

## c. The king was constantly under attack

Readers of the psalms, especially Books 1 and 2, may well feel references to enemies are over-done and that at times the psalmist seems positively paranoid. Understanding starts to come however when we notice how much space is taken up in 1 Samuel by the story of Saul's persecution of David, and in 2 Samuel by the story of his banishment from Jerusalem when Absalom reigned as usurper. Certainly David was not king when Saul was in pursuit of him, but he was king-elect, already anointed for kingship by Samuel (1 Sam. 16:13).

In view of this, the placing of 2 before this long group of psalms may be intended to reassure the reader.[17] The king will be attacked, but God will support him, for he is his king.[18] The attacks severely tested the king's faith, and we will examine this more carefully in chapter 13. There are psalms in which he looks back on experiences of great trial and praises God for bringing him out of them. In 18, after graphically describing his predicament and the way God rescued him, he says: 'You delivered me from strife with the peoples; you made me head of the nations, people whom I had not known served me' (v. 43).

When afflicted for their loyalty to Christ, Christians may find comfort and strength in God's support of their King as they share just a little of his sufferings. When they were under assault, Martin Luther used to say to his friend Melanchthon, 'Come, Philip, let us sing Psalm 46.'[19]

**The Messianic king**

The presence of so many psalms of the king in the book makes it an important part of the Old Testament for the messianic hope, for Judaism thought of the Messiah predominantly as a great king of the future.[20] No matter how this concept is modified in the New Testament by its combination with the Suffering Servant passages and model, kingship remained an important concept in the New Testament understanding of Jesus as the Christ.

In modern times there has been a widespread retreat from the idea that some at least of the psalms were written as prophecies of the Messiah. Today even conservative writers show great caution. Longman, having said that all psalms are broadly messianic in anticipating the Messiah in some way, goes on to say: 'some people, though, believe that a few psalms ... are prophetic and have no direct message of significance for the Old Testament period. They only predict the coming Messiah.' A little later, after discussing the interpretation of 16, he says: 'no psalm is exclusively messianic in the narrow sense'.[21]

This is acceptable if we give full weight to the word, 'exclusively'. Peter certainly argues in Acts 2:25-32 that the words of 16:8-11 were not true of David himself but of the Christ of whom he spoke. When we set them in their Old Testament context, however, it does seem they must have some kind of application to him. We note both a real parallel and a real distinction here, for the author was rescued either from enemies or from illness and so from the grave, while Christ was delivered from it in a deeper sense by being brought out of the tomb at his resurrection. We might compare Hebrews 5:7, about Christ praying to the one who could deliver him from death and being heard, which may be based on 22.

Then there is 110. This was applied by Jesus to himself, and he argued on the basis of a messianic interpretation of it. But did this exhaust its meaning? Perhaps, although there could be some application to David and his dynasty, because they were located in Jerusalem, the city of Melchizedek the priest-king.

The phrase 'forever' (110:4), however, certainly goes beyond the Old Testament dynasty.[22]

De Vaux's view is worth serious attention. He says:

> It has been maintained that Pss 2, 72 and 110 were at first royal psalms, and were modified after the Exile in a messianic sense; but it is very hard to say what the revisions were. It is more reasonable to suppose that these psalms, like Nathan's prophecy and other texts referring to royal Messianism, had a twofold meaning from the moment of their composition: every king of the Davidic line is a figure and a shadow of the ideal king of the future. In fact, none of these kings fulfilled this ideal, but at the moment of enthronement, at each renewal of the Davidic covenant, the same hope was expressed, in the belief that one day it would be fulfilled. All these texts, then, are Messianic, for they contain a prophecy and a hope of salvation, which an individual chosen by God will bring to fulfilment.[23]

This really combines typology, with a succession of kings, and a prophecy focusing on a specific king, in the one interpretation.

Murphy maintains that these psalms came to be reinterpreted after the Exile as messianic, because the Davidic dynasty had ceased to be represented by a ruling monarch.[24] He also asks:

> Was this merely wishful thinking? No, because of the divine promise to David in 2 Samuel 7 that he would always have one of his descendants upon the throne in Jerusalem. This promise is clearly reflected in 89:40, where it is called a *covenant* with David and it is so referred to again in Psalm 132:11. Royal messianism never faded out in Israel's difficult history. It is nourished by many references in the prophets (e.g. Amos 9:11; Hos. 3:5; Jer. 23:5-6) and especially in the so-called 'Book of Immanuel' (Is. 7-11).[25]

If De Vaux is right, then the post-exilic interpretation, which may have seemed new at the time, was actually the discovery of a deeper significance always available to the interpreter but which came into clearer focus when there was no longer a Davidic king on Judah's throne.

The way the Book of Psalms was eventually structured was calculated to foster such a hope, and it must have furnished a major part of the Old Testament's preparation for the coming of Jesus the Christ. We will examine this in chapter 15.

# Chapter 8

## God speaks to his people

Divine revelation has been much debated in modern times, especially since the first edition of Karl Barth's commentary on the Epistle to the Romans published just after the First World War, as this stimulated fresh theological thinking. Prior to the modern critical period, revelation from God was normally assumed to be verbal. There was also, of course, the concept of Christ as the living Word, but it was assumed that we have access to him only through the word written.

Since Barth, all kinds of questions have been raised. These go back at least to Kant, for they raise major epistemological issues and it was Kant, more than anybody, who set modern philosophy moving along the epistemological path. So there have been discussions on the relationship between knowing words and knowing a person, between knowing a person through his words or his deeds, and also whether a piece of literature can be said actually to be the Word of God or to contain it or to be God's Word potentially rather than intrinsically.

This has an important bearing on the Book of Psalms, not only because the concept of revelation occurs within it, but also because recent research has emphasised the teaching character of the book as a whole.

### The voice of God

Israel had heard God's audible voice at a moment of supreme drama when her tribes were gathered before him at Mount Sinai (Exod. 19, 20). The Decalogue and other legal material associated with it were to become central to Israel's conception of her relationship with him. So much of later divine revelation rested on, or developed from, or called God's people back to the Sinaitic Law. It is strange then how little reference there is to this event in the psalms, when it was fundamental to the whole concept of divine revelation to Israel.

The voice of God in this audible sense was heard also, at least three times, in the ministry of Jesus, at his baptism and transfiguration and just a few days before the crucifixion (Mark 1:11; 9:7; John 12:28), and, of course, the New Testament sees him as the supreme revelation of God (John 1:1, 14).

There are at least two references to the voice of God speaking to the people at Meribah (81:11; 95:7) and to Israel's refusal to listen to God there. This was a most significant event in the wilderness, because it revealed the attitude in the hearts of the people. It is treated in Hebrews 3 and 4 as the reason they were not allowed into the land, and so as a warning to the epistle's readers not to show the same attitude.

God's voice was heard in a different way in the natural elements. In Exodus 9:28, Pharaoh heard him in the thunder, and 77:18 speaks poetically of God as thundering at the Exodus from Egypt. Elihu too calls the thunder the voice of God (Job 36:27-37:13). The voice of the Lord which completely dominates Psalm 29 is the thunder.[1] There we trace the passage of a great storm across the country from Lebanon in the north to the southern desert. What are we to learn from this? Perhaps the power of the God of thunder (cf. 68:33,34 'listen, he sends out his voice, his mighty voice. Ascribe power to God'). Perhaps too it is a reminder of the thunder at Sinai, so that we take his word in the commandments seriously.

In some other passages, the voice of the Lord seems to be figurative for his power, for instance in 18:13 (another reference to the thunder) and in 46:6, where the psalmist says, 'he utters his voice, the earth melts.' This is not surprising, for the great power of that voice actually to execute God's plan is manifest in the creation account of Genesis 1, where so often the simple yet awesome words occur: 'And God said ... and it was so.'

Psalm 19 also features the voice of God in the created universe, but this is no longer the noise of the thunder. Indeed, depending on translation,[2] it is probably not an audible voice at all, but a revelation presented to sight rather than to hearing. For Israel revelation was so much tied to hearing and to the word that it would be natural to express it in these terms. The whole human race has had access to God's 'speaking voice' through the observable universe. Paul says something similar in Romans 1:18ff and also refers to another part of this psalm in Romans 10:8. Perhaps this psalm was one source of his thought in the first chapter of this letter.

**The word and law of God**
The term 'word of God' is important in the psalms. It is not particularly frequent, but it comes at very significant points in the book and the concept completely dominates its longest psalm.

The word of the Lord is mentioned twice in 33. In verse 6, it is powerfully creative in the formation of the world, but in verse 4 it seems to be the written word: 'for the word of the LORD is upright, and all his work is done in faithfulness.' If this is the written word, the psalmist obviously sees a connection between the word in creation and that in Scripture. This reminds us of 89:1-14, where God's faithfulness to the Davidic covenant is likened to the stable nature of the universe he has brought into being, as if to say that God's word to David is as likely to fail as the order God has established in creation. Here is a very high conception of God's written word. No wonder its wholehearted reception brings divine order into life!

God's word is contrasted with human speech, which is so often lying and deceitful and unreliable, as James says in chapter 3 of his epistle. Unlike such words, the psalmist says:

The promises of the LORD are promises that are pure,
 silver refined in a furnace on the ground,
 purified seven times (12:6).

There are three important psalms of the word of God or, more specifically, of God's Law: Psalms 1 and 19 and 119.[3] There has been some debate as to whether the word *tora* as used in these passages has its general (instruction) or its more specific (law) sense. In other words, does it simply refer in a general way to all God says to his people or quite specifically to the Mosaic Law? There is no general agreement.

Probably it meant 'Mosaic Law' for the actual author of each psalm,[4] but its wider meaning was probably in the minds of those who ultimately compiled the Book of Psalms, so that it could be re-applied in a wider way as an encouragement to read this book itself as instructional revelation from God. The legal nature of the term is not unpacked in 1 as it is in 19 and even more markedly in 119. This would then make 1 particularly fitting as a general introduction to the book. A quotation from the psalms (82:6) is referred to by Jesus in John 10:34 as being in 'your law' as well as being 'the word of God'.

In 119, the supreme *tora* psalm, the psalmist constantly rings the changes between various synonyms, although *tora* itself is the most frequent, occurring twenty-five times, including the first verse, suggesting that for him it was fundamental. He may have viewed its synonyms as providing exposition of its many-sided significance. Soll has written a thorough study of this psalm. He holds the narrower sense to be the correct one here,[5] and he contrasts the outlook of the psalmist with that of the Pharisees. He says:

> The psalm's high regard for Torah [in a post-Deuteronomic context] has led many to associate this psalm with the Pharisees. But these verses are very un-Pharisaic in view of their respect for tradition and for their own teachers ... They scarcely constitute an argument for professional teaching. It is not just that YHWH himself is the teacher in Psalm 119, but that such teaching is contrasted to the instruction of human teachers and elders within the psalmist's own community, rather than presenting human and divine instruction as complementary.[6]

He is referring here to verses 99 and 100. This reminds us of our Lord's own attitude of great respect for the written Law but rejection of 'the tradition of the elders' (e.g. Mark 7:5-8).

All three *tora* psalms show great delight in it (1:2; 19:7-11; 119:16, 35, 70, 72, 77, 97, 103; cf. 112:1), comparable with passages in the written prophets where the prophet is given the word of God – in these cases for utterance to the people – and, on 'eating' it, he found it to have honey sweetness (Jer. 15:16; Ezek. 3:3). Paul also shows delight in the Law (Rom 7:22; cf. 7:12), although in his case the context makes it clear he has the Mosaic Law and not simply divine instruction in view.

In 119, the psalmist commends the importance and value of meditating on the *tora* (119: 15, 27, 48, 97, 148). Also we get the impression from 1:2, not only that the *tora* stands in complete contrast to the counsel of the wicked (v. 1), but that it is the root cause of the fruitful life depicted in verse 3.

Is the intention, expressed several times in the psalms, to meditate on God's works and his wonders (77:12; 143:5; 145:5), itself an implicit intention to open the word of God and consider the wonders recorded there? This would be particularly significant for 77:10-20, for the language of Exodus 15 (especially vv. 11-13) appears to play an important part in the thought of the psalmist in that part of his psalm. In fact, this was probably the way God renewed his faith which appears to have been almost in eclipse in the first half of the psalm. For the Christian, the cross and resurrection of Jesus have taken the place of the Exodus as the heart of God's mighty activity and so faith's renewal can come through meditation on them.

The qualities of the *tora* are extolled both in 19 and 119, and one reason for the psalmist's delight in it is its trustworthiness. In a number of psalms the psalmist is the target of the lying and deceitful words of men (e.g. 5, 12, 140). This kind of language is so frequent, in fact, that some commentators relate many psalms to the law court, and the fear of the righteous that they will not get justice there because of the lying testimony of enemies. If, however, we accept the Davidic ascription in the headings, it is unlikely that somebody with the king's status would be arraigned before a judge in this way. These lying and deceitful words are contrasted with the true and faithful utterances of God, for example in Psalm 12, parts of which may have furnished an Old Testament basis for James 3, with its strong indictment of bad speech.

The verbal revelation is intimately related to the acts of God, especially in redemption and judgment. In Exodus both Israel on the one hand and Pharaoh and his Egyptians on the other come to know the Lord. In Israel's case it is chiefly knowledge of his redeeming love, for in Exodus 6:7 he says:

> I will take you as my people, and I will be your God. You shall know that I am the LORD your God, who has freed you from the burdens of the Egyptians.

For the Egyptians, however, it is knowledge of him as a God of judgment. In Exodus 9:14, he says to Pharaoh:

> I will send all my plagues upon you yourself, and upon your officials, and upon your people, so that you may know that there is no one like me in all the earth.

In both cases Moses acted as interpreter of the acts of God. Is this what 103:7 means: 'He made known his ways to Moses, his acts to the people of Israel'? We cannot be sure, for this could simply be stylistic variation within the poetic parallelism. The Book of Psalms is, however, itself interpretative of the acts of God in historical psalms like 105 and 106, often confirming the interpretation given in Deuteronomy and elsewhere.

## God as Teacher and Light

The word of God, spoken and written, often goes out to all within its range, without particular tailoring to the individual hearer or reader, although, of course, Christians are aware that the Holy Spirit makes it relevant to individual believers. In line with this, it has been well said that no two Christians ever hear quite the same sermon. In the psalms too God is Teacher and Guide, showing the way ahead. This idea is prominent at the heart of Book 1 where, in 23:2, 3 the psalmist affirms the guidance of God and in 32 God speaks to him, assuring him 'I

will instruct and teach you the way you should go; I will counsel
you with my eye upon you' (32:8). In 27:11 he appeals: 'Teach
me your way, O LORD; lead me on a straight path because of
my enemies.'

In this part of the Psalter, the idea is most prominent in 25,
where it governs the heart of the psalm in verses 4 to 15. As the
psalmist is in the midst of enemies, guidance and protection
become almost synonymous. He also asks for or comments on
God's teaching later in the book, as a perusal of 86:11 ('Teach
me your way, O LORD, that I may walk in your truth') and 143:8-
10 will show. Not unexpectedly, the idea is very prominent in
119.

When God is spoken of as Light (27:1), and as sending out
his light to guide his servant (36:9; 43:3; 97:11; 118:27), this is
the same idea differently presented, for God's light cannot be
detached from God himself. Psalm 18 is often regarded as
authentically Davidic even by those who accept few others, and
it occurs in almost the same words in 2 Samuel 22. One of the
few variations between the two versions is to be found in verse
28 (the psalm) and 29 (2 Samuel). The latter reads: 'Indeed,
you are my lamp, LORD; the LORD lightens my darkness', while
the former: 'It is you who light my lamp; the LORD, my God,
lights up my darkness into light.' There is an interesting parallel
here with two sayings of Christ, 'I am the light of the world'
(John 9:5) and (addressed to his disciples) 'you are the light of
the world' (Matt. 5:14).

The teaching is very practical and is often related to the
psalmist's need to be shown the right way to walk. Having
learned some hard lessons about himself from God, he then
becomes a teacher of others, showing them God's way as a
witness to his truth (51:13).[7] In 34 he seems like Solomon in
Proverbs, especially when he says: 'Come, O children, listen to
me; I will teach you the fear of the LORD' (v. 11; cf. Prov. 4:1).

Christians are often indebted to many teachers, but all truth
comes ultimately from the God of Truth, the supreme Teacher,
and we need especially to learn from him through his Word.

**The wisdom of God**

Proverbs is the main Old Testament book about wisdom, but the vocabulary and idea of wisdom is also found in some psalms. If the compilers of the Book of Psalms intended it as Holy Scripture for believing and obedient meditation, this should not surprise us.

No psalm is more like Proverbs than 37. If we take seriously its Davidic ascription, it makes us wonder how much Solomon may have learned about true wisdom from his father. Wisdom for Solomon was a gift from God, but God could have used the memory of David's teaching and example as a means to this. Wisdom is about real life, and in this psalm there are a number of references to the antagonism and violence of the wicked, yet its whole atmosphere is one of calm trust and waiting on God. The opening verses of 49 (especially v.3, 'My mouth shall speak wisdom') mark it as a wisdom psalm. The theme of worldly futility in this Korah psalm is not unlike that of Ecclesiastes.

The historical psalms present the reader with lessons from history and it is not surprising therefore to find explicit exhortations to learn from what has happened in the past (78:1-8; cf. 107:43). Our present generation often shows reluctance to learn from history.

**The prophetic dimension in the Psalms**

In recent times there has been much interest in the possibility that some psalms may contain material originating in prophetic oracles. This is linked to the view that the temple or the royal court, or both, may have had prophets or teaching priests in residence who were able to give oracles or teaching. Possibly we may discern something like this where the author makes a plea, perhaps an agonised prayer, to God, and where there is a real change with a word from God coming into the psalm. This is however somewhat conjectural and evidence falls short of proof. It certainly adds to the drama of a psalm like 2 to suggest that the words of the divine decree were actually recited by a court prophet, but we cannot be sure.

Davidson says:

> It is important not to underestimate the *teaching element* in Israel's
> worship from an early period, not simply teaching as in the recital
> of the past mighty acts of God in Israel's history or in creation ...,
> but teaching on the fundamental questions of human life with
> which the wisdom teachers wrestled. Too little attention has been
> paid to this educative function of the cult, in a context where people
> are being reminded that they are not only searching but receiving,
> not only reaching out for God but being grasped by God.[8]

## Responding to God's word

As we have already seen, the religion of the psalms is responsive.
So in principle it is not humanly created but divinely given.
Real prayer acts on the basis of God's self-disclosure. In New
Testament terms, it is activated by the Holy Spirit, as we see in
Romans 8. As George Herbert said, prayer is God's breath in
man returning to its birth.

The response needs to be not only devotional but ethical. So
the three important *tora* psalms (1, 19 and 119) each indicate
clearly that God's instruction needs to take a practical, ethical
form. As the first psalm, setting the tone for the whole psalmic
corpus, declares:

> Blessed is the man
> who does not walk in the counsel of the wicked
> or stand in the way of sinners
> or sit in the seat of mockers.
> But his delight is in the law of the LORD (1:1, 2, NIV)

So, delighting reveals itself in walking, standing and sitting,
in other words, not simply in thinking godly thoughts but living
in the light of and in obedience to God's word. As Jesus said at
the conclusion of the Sermon on the Mount:

> Everyone who hears these words of mine and puts them into
> practice is like a wise man who built his house on the rock (Matt.
> 7:24, NIV).

# Chapter 9

## God meets with his people

When most people think of the Book of Psalms, they view it as a worship manual. It was certainly this for the Jewish religious community, as also for the Christian church from its earliest days (Eph. 5:18-20). Not only have the psalms been used as chants[1] and in metrical form,[2] but many hymns and modern Christian songs show their influence. Some hymns are virtual psalm paraphrases, while others interpret psalms in terms of Christ. Take, for instance, two versions of 23. 'The Lord's my shepherd' is a simple psalm paraphrase which follows the language of the original fairly closely, while 'The King of love my Shepherd is' interprets the psalm in terms of Christ, for not only are the rod and staff there but also the cross. The psalms are not only relevant to worship but of great value for this purpose in every age and place.

The marvellous presupposition of this is that God seeks fellowship with his people, that he has made provision for this, and that, in the psalms, there is material for worship and for use in personal prayer.

Worship is an important theme in other Old Testament books also. Genesis shows us early family worship, Exodus to Deuteronomy God's prescriptions for Israel's worship,[3] 2 Samuel quotes psalms, Kings estimates monarchs largely by worship criteria, Chronicles emphasises worship in the context of Old Testament history and records some psalms, the prophets condemn merely formal, shallow and insincere worship, and one of their number, Ezekiel, tells of the new temple to come.

The distinctive worship feature of the Book of Psalms is that it gives Old Testament worship its vocal poetic content.

## Praise and prayer

This volume is called *Prayer, Praise and Prophecy* and we now address two of these elements directly. Even here though we should not forget the elements of divine revelation and inspired reflection. The Book is deeply theological and perfectly blends worship and theology.

Gunkel distinguished hymns and individual psalms of thanksgiving. Westermann described virtually the same list as descriptive and declarative psalms of praise respectively, pointing out that the declarative ones praise him 'for a specific, unique intervention' and the descriptive 'for the fullness of his being and activity'.

This means that praise does not begin with speculation about God's being and nature, nor does it take its rise from abstract conceptions of him. It is deeply moved by what God has done for his people and fashions its praise accordingly. Westermann, writing of the descriptive psalms of praise, says:

> It is speech directed toward God in the sense that it looks away from the unique occurrence of a specific deliverance and speaks of God's majesty and grace in a summarising, recapitulating and descriptive manner. But in Israel this recapitulating praise which brings together descriptions never lost its connection with the unique, concrete intervention which was experienced in the history of the people or of the individual.[4]

We might take 145 as an example. It is true that God is here praised for his greatness, goodness, faithfulness, righteousness and much else, but are these really simply abstract qualities? Hardly, for the psalmist, writing of God's greatness, goes on immediately to refer to his wonderful and awesome works. These are the evidence of his greatness. No doubt he could have done just the same in connection with the other divine attributes to which his psalm makes reference. In line with this, the New Testament focuses on God's great works in Christ and the revelation they give of his character.

Praise must be theological to be authentically Biblical. Brueggemann describes our relation to God as 'a reciprocal but not symmetrical relation', and he then says:

> It is precisely the children of John Calvin who are so clear about God's majesty, who understand praise best. He also refers to the genuinely theological character of the act of praise.[5]

Westermann makes a very important point when he says:

> The relationship of descriptive to declarative praise may perhaps help us to understand the relationship of proclamation and teaching in the church. Proclamation corresponds to declarative, teaching to descriptive, praise.... All 'dogmatics' of the church will be only development of the confession of Jesus as the Christ.

He then says:

> Theology, that is, speaking about God, statements about God, can exist only when surrounded by praise of God.[6]

Ephesians 1:3-14 provides a striking New Testament example of this, for it is theology in the context of praise. Paul begins, 'Blessed be the God and Father of our Lord Jesus Christ' (v. 3) and punctuates this passage with three references to praise (vv. 6, 12, 14). James Denney used to say that he was not interested in a theology which could not be preached. Neither should we be interested in a theology which does not lead us to praise and prayer.

The psalms constantly praise God for his acts in history, but they recognise too that he has made himself known in the natural creation. Psalm 104 extols God's greatness as seen in what he has made, although the use of Yahweh rather than Elohim (which occurs only once) reminds us that it is still the God active in historical redemption to whom he comes. Also there are many psalms which give praise for personal rather than great historical blessings.

What overflowing exuberance there is in a psalm like 98! This man cries out: 'Make a joyful noise to the LORD, all the earth; break forth into joyous song and sing praises' (v.4). Nothing less than worldwide worship of such a great and good God will satisfy his sense of what is fitting. In fact, in the closing verses he even calls inanimate elements like the sea, the floods and the hills to join in. The closing verses of Paul's great theological exposition in Romans 1-11 (11:33-36) form an impassioned ascription of praise to God, and in Romans 15:9-12 he quotes 18:49 and 117:1 ('Praise the Lord, all you Gentiles, and let all the peoples praise him') in calling Gentiles, through the gospel, to joyful praise.

This desire for all creation to engage in praise finds expression in a number of psalms and most comprehensively in 148, where the psalmist calls both the heavens and the earth to praise the Lord. Such invocations are in fact major utterances of faith. The post-exilic community must have been aware of its numerical insignificance. They knew too of the strong commitment to paganism of other peoples, and yet they visualised the whole world with all its nations uniting to praise their God. No doubt the disciples of Jesus, faced with the challenge of worldwide evangelisation, will have warmed to such visions of a world worshipping the one true and living God, and many a missionary must have taken heart from them.

The psalms also show us the people at prayer. In some, the writer utters petitions on behalf of the whole community (e.g. in 74), but many are individual prayers. There is a major concentration of these in Books 1 and 2, many of them obviously stemming from the psalmist's own devotional experience. They often arose from representative situations typical of the people's spiritual life, and so could be used more generally. Their worship potential was recognised in the larger religious community by their incorporation in the Book of Psalms. Their value for Christian prayer is enhanced because in them truth is always expressed in devotional form.

These psalms are very honest. Their authors talk frankly to

God about their concerns, not only with enemies and trouble, but with his own government of the world (26:1, 11; 22:1; 44:23, 74:1). Murphy says, 'The psalms form the heart of Israel's prayer. In fact they are a "school of Prayer" in the sense that they teach one how to pray.... The variety of the Psalms conveys the entire range of human emotions before God.... Prayer is not simply asking for things: it is the varied expression of the human condition in the presence of God.'[7] He says too, with reference to the imprecations, 'One does not pray simply in order to cultivate "pious thoughts," or in order to enter an unreal world that is not shadowed by human sinfulness. Prayer is best geared to reality, which is imperfect and sinful.'[8] We will be examining many of them in chapter 10.

Prayer is not stereotyped here. Craven has well said:

> The psalms are not one hundred and fifty models of the most correct or most perfect ways to pray. Their 'rightness' about prayer is not in their individuality, but rather in a pattern their totality suggests. As a whole, the psalms legitimate multiple modalities of conversation with God, and model the 'rightness' of every voice that speaks in faith to God.[9]

This was worth saying, for the fact that everything about priesthood and sacrifice was made the subject of strict regulations might make us wonder if there was any room left for spontaneity. Here it is, where it is most to be valued, in individual prayer, and this encourages us too to 'take it to the Lord in prayer'.

## The holy hill and the sanctuary
This was a busy area, with constant activity, with communal and individual acts of worship and prayer going on, and there was much to see and hear in terms of sacrifices, playing, singing and dancing. It was however a somewhat different world from the modern Christian church, even though there is some overlapping. Incidentally, there were basic festivals of the family

which were not held there but in a home environment.[10]

How should worshippers come? People were set apart for offering sacrifice (the priests) and doing other work connected with the temple (the Levites). So, when the psalmist asks:

> O Lord, who may abide in your tent?
>     Who may dwell on your holy hill? (15:1),

we expect the answer to be in terms of genealogical qualifications. There is however no reference to these but rather, in line with the prophets with whom the psalmists have so much in common,[11] to moral and spiritual qualifications. Here then are the true worshippers:

> Those who walk blamelessly and do what is right,
>     and speak the truth from their heart;
> who do not slander with their tongue,
>     and do no evil to their friends,
>     nor take up a reproach against their neighbours (15:2, 3),

and so on.

Psalm 24 takes the same approach. Again there is a question:

> Who shall ascend the hill of the Lord?
>     And who shall stand in his holy place?

and the answer is:

> Those who have clean hands and pure hearts,
>     who do not lift up their souls to what is false,
>     and do not swear deceitfully (24:4).

In both these psalms, we are reminded of the words of Jesus: 'Blessed are the pure in heart, for they will see God' (Matt. 5:8).

Some writers, notably in psalms attributed to Levites, show great wistfulness for the house of the Lord at Jerusalem. A Korahite psalm likens the psalmist to a deer panting for streams of water (42:1), and his desire to be at God's house and to meet with God appear to be identical ways of saying the same thing. This shows an attitude in which worship was no mere formality, but rather a real means of grace to those worshipping in spirit and truth, the kind of worship of which Jesus spoke to the woman of Samaria (John 4:21-24). Psalms 63 and 84 strike the same kind of note.

Even after Jerusalem and its temple had been razed to the ground and rebuilt, the psalms of Zion were still sung. As Hayes puts it:

> The Zion theology was not smothered in the ashes of Jerusalem. It was transposed to a new key.... The Zion psalms with their marvellous claims and promises were not discarded but were no doubt sung in anticipation of the new, the true, the ideal Zion to come. These psalms are undoubtedly part of the background to the picture of the new Jerusalem in Revelation 21,22, the perfect place of worship under the new covenant, which will have no temple because 'the Lord God Almighty and the Lamb are its temple' (Rev. 21:22).[12]

Here is perfected worship which takes up the old terminology but goes beyond it.

## Festivals and fasts

Form criticism takes much interest in public occasions for worship because they tend to be somewhat stylised. This was not however true of their content. There are two large collections of psalms which were sung at the Pilgrim Feasts, the Egyptian Hallel (113-118), sung especially at the Passover, and the Songs of Ascents (120-134).

These two groups may have been chosen from a much larger number of psalms, for there are certainly others which refer, for instance, to the redemption from Egypt. Is there a thread of consecutive meaning running through each series? Possibly, and if objective criteria for such an understanding of them could be identified and agreed, such a study would be very profitable, even giving some pointers to the way Christian services, especially special celebrations, might be structured. What we can see quite clearly in both series is that the hearts of the people of God were full of joy as they celebrated the redeeming love and redemptive acts of their God.

Psalms 42 and 84 refer to the delights of pilgrimage. The latter is especially interesting as its expressions of longing to be in the temple at worship are combined with a representation of the people on pilgrimage and their strength and joy as they set out to do God's will by going to worship.

Zion Psalms like 46, 48, 76, 87 and 125 centre in Jerusalem and its temple as the place where the true God is worshipped,[13] and they too were probably often sung by the crowds who thronged the city at festival times. Some of the more martial psalms like 18, 68 and 118 may have been sung after great victories, such as those that occurred during the Maccabean struggle. Also, of course, there would be worshippers at the house of God every day, bringing their sacrificial animals as offerings to the Lord.

The Pentateuch provides for one communal fast day, the Day of Atonement, its regulations given in Leviticus 16. No doubt some penitential psalms would be sung then. Laments such as 44, 60, 74, 79, 80, 83, 85, 89, 90, 137 would probably be sung on some of the fast days associated with the destruction of Jerusalem by the Babylonians, which are referred to in Zechariah 7.[14] Some individual penitential psalms would be very suitable for those coming to make sin and guilt offerings.[15] They can still give words to a conscience made sensitive to sin by the Spirit of God.

## The engagement of the whole person in worship

True worship is the response of all that I am to all that God is, or at least to God as he revealed himself to me. We see in the psalms how the whole person was engaged in the praise of the great God of Israel.

Worship has an emotional dimension. Real praise comes from the heart (Isa. 29:13), whether it is joyful (98) or profoundly penitent (51). The psalms show us deeply felt worship. In 103:1 the author calls everything within him to engage in the Lord's praise and in 150 every available musical resource is put to service for this purpose. How joyful God's praising people were when they came before him! One writer says:

> Praise the LORD.
> How good it is to sing praises to our God,
>> how pleasant and fitting to praise him! (147:1, NIV; cf. 92:1-4).

We see too that worship has a physical dimension. All kinds of postures and physical gestures are referred to, as a perusal of the following passages will reveal: 24:3; 42:4; 47:1; 63:4; 95:6; 107:22; 150:3-5. Confronted with such variety, it would be difficult therefore to prescribe any one form as mandatory for our worship.

Worship also has a volitional dimension. As we have already noted, it expresses 'all my inmost being' (103:1). Worship is not simply what we do when we come together at the house of God, but is co-extensive with life itself. As 40:6-8 affirms, it means not simply the making of a tangible offering, but the surrender of our wills: 'I delight to do your will, O my God; your law is within my heart' (40:8). How deeply demanding this could be is shown in the Epistle to the Hebrews, where the writer quotes this passage and shows its fulfilment in the sacrificial death of Christ.

The compilers of the book *Hymns and Psalms*[16] wrote in their preface: 'Hymns and Psalms have been in the past, and still are today, distinctive features of Christian worship. They unite the intellect, the emotions, the will and the voice, in the human response to God's grace, and they also point beyond our human faculties and abilities, for God addresses us in them, and through them applies the good news of Jesus Christ to our lives.'

# Chapter 10

## God distinguishes his people

Who are the people of God?[1] The question is of major importance because the psalms are all about relationships, for they are concerned with real life and that is what life is about. The Book of Psalms is a prayer and praise book, and both are relationship matters. So, for instance, in 22 we find references to trusting God (vv. 4, 8, 9), praising him (v. 22), honouring and reverencing him (v. 23), fearing him (vv. 23, 25), seeking him (v. 26), bowing down before him (v. 27), worshipping him (v. 29), serving him (v. 30) and declaring his name and his righteousness (vv. 22, 31), and the psalm is of course compounded of prayer and praise.

In fact it is doubtful whether the psalms say anything about God that is not in the context of relationships, either explicitly or by implication. To the psalmists he was not an abstraction, more akin to the God of the philosophers than of the patriarchs and of Christ, as Pascal would have put it. Certainly he is eternal and exalted, but he is not abstracted from either time or space, but deeply involved at every point in the story of his people.

The Book of Psalms, like the rest of the Old Testament, is the product of faith. It is the virtue of Childs that he has emphasized that the canon is the literary corpus of a faith community. So even when the psalmist is sceptical, as in parts of 77, this can never be his deepest nor his ultimate attitude, for he is a believer.

### Israel and the nations
Israel is God's special people, specially related to him, chosen by him, brought into a covenant relationship with him and experiencing him in his acts of redemption and chastisement. He created this nation for himself, brought them out of the fiery

crucible of Egypt, gave them a land to live in, spoke to them, blessed them, chastised them, ejected them from the land and yet still did not forsake them but brought them back to it. Christians too are chosen in Christ and brought into a new covenant through his redeeming death, and they too may experience chastening if they go astray. All this comes to them from the same God, who in the fulness of time sent his Son to bless them and others through him and them.

Israel's distinction from the nations as God's own people does not mean that all Israelites were looked on with favour by God. Certainly they had special privileges. Whether godly or ungodly, they were heirs of all God had done in making their nation his people: they enjoyed liberty from Egyptian bondage; they lived in the land with all its material blessings; the Old Testament means of grace were available to them – although God's displeasure at abuse of these privileges is patently clear in passage after passage.

**Godly and ungodly, righteous and unrighteous**
The concept of two ways, those of the godly and ungodly, is not confined to the psalms. It runs right through Proverbs and is also important for the prophets, where the ungodly are seen not only to be foreign nations antagonistic to God's purposes but also those in Israel who refuse to hear God's word. The godly are not simply worshippers of Yahweh, but those who are concerned to live in the light of his revelation. They will not go after other gods, and, for all his imperfections, David is treated in the Books of Kings as the exemplary king, for he was never an idolater.

The theme is really woven through the whole Bible story and all its literary genres from Genesis 4, the murder of Abel by Cain, onwards. It comes to its dramatic and profoundly moving climax in the story of the passion and death of Jesus, a story with strongly paradoxical elements, for it was deeply religious men who were his chief antagonists.

In the Old Testament there is no real difference between

godliness and righteousness on the one hand and ungodliness and wickedness on the other. In the psalms righteousness is grounded in relationship with God. The concept of righteous but ungodly people is quite alien to the Old Testament in general and so to this Book in particular. Paul too links ungodliness and unrighteousness very closely when he says:

> For the wrath of God is revealed from heaven against all ungodliness and wickedness of those who by their wickedness suppress the truth (Rom. 1:18).

The fundamental religious and moral distinction of the righteous and the unrighteous is clearly laid down in the very first psalm. If there is a theological rationale in its present arrangement, this distinction is quite fundamental to the book's whole theme and purpose. In 2 the distinction becomes Messianically orientated. The terms, 'godly and ungodly', are not used in it, but it is clear that the rebellious rulers of verses 2 and 3 are fundamentally ungodly. These rebellious kings are called to repentance, which, it is implied, will save them from wrath. These two psalms are fundamental to the whole book. It is sobering to find 2 applied in the New Testament to an alliance of ungodly rulers and deeply religious Jews (Acts 4:25-28).

Psalm 11 has points of similarity with 1, especially in verses 4 to 7. God's discrimination between the righteous and the unrighteous here is grounded in his own character, for, the psalmist says (v. 7): 'The LORD is righteous, he loves righteous deeds; the upright shall behold his face.'

The two ways are strongly presented in 14-17, which appear to have been arranged to expound this theme. Psalm 17 virtually summarizes 14-16. Here is aggressive evil, as in 14, directed against total commitment to God, as in 15 and 16. Here too is the certainty of awaking from death to find oneself in God's presence, as in 16. How completely all this was fulfilled in Christ's experience and his triumph over death!

The godly have been set apart by God for himself, with the

important consequence that he hears their prayers (4:3). So the psalmists engage in a prayer-life in which they bring everything, even their complaints about him, into his presence. Godliness and prayerfulness necessarily belong together, for godliness is based on confidence in God, and this finds expression in prayer.

What then of ungodliness? The psalmists never represent it as mere indifference. The nearest we get to this is the assertion by 'fools' that there is no God (14:1 and 53:1), really a kind of practical indifference to God, probably even more offensive to him than theoretical denial of his existence. Also in 94:7, the psalmist represents the wicked as saying, 'The LORD does not see; the God of Jacob does not perceive.' Even here, however, the remainder of the psalm shows this to be a cover for very active and aggressive wickedness against God's servants, for, the psalmist says: 'they band together against the life of the righteous, and condemn the innocent to death' (v. 21). The ungodly are essentially active and aggressive in their wickedness. There are no grounds in the psalms for a merely privative view of sin.

Throughout much of the first two books (and the idea is not absent elsewhere) the antagonism of the wicked to God is focused on the king. This is what 2 leads us to expect. If the king represents the centre of God's purpose for Israel and the world, as we see in that psalm, then the reader should not be surprised to find this.

This antagonism is implacable and bitter. The picture given in 52 (related in the heading to the antagonism of Doeg the Edomite) is fairly typical. Here the wicked man is boastful, with a destructive tongue, and loving evil rather than good. So we see a further feature of ungodliness, for instead of trusting in God this man 'trusted in abundant riches, and sought refuge in wealth' (v. 7). It is not simply that he was an unbeliever (in the normal biblical sense of the term), but that his faith was placed in something other than the true and living God, just as in some psalms it is idols which are the misplaced confidence of the ungodly (e.g. 135:15-18). In fact, in every age it is true that if people refuse to believe in the true God they never simply believe in nothing. Always they find some supposed substitute.

The ungodly are anything but wise, for true wisdom is a quality of God and of the godly, but they do have a certain shrewdness, a cunning and an ingenuity which makes them resourceful in their plotting against the psalmist and others who stand for the Lord's purposes. They are deceitful and they do a great deal of plotting. All this comes into full view in the Second Psalm (v. 1; cf. also 21:11). Here we see this happening on an international level, and the same kind of thing emerges also in 83, where nation upon nation (see vv. 5-8) is allied against Israel. These plots sometimes seem to succeed, but these psalms also show that they are doomed to fail, for God will judge the plotters.

Sin has a social quality. It is not just a matter of isolated individuals refusing God's will, but there is a kind of community of sin, rather as 'the world' is viewed in the Johannine literature and Babylon in the Book of the Revelation. In 1:1, the succession of the words, 'counsel', 'way' and 'seat' implies that evil thinking, which leads to evil living, can have a malign influence on others, so that the way of sin keeps spreading.

Is there then no hope for the wicked? Not if they continue in their wickedness, but sometimes they are exhorted to repent and serve God. This is clear in 2:10-12, which ends with a call to rebel rulers to repent in response to God's word and to submit to the king, his vicegerent. New Testament gospel preaching sounds the same note. So Paul, preaching the gospel of Christ, declared that 'God ... now commands all people everywhere to repent' (Acts 17:30).

Do the psalmists ever claim to be totally without sin? On the face of it, it seems so. In 26, the writer not only claims he does not associate with evildoers but also that he washes his hands in innocence (vv. 4-6). A claim to perfection? It is difficult to read it that way. If the compilers of the Book of Psalms[2] understood it this way, why did they put it together with 25? Both psalms are attributed by them to David, and yet in 25 the psalmist asks God not to remember the sins of his

youth and to forgive his iniquity which, he declares, is great
(25:7, 11). If they had understood 26 in terms of perfection, the
contiguity of the two psalms must surely have offended their
sense of fitness!

In 26, the writer says: 'Vindicate me, O LORD, for I have
walked in my integrity, and I have trusted in the LORD without
wavering' (v. 1). If the first of these assertions is defined by the
second,[3] then David is claiming what the Books of Kings claim
for him, consistent faithfulness to the one true God. That book
even says he did only right in God's sight (1 Kings 14:8), despite
the fact that the writer must have known of his character flaws.
Scripture puts great emphasis on commitment to the one true
and living God.

This is what the psalmists seem to be claiming: they are
committed to God and his purposes and standards. In 143:1, 2,
the writer calls God to come to his relief, and he says:

Do not enter into judgment with your servant,
    for no one living is righteous before you.

Sinless he is not, but God's servant he is, so he can call on
God in this way. Again, in 18:20-24, the key sentence seems to
be, 'I have ... not wickedly departed from my God.'

We may perhaps compare what John says in 1 John 3:9,
'Those who have been born of God do not sin', while the writer
also says, 'If we say that we have no sin, we deceive ourselves
and the truth is not in us' (1 John 1:8). Here is a decisive break
with sin, a wholehearted commitment to God, a refusal of the
ways of evil, the marks of true godliness in both testaments and
in every age.

## Friends and enemies

We have noted the preoccupation of many psalms, especially
Davidic ones, with enemies. The Bible is a realistic book and
nowhere more so than in the psalms. The psalmists knew this
world to be the scene of a conflict, and that God's will, such a

delight to the godly, is rejected and strenuously opposed by others. So then to commit oneself to God is to become an enemy of God's own enemies.

Mowinckel held that the enemies in the psalms were sorcerers, but he has not convinced most other Old Testament scholars, as it is not easy to find clear references to the use of evil magical powers. Normally they are presented simply as plotters trying to engineer the psalmist's downfall, or hunters intent on destroying his life, or accusers telling lies about him. Perhaps in this last case, they tried to pursue their aims through judicial procedures, although this is unlikely if the Davidic psalms are in fact by David himself, as it is difficult to think the king was subject to the judges when he was himself the supreme judge in the land.

Psalm 1 simply sets the two ways side by side, while 2 shows the rebelliousness of the wicked and their antagonism to God's servant, the king. In this psalm they are rebel kings, but it is not easy to view the enemies of God and of the psalmists as exclusively non-Israelite. In 55, the writer's own close friend joins the ranks of his enemies. His speech is as smooth as butter but there is war in his heart (v. 21). There are psalms related to Saul's pursuit of David (e.g. 59) and also to Absalom's rebellion (3), while one other (7) is about Cush, a Benjamite. Each of these refers to his enemies, and so those who gave these psalms their headings must have realised that the enemies referred to would need to be understood to be Israelites.

This brings us to the difficult issue of the imprecatory psalms. In these, the psalmist curses his enemies or asks God to judge them. Zenger, whose book deals specifically with them, selects 12, 44, 58, 83, 109, 137 and 139 as representative (1996). There are also brief imprecatory elements in many other psalms and it is difficult to read the Psalter consecutively without coming across such elements fairly frequently.

It is striking that they sometimes occur in psalms where the authors show deep spirituality. What a shock we get, for instance, when in 139:17-19 we find the writer saying:

How weighty to me are your thoughts, O God!
　　How vast is the sum of them!
I try to count them, they are more than the sand.
　　I come to the end – I am still with you,

immediately followed by:

O that you would kill the wicked, O God,
　　and that the bloodthirsty would depart from me.

Perhaps this very feature may give us a clue to help us understand them. The psalmist loves and praises God, and he cannot tolerate the thought that there are people working against God's purposes and refusing to give him the glory he deserves. Such people are not fit to live, and so he expresses this in imprecatory fashion. C. S. Lewis points out that this goes beyond anything in Greek, Latin or Norse paganism, because the worshippers there did not care enough. He says that absence of anger in the presence of evil is a very disturbing thing, and so it is.[4]

Zenger has well said:

When those who pray call to their God as the righteous judge, they avert 'vengeance' from themselves.... They appeal to a God who, as the God of justice, considers, decides, and punishes, this last not out of pleasure in punishment, but in order to restore and defend the damaged order of law.[5]

What often prevents us from viewing such psalms aright is the fact that in them the enemies referred to are not simply foes of God but also of the psalmist. If he was truly committed to God, so becoming the object of their hatred, God's enemies and his were the same people. This may help us with 137, the most difficult of them all. Here the last two verses are truly horrifying, for the psalmist says:

O Daughter of Babylon, you devastator!
  Happy shall they be who pay you back
  what you have done to us!
Happy shall they be who take your little ones
  and dash them against the rocks.

It is difficult to read such words without a shudder. Candidates for the post of Old Testament specialist at one theological college were required at their interview to provide an interpretation of this passage, because it was felt to be the most difficult in the whole Old Testament.

Zenger deals in detail with the problems of this psalm,[6] and he says:

> Psalm 137 is a political psalm: It deals with the end of Babylon's reign of terror. This is also important with respect to the image of the children of the daughter of Babylon, who are to be smashed against the stone pavements of the capital city. 'The children' are those of the royal house, that is, of the dynasty (cf. Isa. 7:14-16; 9:1-6). The horrible image means to say that this dynasty of terror ought to be exterminated completely ('root and branch').[7]

Remember too that the Hebrew tended to concretise much that others would present less vividly. This is most valuable for the way it engages the imagination, but here the modern reader's imagination can hardly cope with what is being presented to it. Such a reader would prefer a more general statement like, 'It will be just and right when this evil Babylonian dynasty has come to its end,' but, as we do not have this, we need to ponder what message the shocking words are intended to convey, and it is virtually this in more concrete form. Keel, writing of the same language, says: 'The inhabitants of the oppressor-city or the children of the ruling dynasty concretise the continuation of the unrighteous empire.... In this vein, one might translate, "Happy is he who puts an end to your self-renewing dominion".'[8]

Such passages, difficult as they are, have the virtue that they stab us awake, forcing us to think deeply about God and his ways.[9] How many readers of the Gospels must have been stimulated to deep thought about the meaning of the cross by the awful question of Jesus, 'My God, my God, why have you forsaken me?' (Matt. 27:46; Mark 15:34)

# Chapter 11

## God protects his people

How often the psalmists seem to be in danger and cry out to God to save them! This is a strange feature of the psalms for modern western Christians, most of whom live in relatively unthreatening situations. Novels have been described as 'real life, with the boring bits left out'. The same may be said of biography, and a great many of the psalms are biographical. There is certainly nothing boring here, for the psalmists often write under pressure, especially from their foes. No wonder the psalms often mean so much to Christians in lands where the open confession of Christ may carry severe penalties!

Not surprisingly, there is a plenitude of graphic imagery in such psalms. For instance in 124, the enemy is an all-engulfing torrent, a ravenous beast, a fowler's snare. As we will see, the images of God's protection are similarly graphic, often reflecting the natural and cultural background of the psalmists.

This is particularly true of those attributed to David. When he was on the run from Saul, he must have become well acquainted with hiding places in the rough terrain of Judah. He had a second spell as a fugitive when Absalom reigned as a usurper in Jerusalem. It is not easy to link many of these psalms with recorded incidents in his life, but not difficult to take their ascription to him as authentic, especially in Books 1 and 2, as so many would fit this general background very well. The heading to 57, for instance, relates the psalm to 'when he fled from Saul, in the cave'. He must have felt just like a bird or animal pursued by hunters, as the psalm indicates. Psalm 142, another 'cave' psalm, uses the same sort of language.

### Geological imagery

The term 'rock' occurs quite often and is used in various ways. Sometimes it appears to be a rock to hide in (71:3, 'Be to me a rock of refuge'), perhaps with the cave of Adullam (1 Sam. 22:1) or the rocks at En-gedi (1 Sam. 24:1-3) in mind. At others it is the high rock, desirable because difficult of access and because it puts the foe at a disadvantage (61:2, 'Lead me to the rock that is higher than I'). Sometimes the rock is presented as a divine provision, but much more often God is himself his Rock of refuge (19:14; 28:1; 31:2, etc.). God uses means to secure his people's safety, but their trust should not be in the means but in the God who provides them.

This kind of imagery occurs elsewhere in the Old Testament, with Deuteronomy 32 as the classic passage. Rocks would have been important for the people wandering in the 'howling wilderness waste' (Deut. 32:10), not simply to shelter from enemies but from the merciless desert sun. Not only so, but historical events were connected with rocks and with the divine provision (Exod. 17:6,7; Num. 20:1-13; cf. Ps. 95:8,9). It is not surprising therefore that the Rock became a standard image for God as Protector and Provider. Paul applies it to Christ in 1 Corinthians 10:4, although more with the thought of provision than of protection.

## Political, social and occupational imagery

Israel's God entered into covenant with them, and covenant-language is also used of his promise to David of a lasting dynasty. This kind of language, because probably based on the suzerainty treaty model common in the ancient Near East, would itself imply protection, especially if based chiefly on Hittite rather than Assyrian models, for the Hittites offered protection in return for a vassal's faithfulness. Longman points out that although only twelve psalms explicitly use covenant language and only two (89, 132) have covenant as a central theme, yet the psalms in general speak out of the context of covenant.[7] This means God as King is like the great king of the treaties, and the Law is like the treaty stipulations, while Psalm 1 refers to blessings and curses, which were always included by the Hittites in their treaties with their vassals.

The word normally translated 'steadfast love' in the NRSV and 'unfailing love' in the NIV[2] occurs sometimes when the psalmist feels under threat. For instance, in 6:4 he is suffering in some way and is deeply aware of his personal sinfulness, and he says, 'Deliver me for the sake of your steadfast love.' In 31:16 he invokes the same steadfast love when threatened by his enemies, while in 44:26, in a psalm of the sons of Korah, the nation's deep concern that God has apparently surrendered them to their enemies is expressed in a poignant cry which combines covenant and redemption language in the words, 'redeem us for the sake of your steadfast love'.

The family was important in Israel, as in all ancient eastern societies, and the divine revelation took up elements in the family concept to illustrate spiritual truth. A kinsman was to act as redeemer when the land of a family member, which was viewed as a family possession, or even that person's personal freedom, had to be surrendered to others because of poverty.[3] When God is called Redeemer this means that, as the God of Israel, he virtually treats his people as his kin, and takes their part to secure their freedom.

So God is not only the psalmist's Rock but his Redeemer (19:14). The redemption referred to is normally from captivity or danger or trouble (25:22; 77:15; 107:2). In the New Testament, redemption language is taken up into atonement theology, so that it is predominantly from sin and by means of the sacrificial death of Christ.[4] This combination of ideas is infrequent in the Old Testament, but is found occasionally in the psalms. Psalm 130:7, 8 identifies full redemption as redemption from sin. Here then the psalmist recognises that there may be a deeper danger than that posed by human foes, and from which God may give deliverance. Psalm 34:21, 22 too seems to relate to redemption from sin. Here the psalmist says:

Evil brings death to the wicked,
  and those who hate the righteous will be condemned.
The LORD redeems the life of his servants;
  none of those who take refuge in him will be condemned.[5]

The image of a shepherd was immediately meaningful to the Jewish reader of the psalms because of the pastoral setting of the Holy Land. It was a picture of provision, care and guidance but also of protection, for wild animals were always looking for food and sheep were utterly defenceless against them. In conversation with Saul, David argues his fitness to fight Goliath from his early shepherding experience of fighting lions and bears when defending his sheep (1 Sam. 17:33-37).

The Old Testament often uses this imagery for the leaders of the people,[6] who were charged with responsibility for their care. Often they are accused of negligence and self-seeking.[7] Perhaps there is a suggestion of implied contrast with them in a psalm of Asaph in the words, 'With upright heart [David] tended them, and guided them with skilful hand' (78:72). This reminds us of the way the Books of Kings use David's faithfulness to God as a yardstick for measuring the quality of later monarchs.

Just as God is the great Redeemer, so he is also the supreme Shepherd. In the Davidic Psalm 23:1, the writer says, 'The LORD is my Shepherd'. God gives him food in the very presence of his enemies, thought of perhaps as hungry wolves looking on helplessly while the armed shepherd, maybe using their fear of a fire, sees that his sheep can feed in safety (v. 5). In his role as Shepherd of his people the psalmists sometimes appeal to God to save them, as in 28:8, 9 and 80:1, 2, where the psalmist says,

Give ear, O Shepherd of Israel,
    you who lead Joseph like a flock! ...
Stir up your might,
    and come to save us!

Jesus applies this imagery to himself in John 10, with special emphasis on the shepherd's protecting role. As Deliverer he lays down his life. There may be a suggestion of the shepherd role too when he called the tax-collector, Zaccheus, and said, 'The Son of Man came to seek out and to save the lost '(Luke 19:10), especially as Luke had already recorded the parable of the lost sheep (Luke 15:1-7).

## Military imagery

Psalm 68 commences with an echo of Numbers 10:35, 'Let God rise up, let his enemies be scattered.' The ark going in front of Israel was a symbol of God the warrior and 68 is full of military language and the sound of battle. Here God is on the offensive, bringing his people from Sinai, the mount of God, through the desert and settling them in Canaan, with the ark at last finding rest at Zion, another great mount of God (cf. 132:6-8).[8] In Ephesians 4:8, the ascent to Zion is seen to typify Christ's ascension, after his victory over his foes at Calvary, which led to the giving of the Spirit at Pentecost.

The term, 'Yahweh of hosts', is distinctly military,[9] and its origin has been variously linked with God's command of Israel's forces or of the angelic armies. In the psalms it usually occurs in the Zion group in passages like 24:10; 46:7; 48:8 and 84:1, 2, 12. Psalm 59:5 is an exception. Its heading relates it to an incident in David's early life and it appears in a context where David is asking for deliverance from his enemies.

The shield was important in a soldier's defence, so its figurative application to God in his defensive role is no surprise. It is one item in a whole series of military images in 18:2 and 144:2. It can only protect the warrior from attack at the front, but two psalms speak of God as a shield right round his people, suggesting his protection is more comprehensive than that of any literal shield (3:3; 5:12). 'Shield' is often linked with another word in a twofold designation of God as 'my strength and my shield' (28:7), 'help and shield' (33:20), 'sun and shield' (84:11) and 'my hiding place and my shield' (119:114), but it is not easy to suggest a reason for this.

Terms like fortress and stronghold (18:2) probably refer to rocky caves, like the cave of Adullam, and so would have a geological flavour, but they also suggest places regularly used for military purposes. The tower, however (61:3) will be purpose-built for use in war. Such a tower still standing in Jericho is one of the world's oldest buildings and must have been well made.

## Imagery from the animal kingdom

In the Old Testament (e.g. in the visions of Daniel) the horn is a symbol of strength and is so employed in some psalms (e.g. 75:4, 10; 132:17), but in 18:2 it is God who is the psalmist's horn of salvation. This suggests perhaps a wild animal or bull standing guard over its family and using its horn to protect them.[10]

The sheltering wings of a mother bird, protecting her young from predators, are employed in connection with divine protection, as in 63:7, where the psalmist says:

> for you have been my help,
>     and in the shadow of your wings I sing for joy.

The psalmist links this to dwelling in God's tent (61:4), and this suggests that he may have temple sanctuary in mind, with the tent standing for the temple and the wings for the cherubim. Adonijah sought and found sanctuary there (1 Kings 1). Might this have been suggested to him from his father's own references to the wings of the Lord in some of these psalms?

Jesus employed this analogy when referring to the hen in Matthew 23:37. He speaks of gathering the vulnerable under his wings. Most surprisingly, the reference is not to his disciples but to the people of Jerusalem, although the Bible has many surprises for the reader, especially in terms of the grace of God.

## The imagery of light and shade

Sometimes very different and even opposite images may illustrate the same basic truth. This is found in the New Testament when birth and adoption are both used to illustrate God's acts when someone becomes a Christian. Normally one is not born and adopted into the same family!

Light is perceived to be a protection, for to go out at night without a light is to court danger. Light brings a measure of security and assurance and this feature of it seems to be in view in 27:1: 'The LORD is my light and my salvation; whom shall I fear?' Jesus spoke about people walking in darkness and promised his disciples they would have the light of life (John 8:12).

There are circumstances, however, when the sun may pose a threat, as in 121:6, 'the sun shall not strike you by day'. In such a case, the psalmist desires shade and he finds this in the Lord. So the contrasting imagery of light and shade serve to represent the divine protection.

## Religious and historical imagery

Creach has shown how important is the theme of refuge in the Book of Psalms.[11] So important does he see it to be that he has explored its use, not only in particular psalms, but also as a key to the actual arrangement of the book as a whole.[12] He takes 11 as a key psalm and on the basis of it sees that the place of refuge is often the sanctuary that can be found in God's house.[13] His research will be taken into account in chapter 15.

In 61, David is away from home and he seeks safety in God. He uses several different images of security and the word 'tent' may suggest wistful longing for God's house in Jerusalem, for God's dwelling place among his people was in fact a tent during their wilderness wanderings.

Psalm 18 is more often regarded as authentically Davidic than is any other, and much of it is dominated by David's experience of divine rescue. Not only is there great variety of imagery reflecting the psalmist's experience, but God coming to the rescue of his servant is described in ways that call to mind Israel's history. In verses 7-15 we are reminded of great events like the Exodus (v. 15, 'the channels of the sea were seen'), the Sinai theophany (references to thunder, lightning and clouds) and perhaps also God's intervention in the Valley of Aijalon (v. 12, 'hailstones and coals of fire'; cf. Jos.10:11). The psalmist is saying that his rescuer was the God of Israel, being faithful to his character and showing that he has not changed since the days of the fathers. All the power of the Almighty One revealed in these great past events was now focused on that one man, to rescue him from danger. What great encouragement for the individual Christian!

## The psalmist's appropriation of God's protection

It is impressive to find how many images are marshalled within a few verses. This often shows the intensity of the psalmist's prayers or praises and functions as strong emphasis. Here then is the objective basis for his strong confidence in God as his Protector.

The shape taken by the life of faith in the experience of any one believer is determined by his or her personal circumstances. As Hebrews 11 shows us, Noah built an ark, Abraham left one country for another, Moses brought the people out of Egypt and Joshua led them into Canaan. David too is mentioned in Hebrews 11, but not with clear reference to details of his life (Heb. 11:32ff.). If the writer had gone into more detail, what would he have highlighted? Perhaps David's experience of God's protection.

The psalmist needed to place his confidence in God. If God provides a tent, he must take refuge in it (61:4). What in fact we see him doing in psalm after psalm is calling on God for help, and in 18 especially this help comes in the most convincing of fashions. It is in prayer that we express our confidence in God our Refuge, and our experience of God's answers to prayer makes that confidence stronger and stronger and becomes, as in David's case, an important part of our testimony to God's faithfulness.

# Chapter 12

## God judges and blesses his people

It may be truly said that a human being is the sum-total of his or her attitudes. Relationships between people are certainly all about attitudes and nothing could be more important when we are thinking about God and our relationship with him. The gospel is really a call to those who hear it to come into a new attitude, a faith relationship, with God. In this chapter we are thinking about the witness of the psalms concerning God's own attitude to his people and the consequences for them which follow from this.

### God as Judge of his people

God is the great Judge of all he has made and everybody is responsible to him for his or her actions and attitudes and will have to face his judgment in due course. In Scripture, however, judgment is not exclusively a divine function, although it is supremely so, and all other legitimate judges are so only because he has given them this office. So the theme occurs at times when the king is viewed as judging, or when reference is made to other human judges. For instance 72 is dominated by the picture of a king ruling with a deep and practical concern for justice. Psalm 101 too is deeply impressive, for in it the writer, called David in the heading and with very obvious judicial responsibilities, solemnly commits himself to justice and spells out this commitment in some detail. Predominantly, however, judgment is seen in the psalms as an activity of God himself. In 76:8, 9 he dispenses justice from heaven and in 89:14 righteousness and justice are the foundation of his throne.

### a. The nature of his judgment

It may seem strange to link judgment and blessing together in one chapter, but it would not have seemed so to the people of the Old Testament. There judgment and blessing are often two sides of one coin.

Judgment does not refer only to an adverse verdict or to condemnation merited by guilt and leading to punishment. God's judgment is the product of his righteousness or justice, and this means he will put things right where they have been wrong, so that in many cases this will mean that those denied proper justice from human beings receive it from God. For them therefore justice is transformed into blessing, and can even be synonymous with it. It should not therefore be assumed that the judgment about God's people will always be adverse.

In 98, when God reigns in the world, this results in joy for its people but also judgment, as the psalmist says:

> Let the sea roar, and all that fills it;
>     the world and those who live in it.
> Let the floods clap their hands;
>     let the hills sing together for joy
> at the presence of the LORD, for he is coming
>     to judge the earth.
> He will judge the world with righteousness,
>     and the peoples with equity (vv. 7-9).

Here judgment and joy are by no means mutually exclusive, for the first is productive of the second.

Of course, there are places where judgment and blessing are opposites, as for instance in 129. Here the psalmist does not actually use the terminology of judgment, yet he does call on God to act against wrongdoers when he says:

> May all who hate Zion
>     be put to shame and turned backward ...
> while those who pass by do not say,
>     'the blessing of the LORD be upon you' (129:5, 8).

Psalm 96 is a joy-filled praising psalm, and we see that when God comes to judge the world, both the heavens and the earth will rejoice. All has been put right and so the creation, which came in perfection from God's hand, can rejoice once more. 1 Chronicles 16 quotes this psalm in connection with the triumphal entry of the ark into Jerusalem, which was a kind of foretaste of this judgment, just as the Transfiguration was of the resurrection of Jesus. In this psalm the earth is called to praise him.

In fact not only the human creation but the heavens and the earth, with all that is in them, will sing his praise when he comes to judge, as the New Testament declares Christ will do. In one of the most solemn passages in the whole Bible, the judgment of Babylon, the symbol of humanity organised in opposition to God, is greeted by a great paean of praise from a great multitude in heaven:

> Hallelujah!
> Salvation and glory and power to our God,
> for his judgements are true and just (Rev. 19:1).

God has put all things right and so he receives praise for this.

In 140, the psalmist expresses confidence in God's justice, including his championing of the poor and needy. In a sinful and greedy society this is often the acid test of true justice. Mason says:

> A God who never judged could never be the ground of trust nor the deliverer of the poor and oppressed. For the Old Testament this is an attribute of God which is at the heart of faith, worship and hope.[1]

He says it is surprising to us to find the idea of God as Judge given such a welcome in the Old Testament, e.g. in 50:6 and 94:2:

> The belief that God is the ultimate and faithful judge who is determined to establish *mishpat*[2] in society is a source of constant joy in the Old Testament. No evil-doers are too strong to oppose

him. No one can deceive him nor blur his judgement by bribery. He will champion the cause of the poor and needy. His justice is perfect, his judgements all-wise. For the widow, the orphan, the poor and the immigrant, the God who is judge is in a real sense the God who is their deliverer.[3]

That Yahweh is a God of justice might appear to be denied by experience. Otherwise why do so many psalms cry out to God for justice? In 10:1 and 12, for instance, the psalmist cries out:

Why, O Lord, do you stand afar off?
    Why do you hide yourself in times of trouble? ...
Rise up, O Lord; O God, lift up your hand;
    do not forget the oppressed.

In such psalms believers are facing experiences that might not have been expected in a world governed by a just God, although sometimes in the same psalm they express their confidence in his justice. So, after the words just quoted, the psalmist goes on to say (v. 14):

But you do see! Indeed you note trouble and grief,
    that you may take it into your hands;
the helpless commit themselves to you;
    you have been the helper of the orphan.

Increasingly the hope is expressed that he will establish full justice at some future time when all will be put right and so will show how deeply founded is his moral order, as in 96:10:

The world is firmly established; it shall never be moved.
He will judge the peoples with equity.

In 1:6, the psalmist says:

For the Lord watches over the way of the righteous,
 but the way of the wicked will perish.

This should not be mistaken for facile optimism, as verse 5,
which is logically connected with verse 6, shows that it should
be understood eschatologically:

Therefore the wicked will not stand in the judgment,
 nor sinners in the congregation of the righteous: for ....

The regular use of psalms which have this kind of conviction
in worship must have reinforced this hope in the hearts of those
who sang them.[4] The call to him to rise up in judgment (9:19;
82:8; 12:5) is a call for a kind of realised eschatology in which
the God who will put all right at the end is asked to do so here
and now.

This is still an issue in the New Testament, as we see in
Revelation 6:9, 10:

I saw under the altar the souls of those who had been slaughtered
for the word of God and for the testimony they had given; they
cried out with a loud voice, 'Sovereign Lord, holy and true, how
long will it be before you judge and avenge our blood on the
inhabitants of the earth?'

That book too makes it abundantly clear that in judgment God
will put all things right.

## b. God as the Judge of the world and of the nations
He is the Judge of the heavens and earth, which implies of course
that he judges all the personal inhabitants of both realms, that
is, the angels and the human race. This concept of God as the
universal Judge can therefore be broken down into two spheres.
  Psalm 82 has sometimes been applied to God judging angelic
judges, presumably those who have fallen out of fellowship
with him. If so the term 'gods' is used here as a true plural

employed of them because of their superhuman status. On the other hand, the psalm may be about human judges who have been granted, in their work, one of the prerogatives of deity, although of course, without divine standing.

The psalms call God to judge the enemies of Zion, as in 83 and 129. A purpose of this is to 'let them know that you alone, whose name is the LORD, are the Most High over all the earth' (83:18). This was the way Pharaoh and the Egyptians knew the Lord, for they too experienced his judgments (Exod. 9:14). Sometimes, as in 149, Israel and its people are the very instruments of God's judgment on the nations.

### c. God as the Judge of Israel
Psalms 105 and 106 are companions. Both survey Israel's early history, but while 105 sees it as a record of God's faithfulness, 106 views it as the story of Israel's unfaithfulness and ingratitude. This psalm gives some examples of the Lord's displeasure and of the judgments that fell on Israel as a result of it.

Psalm 90:7-11, part of a psalm entitled, 'a prayer of Moses, the man of God', sees the life of the people as being lived under God's anger. This cannot be a reference to mankind as a whole, at least in such a way as to exclude Israel, for the psalmist goes on to say: 'Turn, O LORD! How long? Have compassion on your servants' (v. 13). Perhaps it was written when God was showing his displeasure with the people by some specific act or acts of judgment.

The anger of God against his people because of their folly, shown in a bad harvest, is the subject of 85, and the psalmist calls out to God to show favour to them once again. God says he will faithfully dwell amongst them in glory and give them good harvests.

### d. God as the Judge of individuals
Psalm 1 makes it clear that the wicked will be subject to strong and destructive judgment by God. The righteous have the

strength and stability of an evergreen tree, but the wicked are just like chaff and they will not stand in the judgment. A substantial number of psalms contain prayers for judgment on enemies. In 140, for instance, the psalmist asks God to frustrate the plans of his enemies and to judge them. We have looked at some of the problems connected with these in Chapter 10.

The heading of 52 connects it with the antipathy of one man, Doeg the Edomite, against David. David says he is sure to face judgment, which will encourage the righteous, while he himself will flourish in God's house like an olive tree.

## God as the dispenser of blessing to his people

### a. This is confidently asserted

There are many benedictions in the psalms, e.g. in 1:1; 2:12; 32:1, 2; 41:1; 33:12; 23:8; 40:4; 65:4; 84:5; 89:15; 94:12; 112:1, 2; 119:1; 128:1. These almost invariably relate to God's blessing on individuals or on those in the nation with a particular character.[5] So these psalms are in line with the fundamental psalm of blessing which commences the book. In its final verse, the psalmist says: 'For the LORD watches over the way of the righteous, but the way of the wicked shall perish' (1:6 NIV). Although blessing is only for the righteous (18:19-27), it can be the portion of those formerly under God's wrath for rebellion, for 2 follows a call for repentance with, 'Blessed are all who take refuge in him' (2:12 NIV).

In what does this blessing consist? In 1 an analogy is employed. The tree, with its resources of refreshment, its production of fruit and its evergreen foliage, symbolizes the prosperity of the righteous. Jeremiah seems to take up this language in Jeremiah 17:5-8.[6] Joseph in Genesis 39:2-5 is a good illustration of this principle. So we can see that there is a special providence of God for the righteous: 'The LORD watches over the righteous' (1:6 NIV).

God's blessing comes because he looks favourably on the person he blesses. In 4:6-8 the psalmist says:

There are many who say, 'O that we might see some good!
   Let the light of your face shine on us, O Lord!'
You have put gladness in my heart
   more than when their grain and wine abound,
I will both lie down and sleep in peace,
   for you alone, O Lord, make me lie down in safety.[7]

If the Book of Psalms has an overall plan and the first two psalms are a joint introduction to the whole book, the offer of blessing in both is surely significant. The reader is learning that the way of experiencing blessing is to walk in God's ways and not to rebel against him or his appointed king.

The New Testament too contains many benedictions, beginning with the Beatitudes (Matt. 5:1-12). In a staggeringly comprehensive expression, Paul says that God 'has blessed us in Christ with every spiritual blessing in the heavenly places' (Eph. 1:3) and again, expressing the same thought without the actual language of blessing, he says: 'you have come to fullness in him' (Col. 2:10)

### b. It may result in prosperity but this is not invariable

Prosperity is an important Biblical theme, and there are several prosperous godly people in the Old Testament. These include Abraham and Job, and in the book that bears the latter's name, we note his material prosperity both before and after his profound experience of suffering. Deuteronomy promises the whole nation prosperity in a good land if they will be faithful to God and obey his laws.

This theme also occurs in the psalms. In many the blessing of God is conceived in terms of prosperity. Psalm 128 is an example of this, for in verses 1 to 4 (NIV) the psalmist says:

Blessed are all who fear the Lord,
   who walk in his ways.
You will eat the fruit of your labour,
   blessings and prosperity will be yours.
Your wife will be like a fruitful vine
   within your house;

your sons will be like olive shoots
    round your table.
Thus is the man blessed
    who fears the LORD.

Is this true to experience? Sometimes the psalmist says it is. For instance, in 37:25, 26, he declares:

I have been young, and now am old,
    yet I have not seen the righteous forsaken,
    or their children begging bread.
They are ever giving liberally and lending,
    and their children become a blessing.

This is the kind of passage quoted by present-day prosperity theologians. There is, however, another side to the matter. Sometimes blessing for the psalmist is linked with adversity. This seems to be the case in 4, where he faces the antagonism of his foes and yet asserts that God has given him great joy and that he would lie down in peace. At other times however the problem is really deep and the complaint goes up that it is the wicked, not the righteous, who appear to be prospering. In 73, the psalmist tells us this was a real trial for his faith:

Such are the wicked:
    always at ease, they increase in riches.
All in vain I have kept my heart clean
    and washed my hands in innocence.
For all day long I have been plagued,
    and am punished every morning (73: 12-14; cf. Job 21:4-21).

In his case he got a new perspective on things when he went into the sanctuary of God and perceived their end (73:17).

At other times there is delay in God's action to put things right and deliver those who face sore trials. The prosperity comes, but not immediately. It often comes in answer to prayer, and prayers in the psalms are based on the special relationship the people had with their covenant God, with all that meant for access to him. So the fundamental blessing of the covenant, which was of course a spiritual one, was the source of so much more. So we can give plentiful Old Testament documentation for the promise of Jesus, when, speaking to his disciples about their basic needs of food, drink and clothing, he assured them:

> Your heavenly Father knows that you need all these things. But strive first for the kingdom of God and his righteousness, and all these things will be given to you as well. So do not worry about tomorrow (Matt. 6:32-34).

Studies of the overall structure of the Book of Psalms may help us here. Psalm 1 sets the scene for all that follows, showing the two ways of godliness and of ungodliness and expounding them very much in terms of prosperity theology. So we have the illustrations of the fruitful evergreen tree and the light insubstantial chaff. Indeed, it is actually said of the righteous, 'in all that they do, they prosper.' Then this psalm ends with the words:

> For the LORD watches over the way of the righteous,
>     but the way of the wicked will perish.

What are we to make of this in the total context of the book? A superficial understanding of it is challenged immediately, for the king of 2 has to face the machinations of the wicked, but (and this is important) God promises his support. Then, from 3, we are launched into two books of the Psalter which major in adversity, and yet it is evident that the one suffering it is normally viewed as a godly and righteous man.[8] This then balances the prosperity teaching.

As the whole book draws towards its close, it becomes more and more a book of praises, and in 145:18-20, we read:

> The LORD is near to all who call on him,
>   to all who call on him in truth.
> He fulfils the desire of all who fear him,
>   he also hears their cry, and saves them.
> The LORD watches over all who love him,
>   but all the wicked he will destroy.

Here then, as in 1, we are assured that God watches over his people, but there is also recognition that there are times when they need to call on him for salvation.

It looks as if 1:6 should be understood eschatologically, and as if the many psalms of adversity and deliverance have an exegetical function in this respect. Blessing and prosperity will be the portion of the godly, but not necessarily immediately. The God who has spoken, however, may be trusted, for his word is always faithful and true.

When we turn to the New Testament, we find that the only perfect Man, who might have been expected to enjoy the greatest prosperity, in fact endured the greatest affliction and the profoundest suffering. The Fourth Servant Song (Isa. 52:13–53:12), so often quoted and alluded to in the New Testament with reference to the sufferings of Christ, commences with words of strong assurance (Isa. 52:13),

> See, my servant shall prosper;
>   he shall be exalted and lifted up,
>   and shall be very high.

So the resurrection and exaltation of Jesus are the ultimate guarantee to us of the faithfulness of God.

# Chapter 13

## God refines his people

The New Testament gospel calls men and women to respond in faith and it is clear that there can be no salvation without it. There is nothing arbitrary in this, for faith is basic to all personal relationships. There is no purely objective way that another person's reliability may be guaranteed to us. We may learn something from his or her face and speech and general demeanour, and from information we have about his or her history, especially in relations with others. Ultimately however decisions about trusting others are based on our personal estimate of their trustworthiness.

Because of its basic character it is not surprising that faith is a theme of great importance in the psalms. Seybold discusses two important verbs, one meaning 'to flee to the protection of' and the other 'to rest in or on',[1] as important for the Book of Psalms and as representing faith now in dynamic, now in static, terms.[2]

The psalmists however often express their trust in God without using either term or any equivalent. There are typical examples in 3 and 4, where the writer, beset by foes, shows his faith because he is able to sleep, knowing that God is watching over him. In 2:12 and 5:11 one of the verbs does appear, when the psalmist encourages others to flee to God's protection. James Barr's criticism of an approach to theology which concentrates mainly on terminological study and analysis was never more apposite,[3] for throughout the Book of Psalms there are countless passages with an atmosphere of confidence in God without the use of the specific terminology of faith.

Childs has emphasized that the Old Testament canon is a body of faith literature expressing the confidence of the Old Testament believing community in its God. This is certainly true of the psalms. Every one must be a faith product, even when they ask the deepest of questions, reflecting the greatest of problems in the psalmist's mind. This is because faith and problems may co-exist. Nowhere does Scripture promise us that all our problems will disappear if only we will believe. As in the rest of the Bible, the faith of the psalmists is not speculative but based on God's self-revelation. If it rests on God, it is because it rests on truth revealed by God about himself.

Brueggemann makes a helpful distinction, which owes much to Paul Ricoeur's thinking. He distinguishes psalms of orientation, disorientation and reorientation, with some psalms showing more than one of these features.[4]

Orientation psalms affirm or rejoice in the stability of things as God has ordered them, whether this is the stability of the physical universe or of the moral order or of God's purposes for his people. 'God's in his heaven; all's right with the world,' might sum up such psalms.

Psalms of disorientation are quite different. They do not rejoice; rather they agonize. They raise questions about the order of things, questions based on the brute facts of life. They may even deny that such order exists and they cry out, 'Why?' Book 3 is practically dominated by such psalms, but there are many of them too in other parts of the Psalter.

Psalms of reorientation are based on the conflict between the sentiments expressed in the other two types. Here the psalmist looks at life with all its problems. He does not sweep the problems under the carpet, but asserts by faith that such conditions are not ultimate, that God has a purpose of restoration in which the world will be different and God's will done on earth as it is in heaven.

Can anything be of greater personal, preaching or pastoral value than a Biblical book containing all these elements?[5] The Epistle to the Hebrews, although deeply theological, was written with an important pastoral end in view, and its writer loved the psalms. He appears to be operating with this threefold distinction in Hebrews 2:5-10 with reference to Psalm 8. God's original order for human beings, revealing his glory and given dominion over the animal creation, cannot now be seen. Jesus, however, experienced in his death the ultimate in disorientation, but is now crowned with glory and honour, the earnest, the pledge and foretaste, of many sons coming to glory. This is in fact the story of the whole Bible.

### Faith's commitment to God, his revelation and his order

In a psalm of orientation, faith's object is God, his truth and the order he has established. Such psalms are of different kinds.

Some speak of creation, such as 104 and 19. They often stress order, as Genesis 1 itself does both by its statements and its ordered pattern. In 19 a section about God's creative work is followed by one on the Mosaic Law, as if to emphasise the importance of order both in the natural and moral realms. Psalms 74 and 89 both come out of a situation of national anguish. This is almost palpable in 74, where the psalmist says:

> the enemy has destroyed everything in the sanctuary.
> Your foes have roared within your holy place;
>     they set up their emblems there.
> At the upper entrance they hacked
>     the wooden trellis with axes.
> And then, with hatchets and hammers,
>     they smashed all its carved work.
> They set your sanctuary on fire;
>     they desecrated the dwelling-place of your name,
>     bringing it to the ground (vv. 3-7).

In 89, the Davidic dynasty faced apparent eclipse. But, as Seybold has pointed out, in both 74 and 89 faith rested on what antedated both temple and monarchy, the created order of things ('You have fixed all the bounds of the earth', 74:17; 'your faithfulness is as firm as the heavens' 89:2).[6]

Other psalms dwell on God's great act of redemption from Egypt. Virtually all the historical psalms begin there, although some go back to Abraham. It is surely significant that after the close of Book 3, in which we so often see faith under attack, it is a psalm of Moses (90) with which Book 4 begins. Faith's confidence in the Davidic dynasty may have taken a knock, but the believing community reminds itself that their God is the God of Moses and the Exodus.

There are also psalms of the moral order. This is how the Book of Psalms begins, with its indication in 1 of the two ways and the consequences of walking in them. Psalm 15 stresses the spiritual requirements of worship at God's house. Every psalm which tells of blessing for the righteous or judgment for the wicked is a psalm of moral order.

We do not have to characterize this, as Brueggemann does, as originating in the common theology of the Near East.[7] It stems rather from God's own disclosure, for this strong moral order needs the Old Testament revelation of ethical monotheism as its basis. It is because God is who he is that the moral order is what it is. There may be points where the common theology and the Old Testament theology of divine order coincide, for there are basic concepts of God which make discourse about him and the witness of Israel to the nations possible, but there will also be important points of difference.

## Faith's experience of life and its apparent disorder

The Old Testament knows nothing of private religion or a hermit life. The psalmists lived the life of faith in the real world, with all its pressures. This means that faith at times found itself battered and had to come to terms with the apparent conflict of divine revelation and personal experience. Because of this, the psalms can help us when we face such situations.

About one third have been classified as psalms of individual lament, the majority occurring in the first two books, plus about eight or ten others in which it is the community which laments in God's presence. The recognition that the psalms of lament are important, for understanding not only the whole Book of Psalms but also the theological content of the Old Testament as a whole, is a growing point of Old Testament theology at this time. This has highlighted too the lament element elsewhere in the Old Testament.

Westermann's work has proved germinal in this regard.[8] Stimulated largely by his writings, a whole group of scholars has been working in this field, and significant work has been done by such as Kraus,[9] Gerstenberger,[10] Broyles[11] and, most especially, Brueggemann.[12]

What did the psalmists do when they faced problems? They sought God. As we have seen, to trust often means, 'to flee to the protection of', and this assumes the presence of some kind of threat. Not only so, but even when a psalmist is utterly perplexed almost to the point of disillusionment, as in 88, he still comes in prayer to God.[13] Murphy says:

> Psalms 39 and 88 seem to be the most forlorn, with little hope expressed. Yet one must realise that these are prayers brought before God, even if in a given instance the psalmist is without enough spirit to voice the confidence which moved him to compose the prayer.[14]

In some psalms even expressions of disillusionment occur, as in 77, especially verses 7-9, where the psalmist asks:

> Will the Lord spurn forever,
>     and never again be favorable?
> Has his steadfast love ceased forever?
>     Are his promises at an end for all time?
> Has God forgotten to be gracious?
>     Has he in anger shut up his compassion?

These questions turn out to be a stage on the way to a new confidence, born out of the troubles and trials expressed in the psalm, for there is a dramatic change of mood at verse 11 and the reader can see the psalmist's faith being re-established.

Many of these psalms are not simply laments but complaints,

for the psalmist talks to God about his problems with God's ordering of things, yet it is noticeable that even here it is to God he comes. Brueggemann says:

> It is remarkable that Israel's rage against God did not drive Israel away from God to atheism or idolatry, but more passionately into prayer addressed to God.[15]

We find the same kind of thing in the Confessions of Jeremiah, especially when he accuses God of deceiving him (Jer. 20:7-18). Moreover, Broyles is right when he says:

> A lament psalm is not a lamentation. It does more than bemoan current hardship. It seeks change. As H Gunkel notes, 'The aim of the lament is to attain something from Yahweh.'... A lament psalm is primarily an *appeal*. Interpretation of lament psalms must therefore explore how these psalms form an appeal.[16]

The reason for the problem or the suffering is often not clear, but this may increase the personal and pastoral value of such psalms, as, in our different circumstances, we may still identify with the psalmist.[17] Not only so, but we cannot always be sure whether he is writing literally or figuratively. Was he literally drowning in Psalm 69 or is this simply the language of a man in desperate need of help? In this case it is probably the latter, but often there can be no certainty. Hayes says:

> Images and descriptions drawn from a wide range of distress situations can be employed to present one's dire circumstances. This means however that such descriptions cannot always be taken literally.[18]

What then did the psalmists have to face? Many different threats to an ordered life. We will briefly survey these, highlighting particular psalms which express them.

They sometimes faced *danger*. Its cause is usually the psalmist's enemies, as, for instance, in 3 and 7. For years David lived with danger, chiefly in two periods of his life, as a fugitive from Saul and during Absalom's rebellion. The two periods were different, of course, for the second was a punishment for his sin, but, as a penitent sinner who was promised a continuing kingship, he knew that even at this time he could trust God to protect his life. In 3 his foes are after his blood and taunting him for his trust in God, but he goes on trusting. His trust is great enough to give him sleep. In 7 there is another factor, false accusation, so that divine salvation here includes true judgment.

They sometimes faced *defeat*. At times this was military, as in 44, where the psalmist finds this perplexing as he is not aware of national sin, and he calls on God to come to the people's aid. Sometimes it is moral, as in 51, the classic penitential psalm. Here he acknowledges his transgression, sees the Godward quality of his offence, recognises his sinful nature, and cries out to God for mercy. It is worth noting that this psalm found a powerful echo in the hearts of men like Augustine and Luther, showing that it was not only a means of grace for those who were under the old covenant.

There are psalms of *doubt*. The psalmist's experience in 73 seems, for example, to contradict the assurance of 1. He did not voice his doubts to others but took them to God. People who encounter doubt sometimes forsake worship, but this is just when we need to come to God and find the orientation to him which worship brings.

There are also psalms of *depression*. Psalms 42 and 43 appear to have been one unit originally. The psalmist is deeply depressed, and this depression seems circumstantial rather than clinical in nature. His enemies are making the most of it. As in 73, he too looks to God, and he confronts himself realistically and calls on himself to hope in God. Christians too need to be realistic, for depression can come into the life of believers today and they need to face it in the same way as this Old Testament believer, but with even greater assurance because our hope is in Christ.

Sometimes the psalmist is troubled by *delay*. In 13 he has three problems. He has inner sorrow and outward enemies, but over and above these was the fact that God did not seem to be intervening. Nevertheless he turns to God and asserts his trust in him as the God of the covenant.

Most awful of all was the experience of *dereliction*. The profound 22 presents a situation where the sufferer experiences both physical suffering and social ostracism and antagonism, and in which he has no feeling whatever of God's presence. Nevertheless even in this situation he addresses God, for the psalm opens with the words, 'My God'. The use of the possessive pronoun expresses a conviction of relationship despite the total lack of any sense of God. No Christian can read it without reflecting on the experience of Christ, who took its opening words on his lips while hanging on the cross.

We may make some comparisons with the Old Testament Wisdom literature, with Job, Proverbs and Ecclesiastes, as well as the so-called Wisdom Psalms themselves. It has often been pointed out that the great salvation events of Israel's history are notable by their absence from this literature. Now the principle of salvation history, a term first coined by von Hoffman and much used in the past one hundred and fifty years, is a principle of repetition. God the Saviour shows his saving power in a succession of events within Old Testament history and, ultimately in Christ's cross and resurrection. This means that the Old Testament almost views God's actions as predictable. Perhaps the classic passage for this is Judges 2, for the next fourteen chapters are, in a sense, simply so many illustrations of the theme set out in that chapter. Yet, of course, there are mysteries in God's providential dealings with his people and the wisdom literature addresses these,[19] as do the Wisdom Psalms and, moreover, the whole Book of Psalms as canonically arranged.

**Faith looks to God to give deliverance or restore order**

Gunkel identified a number of psalms as individual thanks-givings. Westermann preferred to call them psalms of declarative praise.[20] Remembering that the psalms were used in corporate worship, the comment of Seybold seems appropriate, when he says:

> Their purpose was thanks for an experience of deliverance, and praise for the deliverer in the presence of the community ... Both can be a lesson for all who hear, and this is why the element of reporting plays such an important role.[21]

In some psalms an initial complaint gives place to praise, as for instance in 13, where the complaint of verse 1: 'How long, O LORD? Will you forget me forever?' gives way to the joyful affirmation: 'I will sing to the LORD, because he has dealt bountifully with me' (v. 6)[22] Westermann comments:

> It should be noted that the grief over which the suppliant is lamenting, and for the removal of which he pleads with God, still remains. During the praying of these Psalms no miracle has occurred, but something else has occurred. God has heard and inclined himself to the one praying; God has had mercy on him.[23]

He adds later:

> This group of heard petitions becomes a powerful witness to the experience of God's intervention, intervention that is able to awaken in the one lamenting, while his sorrow is materially unchanged, the jubilant praise of the God who has heard the suppliant and come down to him.[24]

Here faith is refined through experience that is taken into the presence of God. Without doubt the writer received an assurance, like Paul, that God's grace was sufficient for him and that his strength was made perfect in weakness (2 Cor. 12:9).

What actually happened in such a situation? Some scholars

think that such a person, coming to the temple at worship and pouring out his lament, received an assurance from God through the priest.[25] We cannot be sure of this, and it may simply have been that resting on God in faith was used by him to bring a personal inward assurance to the individual concerned. All the objective evidence from the past of God's reliability would be available to the psalmist in such a situation. An examination of 77 shows this happening in practice.

We conclude this chapter with two most appropriate comments by Westermann. Writing of the psalms of declarative praise, he says: 'It is astonishing ... that this category, as far as I can see, is developed so richly and fully only in Israel,' and he adds later that Luke 1:46-55, 1:68-75 and 2:29-32 show us 'that declarative praise was again awakened when God performed the decisive, final deed of salvation for his people in the sending of his Son'.[26] *How could it possibly have been otherwise?*

# Chapter 14

## God fulfils his purpose for his people

Both Biblical testaments look both backwards and forwards, the New back to Christ's first advent and forward to his second, the Old back to the Exodus from Egypt and forward to the eschatological fulfilment of God's kingdom. In this respect, as in many others, the Book of Psalms certainly merits Luther's description 'a Bible in miniature'.[1] It is the forward orientation which now concerns us.

### Yahweh as the universal God

There is a strong universal element in the Book of Psalms, and no suggestion that there is any other 'god' who can challenge Yahweh's absolute sovereignty. This is especially evident as the book moves towards its close. If Book 5 was compiled after the Exile and if Book 4, although probably older as a compilation,[2] was given its place in the developing Psalter during the Exile, this is very impressive, for the post-exilic community was not large and yet its God claimed dominion over the whole world. This fits in well with the fact that the post-exilic Books of Chronicles start with Adam, thus linking Israel's story with that of the whole human race. It would be spiritually helpful for local churches today, especially small ones, to have something of that breadth of outlook.

Psalms 93, 97 and 99 all commence with the simple yet far-reaching statement, 'The LORD is king' (*cf.* also 96:10), and it is clear from their contents that this statement brooks no modification. The whole of creation and all the nations are his. This is true too of the group of praise psalms which concludes the whole book. It is he who is the Maker of heaven and earth (146:6), his name alone which is exalted (148:13).

## Humanity, its glory and its judgment

Psalm 8 commences and concludes with the worshipping exclamation, 'O LORD, our Sovereign, how majestic is your name in all the earth!' The psalmist expresses amazement that such a God, the majestic Creator of the immense heavens, should concern himself with human beings (v. 4, 'what are human beings that you are mindful of them, mortals that you care for them?'), and yet he has, making them little lower than the heavenly beings and crowning them with glory and honour. Now glory is an attribute of God himself, and yet it is used here of humanity.

Psalm 144:3 is quite a contrast with 8. In it the words, 'O LORD, what are human beings that you regard them, or mortals that you think of them,' are followed by, 'They are like a breath, their days are like a passing shadow.' The two psalms taken together present a picture of humanity, very weak and vulnerable and yet with a great destiny from God. Psalm 90 has a similar polarity, for the God who is the dwelling-place of his people in all generations also created human beings from the dust. They are not simply weak and temporal, however, but also sinful, and this psalm has much to say about the anger of God against sinners.

Here then is a most balanced doctrine of humanity.

## Israel and the nations

Like the rest of the Old Testament and indeed the whole Bible, the Book of Psalms combines particularism and universalism. There is no doubt about either God's particular love and care for Israel[3] or his concern that all nations should worship him (e.g. 96).

The nations worship idols (96:5; 115:2-8). They, or at least a group of them,[4] are conspiratorial rebels against Yahweh (2:1-3). It is clear in some of the laments that the enemies of the psalmist are pagan nations. Psalm 9 is particularly strong, for in verse 5 the writer says, 'you have rebuked the nations; you have destroyed the wicked,' and in verses 17-20, closing the psalm, he says:

The wicked shall depart to Sheol,
all the nations that forget God. ...
Rise up, O LORD! Do not let mortals prevail;
let the nations be judged before you.
Put them in fear, O LORD;
let the nations know that they are only human.

This note continues almost to the end of the Book of Psalms, for in 149:6-9 it is said to be the glory of all God's saints that they execute his vengeance on the nations and his punishment on the peoples.

## The universal worship of Yahweh as true God

God's judgment on the nations and their paganism is frequently asserted, but this is only one side of the story. Not only do many psalms, especially in Books 4 and 5, call on all the nations to worship the true God, but we see from time to time clear indications that he has a gracious purpose for them. This is in line with the promises to the patriarchs that all the nations would be blessed through them (Gen. 12:1ff, etc.).

The reader of the Book of Psalms who gets used to the idea of Israel as God's chosen nation, finds some surprises. In 87, just as in Isaiah 19, surely one of the most remarkable chapters in the whole prophetic literary deposit, alien peoples are welcomed into relationship with God. The names amaze us, for Rahab (Egypt) and Assyria, the old and the new oppressors, are there, plus Philistia and Tyre as well as Cush (Ethiopia) to represent the remoter peoples.[5]

Psalm 47, although less detailed, is no less wonderful. Early on there is a particularistic note, for the psalmist says, referring to the people of Israel, 'He subdued nations under us, and peoples under our feet' (v. 3), but as the psalm reaches its climax in verse 9, we read:

The princes of the peoples gather
as the people of the God of Abraham.

For the shields of the earth belong to God;
  he is highly exalted.

Here subordination has been transformed into equality. This is in full accord with what Paul has to say, when opposing the Judaizers, about the inclusion of the Gentiles as children of Abraham (Rom. 4:11; Gal. 3:6-9).

This universal note is frequent in the New Testament, where it occurs in two forms. For instance, in the Book of the Revelation there is a picture of the redeemed as being from 'every tribe and language and people and nation' (Rev. 5:9), while it is expressed in Revelation 11:15 ('The kingdom of the world has become the kingdom of our Lord and of his Messiah') in a passage which shows that the establishment of this kingdom also involves judgement on sin. The proclamation of the gospel is the necessary, divinely-ordained means to the gathering of a church from all nations, and Christ sent his disciples out to commence this task, which as yet still awaits complete fulfilment.

Facing a task unfinished, that drives us to our knees,
A need that, undiminished, rebukes our slothful ease,
We who rejoice to know Thee, renew before Thy throne
The solemn pledge we owe Thee, to go and make Thee known
                                    (Frank Houghton).

## Life after death

The Book of Psalms does have a personal eschatology, although this is not as articulate as that in the New Testament, for Christ's resurrection has now shed a great flood of light on life after death. The Hebrew word *She'ol*, which designates the place of departed spirits, occurs in a dozen or so psalms. This is not surprising, for it is associated with personal destiny beyond death and so many psalms are strongly personal. It has been variously rendered, but most modern translations, including NRSV, often simply transliterate it.

It is portrayed in terms which make it appear most

undesirable, for in 18:5, for instance, David says, 'the cords of Sheol entangled me; the snares of death confronted me.' In 116:3, the psalmist says:

> The snares of death encompassed me;
>> the pangs of Sheol laid hold on me;
>> I suffered distress and anguish.

Is he representing *She'ol* itself as a place of sorrow and pain, or is he expressing rather the pain and anguish experienced by somebody still living but apprehensive because of the apparent imminence of a cruel and untimely death? We cannot be sure. There can, however, be no doubt that the psalmists have no wish to depart and go there. This is so different from the outlook of Paul in Philippians 1:21-23, where he says:

> For me, living is Christ and dying is gain.... My desire is to depart and be with Christ, for that is far better.

In 6:4, 5, for instance, David prays:

> Turn, O LORD, save my life;
>> deliver me, for the sake of your steadfast love.
> For in death there is no remembrance of you;
>> in Sheol who can give you praise?[6]

It is often said that *She'ol* is for the wicked and the righteous without distinction and that it was not until the inter-testamental period that places for the wicked and for the righteous after death were differentiated. This has, however, been strongly challenged recently by P. Johnson. Writing of the Old Testament as a whole, he argues that *She'ol* is predominantly a fate appropriate for the ungodly rather than the godly. He says:

> Psalm 9:18 is typical: 'The wicked shall depart to Sheol, all the nations that forget God.' These reprobate are often described in

general terms, as wicked, or sinners, or the foolish rich, or scoffers, or nations that forget God. Some are named Israelites: Korah and company, Joab and Shimei, while others are national enemies: the king of Babylon, the Egyptians and many other foreign armies.[7]

He gives Old Testament references, including some psalms: 16:10; 30:4; 49:16; 86:13. He also points out that when the righteous do envisage descent to *She'ol* it is normally in circumstances of extreme trial, facing the possibility of 'unhappy, untimely death', or where they are deeply aware of their sins, like the author of Psalm 88. If they envisage a contented death, there is no reference to *She'ol*. He concludes that there is no clear indication that *She'ol* is the portion of the righteous, but it is clear that it is the destiny of the wicked. It is not only in 16:10 that a godly person's soul is not abandoned to *She'ol*, but also in 49:13-15, where, after referring to 'the fate of the foolhardy', the author goes on to say:

> Like sheep they are appointed for Sheol;
>     Death shall be their shepherd;
> straight to the grave they descend,
>     and their form shall waste away;
>     Sheol shall be their home.
> But God will ransom my soul from the power of Sheol,
>     for he will receive me.[8]

Psalm 73 finds the psalmist troubled by the prosperity of the wicked until he is given a changed perspective, when in the sanctuary he perceives their end (v. 17). It is not at all surprising then that he says later:

> You guide me with your counsel,
>     and afterward you will receive me with honor ['will take me
>                                                       into glory', NIV]
> Whom have I in heaven but you?
> And there is nothing on earth that I desire other than you.

> My flesh and my heart fail,
>> but God is the strength of my heart and my portion forever
>>> (vv. 24-26).

Is this an assurance of resurrection? We must be cautious about claiming this, bearing in mind the words of Kraus: 'the emphasis is not on a "resurrection event," but on the confession that not even death can separate a person from Yahweh.'[9] This is itself a wonderful assurance. Here is a conviction of the same order, although perhaps not of the same depth, as that of Paul in Romans 8. There, after quoting one of the deepest and saddest of all the psalms of lament and its reference to the constant threat of imminent death for the godly (v. 36; Ps. 44:22), he goes on to assert triumphantly that nothing, not even death, can separate us from God's love in Christ. The big difference is that for Paul it was Christ's resurrection that gave his assurance such depth and strength, although we should not discount the measure of assurance given to the psalmist.

What about a passage like 17:15, with its confident assertion, 'As for me, I shall behold your face in righteousness; when I awake I shall be satisfied, beholding your likeness'? Kidner, writing on 11:7 ('the upright shall behold his face'), says:

> The psalmists knew the experience of seeing God with the inward eye in worship (*e.g.* 27:4; 63:2); but there is little doubt that they were led to look beyond this to an unmediated vision when they would be ransomed and awakened from death 'to behold (His) face in righteousness' (*cf.* 16:8-11; 17:15; 23:6; 49:15; 73:23ff.; 139:18).[10]

Such passages deserve to be looked at again, with special reference to the significance of awakening[11] and seeing the face of God. Is it possible that in a desire not to claim too much for the Old Testament hope and to understand it on its own terms rather than those of the New Testament, in itself quite right, we have sometimes ended up claiming too little?[12]

## The final state of things

We have already seen much evidence that God is to reign supreme in the future and that all nations are to leave their idols and to worship him. This is of course true for the New Testament as well, as we see in the Book of the Revelation. There, however, the emphasis is on Christ, for the Lamb is in the midst of the throne; it is to him that the keys of the book of destiny are given, and the Lord God Almighty and the Lamb will be the light of God's new Jerusalem. Is this Christological note at all represented in the psalms? Yes, it is.

The Exile brought to an end the long line of Davidic monarchs in Jerusalem, yet the royal psalms found a place in the Book of Psalms in its completed form, which could not possibly pre-date the Exile. A study of the Septuagint and the Rabbinic literature makes it clear that the Jews believed these would find their fulfilment in the reign of the Messiah. For instance 80:17 reads:

> But let your hand be upon the one of your right hand,
> the one whom you made strong for yourself,

but the Targum on this verse substituted 'King Messiah' for 'the one'.

Schaper points out that for both the Septuagint and the Targum on 2, this psalm is about the Messiah. He says:

> Psalm 2 is a royal psalm and celebrates the accession of a Judaean king. On the other hand, it obviously lent itself to a post-exilic messianic exegesis, and the change in perception became a permanent one: with the end of the Judaean monarchy, the hope of the people centred on a future king who would restore Israel to its former glory.[13]

In this and other royal psalms, language is used which would seem extravagant if applied to an earthly king, no matter how great. Kidner, writing on 2, says: 'A greater ... than David or Solomon was needed to justify the full fury of these threats and the glory of these promises.'[14] This is even more true of the exalted language of 45:6, which reads most naturally as translated in NRSV and most English versions: 'Your throne, O God, endures forever and forever.' Everlastingness is also attributed to the king's priestly office in 110:4.

Were the authors of such psalms given an insight into the future which took their thoughts beyond ordinary Davidic monarchs to a transcendent person who would reign universally? Their convictions about God were certainly deep and strong enough for them to believe that such an exalted ideal would one day become a reality. The book in its final form certainly stimulated the messianic hope, and it was this final form which was canonical and therefore authoritative for the Jews of our Lord's day and for himself.[15]

Psalm 2 sets the tone for the whole messianic teaching of the book, and in it God gives a strong guarantee that no rebellion will be able to dislodge his anointed son from the universal throne. This is confirmed in 89:27, where he is to be the firstborn of all the kings of the earth. Jesus himself said to his apostles, after his resurrection: 'All authority in heaven and on earth has been given to me' (Matt. 28:18), and it was to establish the recognition of this authority on earth that he then sent them out to preach the gospel to all nations. This then gives Christian significance to the words of Psalm 72:8, 11, where the psalmist, using language going far beyond anything that could be said of Solomon,[16] declares:

> May he have dominion from sea to sea,
> and from the River to the ends of the earth. ...
> May all kings fall down before him,
> all nations give him service.[17]

So then, the Book of Psalms, like the whole Bible, is fundamentally optimistic, but not shallowly so. Sin does abound on the earth, but God is going to judge it, and his kingdom and his Messianic King, our Lord Jesus Christ, will be established. All nations will come and worship him, to whom all glory and praise is due.

# C. Its Grand Design

# Chapter 15

## The significance of its structure

Is the Book of Psalms simply a library of poetic items used in Israel's worship, or is it an integrated book with a special message when taken as a whole? Many Old Testament scholars think the latter to be true and this has become the subject of considerable scholarly research in recent years.

### The development of the Psalter to its present form

The present form of the Psalter seems to have been arrived at by a lengthy process. There are definite groups of psalms, groups such as the major concentration of Davidic psalms in Book 1, the groups of Korahite (42-49) and Asaphite (73-83) psalms in Books 2 and 3 respectively, the way psalms of Yahweh's universal kingship are grouped together in Book 4 (93-100), the Egyptian Hallel (113-118), the Songs of Ascents (120-134) and the final Hallel group (146-150), all in Book 5. This feature suggests deliberate arrangement at earlier stages in the Psalter's history, although, apart from author groups, the only group heading is 'a song of ascents'. It is difficult to believe though that the other groups had no special significance for those who organised them.

We noticed earlier the interest that there has been at times in link-words and link-phrases, a phenomenon known as concatenation. In some cases, these point to clear links of thought between adjoining psalms, but in others these are less easy to find. A number of interesting pairs of psalms have been identified, two psalms appearing to have a definite theological relationship, with either comparative or contrasting themes.[1] These usually but not always adjoin each other.[2]

Psalms 9 and 10 were probably one originally. Kidner says that the change of mood from 9 to 10 leaves the impression that these are in fact two psalms, written as companion pieces to complement one another, concerned as they are with the twin realities of a fallen world: the certain triumph of God and the present, if short-lived triumphing of the wicked.[3]

Psalms 50 and 51, despite their difference of author, could well have been put together for a theological reason. Psalm 50 attacks a paganised view of sacrifice, while 51 is concerned with sins for which there was no sacrifice, so that David had to cast himself on God's mercy alone.

Psalms 90 and 91 both focus on God as the dwelling-place of his people. Psalms 105 and 106 are a contrasting pair of historical psalms. Psalm 105 tells the story of early Israel as an account of God's faithfulness to his people, while 106 concentrates instead on Israel's unfaithfulness to him. Psalms 135 and 136 have points of comparison, especially between 135:8-12 and 136:10, 18-22.

These examples have been chosen from all five books of the Psalter to show this phenomenon is not confined to one part. Was there some rearrangement at a late stage to produce this feature, or did Book 1 set a pattern which was then followed by later books? We cannot tell.[4]

Each book concludes with an ascription of praise to God. Four of these appear to be editorial, namely 41:13; 72:17-19 (or 18-19, there is some difference of opinion as to this); 89:52 and 106:47,48, while the equivalent for Book 5 or the whole Psalter is 150 or even 146 to 150.[5]

Did the Jews recognise this fivefold division? It certainly seems so, but whether by the inheritance of some oral tradition or from observation of the praise conclusions is not clear. The Jewish Midrash on the psalms says:

As Moses gave five books of laws to Israel, so David gave five Books of Psalms to Israel, the Book of Psalms entitled *Blessed is the man*, the Book entitled *For the Leader: Maschil* , the Book, *A Psalm of Asaph* , the Book, *A Prayer of Moses*, and the Book, *Let the redeemed of the Lord say.*

These are references to 1:1, 42:1, Ps. 73:1, Ps. 90:1, Ps. 107:2, the opening psalms of each of the five books. It is however most difficult to assign any particular date to this. There is an even earlier reference in a badly preserved liturgical fragment from Qumran dating from the turn of the Christian era.[6]

When did the Psalter receive its present shape? We cannot be sure. All the praise conclusions to the five books to be found in the Septuagint, and part of 106:47, 48, the praise conclusion of Book 4, is to be found also in 1 Chronicles 16:35, 36. Of course this raises the question of literary priority, but must be taken into account. There is no need now to date the completed Psalter as late as the second century BC, as earlier critics did.

The headings of the psalms are part of the Biblical text. Their value and authority has been disputed, but their presence in the Septuagint, the translation of the psalms which can hardly be later than the late second century BC, means that they were a recognised feature of the Psalter in our Lord's day. For Christians, that must be significant. It is also of interest that the headings of the psalms found in the Qumran caves, none of which can be more recent than AD 68, are almost uniformly identical with those found in the Massoretic text.[7]

The structure of the book is a stable and fixed one in the Hebrew Massoretic text (and also the Aramaic and Greek and Latin translations), although the order of the psalms exhibits considerable variety in the scrolls discovered at Qumran, for reasons not fully understood.

### Interpreting the structure of the Psalter

Is there a theological intention behind the way the Psalter has been arranged? Many scholars would agree with the judgment of Goulder:

> The oldest commentary on the meaning of the psalms is the manner of their arrangement in the Psalter: that is, the collections in which they are grouped, the technical and historical notes they carry, and the order in which they stand.[8]

If this is true, it opens up great exegetical and hermeneutical possibilities. R. E. Murphy points out that each step in the process by which the psalms were collected yields a context. So, for instance, the story of David is the key to the Davidic psalms and the Pilgrim Feasts the key to the Songs of Ascents. He says:

> There are undoubtedly several contexts for the individual collections, and for the Psalter as a whole we are challenged by a new context, created by the establishment of a cut-off point at 150.[9]

There is also, of course, the narrower context, the individual psalm, and two wider contexts, the Old Testament as a whole and the whole Bible. This means therefore that, in relation to the Psalter we have interpretive riches within the Bible itself which are virtually unparalleled.

This does, however, raise some problems for us. Wilson puts the matter well when he says:

> Very few unambiguous signposts have been erected in this foreign territory, and the wary traveller must constantly guard against going astray by importing meaning to those few that can be found. Despite the difficulty and ambiguity that attaches to this endeavour, I am convinced that such an investigation is possible, valuable and, if pursued with appropriate caution, can be as fruitful as the past century of Psalm research.[10]

When a new and fruitful method of study in any subject develops, it is easy, in the first flush of enthusiasm, to make suggestions lacking sufficient critical rigour. When dealing with literature as important as Holy Scripture, such suggestions must be subjected to thorough examination.[11]

If authorial intention is the main pointer to the meaning of any utterance, whether spoken or written,[12] we need some objective criteria for determining this. Whose intention do we seek? Not that of the authors of the individual psalms, although this is, of course, important in its own right, but that of the ultimate human author of the whole book, the final redactor. We may not know his name, but if this general line of research is correct, he is as important as the unknown author of any other Biblical book, for example the Old Testament historical books.

We will now look at some of the intention markers which have been identified and where the identification seems to be well-based. If commentators can do this with other books of the Bible, as they plainly do, there seems to be no adequate reason for setting aside such an approach to this book.

## The more obvious indications of intentional arrangement

First of all, there are the *superscriptions*. We do not know their age, but there can be little doubt they were intended to aid interpretation. Their place in the final Psalter shows that the redactor had no intention of downgrading the importance of individual psalms. Each was important in its own right, each must be read and prayerfully accepted as a word from God.

Then there are *the consecutive psalm groups.* These reveal not only the minds of those who originally organised them, but also that of the final redactor, who allowed them to remain. The trials of David and of the sons of Korah, the profound concerns of the Asaphite Levites, the acclamation by psalmists of Yahweh as King of the universe, and the thankful praise of those who attended the pilgrim feasts, were all seen by him to have abiding significance. Nothing he had to say invalidated the message each of these groups had been conveying down the years.

*The close of Psalm 72*: 'The prayers of David son of Jesse are ended,' also brings Book 2 to its conclusion. This sentence clearly points to a redactor, for it could hardly have been part of the psalm itself. As there are Davidic psalms later in the Psalter, it must mark the close of a group organised prior to the final redaction. The Davidic authorship of so many of the psalms in this group was surely reckoned to be important. Later we will suggest a reason for this.

What is the significance of *the division into five books*?

Probably it was modelled on the Pentateuch, especially if the reference to the law in 1 has its wider sense of 'instruction' and is intended here to designate the Psalter itself as, like the Pentateuch, an important source of instruction from God.[13]

Why was this modelling done? Because of some similarity of contents between each of the Books of Moses and their psalmic counterparts? It is possible to make out a case for this, although this is much easier with some of the book pairs than with others.

Book 1 has a number of psalms (8, 19, 24, 29 and 33) where creation is a theme of some importance. Psalm 8 shows clear awareness of Genesis 1 in its actual language. In these psalms, too, we see that something has gone wrong, for the presence of sin is fully recognised (8:2; 19:12,13; 24:4; 29:10 if this refers to the historical flood, an act of divine judgment, 33:10). See too the morning/evening theme of psalms 3 to 6.[14] Its psalms of the king remind us of the end of Genesis, for in Genesis 49:8-13 the blessing of Jacob makes reference to the royal status of Judah.

Book 2 is the most difficult to link with its corresponding Pentateuchal book, in this case Exodus. Perhaps the psalmist's depression in 42/43 echoes the feelings of the people in Egyptian bondage. In 68 the Exodus and the revelation of God at Sinai are both featured.

Book 3 consists almost entirely of Levitical psalms, some of them bewailing the demise of the God-given worship system, and of course much of Leviticus is concerned with regulations related to this.

Numbers traces the wilderness wanderings and shows both the goodness of God and the sinfulness of the people. How fitting then that Book 4 of the Psalter should begin with a Psalm of Moses, and end with two psalms that spell out the lessons of the wilderness period in the people's life!

The theory of a thematic link between the two groups of five books is perhaps easiest to sustain in relation to Book 5 and to Deuteronomy. If Book 5 was compiled near the end of the Exile or after the return, we might expect some thematic similarity to a Pentateuchal book. There is in Deuteronomy a focus on the conditions that were to obtain in the land, including the regulations for the pilgrim feasts, which figure so largely in Book 5 of the psalms.

Can we be sure any such book correspondence was intended? Not really. Perhaps the reason for the fivefold structure is simply that the story of God's creative and redemptive acts for his people, the wise laws and gift of worship institutions, all recorded in the Pentateuch, should be taken up into the people's worship as well as being subjects of affirmation and injunction. Both the individual Israelite and Israel as a whole were being called to a God-orientated life of praise, much verbal material for which was given in this book.

## A kingly frame

G. H. Wilson gave careful attention to a phenomenon, already noticed by some earlier writers, but which, largely through him, has now become important in discussions of the structure and shape of the Book of Psalms.[15] This is the high probability that certain psalms owe their places in the Psalter to structural considerations and that this structure was at least partly determined theologically.

He points out that not only does a royal psalm (2) form part of the Psalter's introduction, but that there is one at the close of each of the first three books (41, 72, 89). Psalms 2, 72 and 89 are generally accepted to be royal, and he argues that this is true also for 41, in which David is assured that Yahweh will protect him against his enemies.[16] Certainly there are other Davidic psalms with the same general theme as 41, but this does not invalidate his point.

When the first three books of the Psalter were put together, he maintained, these psalms indicated to the reader that the Davidic covenant was a major theme. This covenant was however a problem also, for 89 shows the psalmist to be utterly perplexed at the demise of the dynasty and it ends with an anguished plea to Yahweh to honour his covenant.[17] He says: 'The three psalms – 2, 72 and 89 – form a covenant frame around the first three books. This frame is concerned with the institution (Ps. 2), the transmission (Ps. 72) and the failure (Ps. 89) of the Davidic covenant.'[18] There is possibly an echo of 2:1 in 89:51, the same kind of reference to enemies being made at both points.[19]

## A wisdom frame

Wilson points out that the book has not only a royal covenantal frame (from 2 onwards) but also a wisdom frame (from 1 onwards). He argues that the wisdom frame was primarily connected with the last two books. Book 4 starts with 90, which has wisdom teaching in verses 11 and 12, and Book 5 with 107, which has a wisdom motif in verses 42 and 43. As we shall see, he holds that the original ending to Book 5 was 145, which in verses 19 and 20 has a wisdom section almost at its end. The wisdom frame was then extended to the first three through 73 (at the start of Book 3) and the wisdom shaping at 2, etc.[20]

This means then that we are not to think only in terms of five books, but of two halves of the whole book, which were eventually united. This idea of two halves to the Psalter is explored also by Mitchell, and he refers both to ancient authors like Origen and Jerome and moderns like Westermann, Wilson and Howard as holding, as he does, that 90 binds the two halves together. He says:

> Psalm 90 is the turning-point of the collection. As a lament psalm, it continues the tone of the preceding sequence of psalms .... On the other hand, it also relates to what comes after it. ... Thus the two halves of the Psalter, which might otherwise seem disconnected, are neatly joined together by this 'Janus-faced' psalm, which, to mix metaphors, binds the whole into a seamless garment. The psalm's fitness to its context suggests that the two major sections of the Psalter were conjoined with consummate and purposeful artistry, and are not simply the result of haphazard pairing. [21]

Psalm 1 shows us that the godly wise man spends time with the Tora so we are not surprised to find that psalms of the word of God are of some special importance for the book. Psalms 19 and 119 are other important examples, and there may well be some significance in the fact that the great 119 comes between the two major pilgrimage groups, as we will see.

The wisdom psalms are like those of the Word in that they focus on divine truth, which was always truth for living. Wisdom psalms occur at various points in the arrangement of the book, and there are also psalms which speak of God as the great Teacher. The book's punctuation by such psalms suggests that the reader is constantly being reminded of the scriptural nature of the material and of the importance of obedience.

Wilson[22] sees a royal, covenantal frame as covering the first three books and then extended to the last two by the inclusion of 144, which he takes to be royal. He also says, very significantly: 'In the final analysis, the shape of the canonical Psalter preserves a tense dialogue (or a dialogue in tension) between the royal covenantal hopes associated with the first two-thirds of the Psalter and the wisdom counsel: to trust YHWH alone, associated with the final third. In conclusion it seems apparent that wisdom has had the last word as demonstrated by the wisdom shaping of the covenantal Psalms 2 and 144 as well as the primary positioning of Psalms 1 and 145 in the final frame.'[23]

Wilson finds Book 4 to be the heart of the Psalter as finally arranged. He points to the large number of untitled psalms in it, and on the basis of this he suggests that it is especially the product of purposeful editorial arrangement.[24] He says: 'As one moves from the first three books into the fourth, a shift is immediately observed. Here untitled psalms predominate.... The preponderance of untitled psalms would have afforded the editor a degree of flexibility in arrangement unheard of in the first three books where author designations are the rule. It is not surprising, therefore, to find here a sustained thematic unity that focuses on the kingship of YHWH.'[25]

## The refuge theme

Several writers have commented on the importance of this theme in the Psalter and especially of the positioning of 2:12, where the psalmist says, 'Happy are all who take refuge in him.'

R. E. Murphy, says that 2:12 makes 2 a fitting introduction to 3–41, or even 2–72.[26] In most of these psalms the writer is in trouble and pours out his heart to God.

G. T. Sheppard says that 2:12, with its reference to refuge, 'specifically thematizes the lamentations in the first half of the Book of Psalms. It marks out a particular theological stance by which laments are to be understood as scripture.'[27] This is a very helpful point, as it is not always immediately clear how the expression of questions, doubts and fears can be regarded as God's message, but this is much easier to see if they are placed there so that the psalmist can be shown as coming with his problem or his afflictions to the God who has promised to be a Refuge for his people.

Seybold too stresses the importance of this verse, where the verb 'to take refuge in'[28] first appears in the Psalter. He says that in the first two books faith is modelled for the reader, and many testimonies are given to the faithfulness of God in the midst of trial. In 2 the king is presented as a model, for, facing rebellious opposition, he takes his stand on the word of God's solemn decree and finds his refuge in him.[29]

The fullest recent study of the refuge concept is that by Creach.[30] He points out how many refuge metaphors there are in the Psalter. This theme commences at the close of 2 and moves through much of the book, especially its earlier parts. The enemies of David and of the psalmists generally are much in evidence, but God is their Refuge.[31]

## Further possible evidence of editing

The conclusion to 72, which is so obviously editorial, raises the possibility that there may be editorial elements in some of the other psalms, although it should be said that this is the only explicitly editorial item in the Psalter.

The theological motive for psalm arrangement sometimes provided good reasons for interrupting a particular sequence of psalms. Allen has some helpful things to say about this, pointing out, for instance, that 86 was put in a group of Korahite psalms because it shared with them the theme that God deserves worship by all nations.[32] Perhaps we should also see 85 and 86 as a pair, with prayer for restoration both in terms of the nation and of the individual.

Various editorial additions to psalms have been suggested. It is widely held that the words of verses 20 and 21 in 51 were added during the Exile, a period when, it is thought, much editing was done. The people were away from Jerusalem and they longed to return and to offer sacrifices to God in the temple once again. Murphy is right though when, in commenting on this psalm, he says:

> It matters little that verses 20-21 may be a 'later addition'. The point is that they are present and add to the richness of the prayer by presenting a creative tension.[33]

If this is correct, David's sin becomes perhaps a kind of parable of Israel's, rather in the way that Jacob's life may be regarded as such a parable in Malachi 3:6:

> For I the LORD do not change; therefore you, O children of Jacob, have not perished.

Although there may be such editorial additions to the Psalter, it is important for us to be cautious in identifying them.

## The Messianic hope

We have already noted the importance of the kingly theme. What though is its significance for the total book? Childs focuses on this final form of the Psalter, and he sees eschatological reinterpretation as the governing motif.[34]

D. C. Mitchell has made a major contribution to the debate about the structure and, in consequence, the leading theme of the Book of Psalms. He points out that 'the figures to whom the

Psalms are attributed were regarded as future-predictive prophets even in Biblical times'. He cites 2 Samuel 23:2-4 (cf. 2 Sam. 7:11-16) for David, Deuteronomy 18:15; 31:19-22 and 34:10 for Moses and 1 Chronicles 25:5 and 2 Chronicles 29:30; 35:15 for Asaph, Jeduthun and Heman. He then says: 'Since David, Asaph, Heman, Jeduthun and Moses were regarded in this way, it is not unreasonable to suspect that psalms bearing their names would be considered future-predictive.'[35] He also says:

> The fact that some of these psalms appear to refer only to historical events need not contradict this. The essence of Israel's view of prophecy was that historic events prefigure future ones. In later times this became a fixed hermeneutical idea.[36]

This is remarkably close to the commonly held notion that many psalms have two senses, an historical and a prophetic one, the first being in the mind of the writer and the second in the mind of God. The Reformers however maintained there is only one *meaning* to a Scripture passage, because in inspiration God worked through the mind of the writer, but that this may have, in God's purpose, a further *significance*. If Mitchell is correct, however, the concept of the one meaning is preserved for the Book of Psalms without the need for the further significance concept, for the historical sense would be the meaning of a psalm's author while the Messianic sense would be the meaning of the Psalter's eventual redactor, and, for a Christian believer, the mind of God would be seen in the inspiration of both.

Mitchell's argument is detailed and focuses largely on the Psalms of Asaph and the Psalms of Ascents, in both of which he sees 'ingathering' to be an important concept. In the former there is much about the judgment of Israel and the nations. In a strongly eschatological context of judgment, God speaks in the first psalm in the Asaph group and says:

> Gather to me my faithful ones,
> who made a covenant with me by sacrifice (50:5).

In the Psalms of Ascents, warfare and judgement are in the past and the people are now gathered for joyful pilgrimage to Jerusalem:

> I was glad when they said to me,
>     'Let us go to the house of the LORD!' (122:1).

For these and other reasons, Mitchell considers that these two sequences of psalms were intended by the redactor to be predictive. He says:

> The dominant figure of the Ascents is David, whose name occurs eight times (122:1, 5; 124:1; 131:1; 132:1, 10, 11, 17). Four lyrics are inscribed or ascribed to him and one to his son Solomon (127:1). The emphasis is on the house of David as a continuing institution, particularly in Psalms 122 and 132, which depict it in full regal authority.[37]

This means then that, far from Books 4 and 5 encouraging the reader to look away from the Davidic dynasty and to look *instead* to God as King, a major point of the whole Psalter is to see the fulfilment of the dynastic promise in a Messianic King of the future as deeply assuring evidence that God keeps his word.

No wonder then that, at the close of his public ministry, Jesus pointed to a psalm (110) as describing his nature and triumph as God's Messiah (Mark 12:35-37) and that, after his resurrection, he particularly highlighted the psalms, along with the law and the prophets, as bearing testimony to him (Luke 24:44)!

# Chapter 16

## The introductory psalms
*(Psalms 1 and 2)*

### A double introduction

Both authors and readers of books are aware of the importance of the start and finish of a piece of literature. The one usually establishes a theme and creates certain expectations in the reader, while the other sums up what has gone before, produces the denouement of a story, or underlines the message the author wants to convey.

Making this kind of point, P. D. Miller instances Deuteronomy, Job, Ecclesiastes, and at least the beginning of Proverbs, as examples from the Old Testament.[1] Perhaps we might also add Judges, for chapter 1 links it with the Book of Joshua, chapter 2 sets out its general theme which finds many illustrations in the main part of the book, while the closing five chapters show the spiritual and moral malady which was the real cause of all the problems Israel faced as described in that main part. Three of these five are Wisdom books, and the historical material in Deuteronomy and Judges and the legal material in Deuteronomy is all, of course, penned not just for its own sake but to teach lessons.

What about the Psalter? It certainly begins with two psalms that may, despite their differences, be categorised as wisdom psalms, for the first shows the ways of blessedness and of perdition, even though it does not actually use the word 'wisdom', while the second counsels wisdom quite explicitly. This suggests that as finally arranged the Book of Psalms was intended to teach lessons. We will consider its ending in a later chapter.

The introductory function of 1 has been long recognised, and it seems probable that it was added at a late stage in the establishing of the book as a complete entity. It has no author ascription. Every psalm in Book 1 is ascribed to David with four exceptions: 10 was probably the second half of 9 originally[2] and 33 is a very obvious companion to 32, which *is* ascribed to David. This leaves just 1 and 2, and 2 is attributed to David in the prayer of the church recorded in Acts 4:25.

If 1 is indeed introductory to the whole Psalter, it seems likely that it is intended by the redactor to indicate that this is a book for meditative reading and for action stimulated by this:

> but their delight is in the law of the LORD,
>     and on his law they meditate day and night.

The word translated 'meditate' suggests mumbling, some kind of quiet word-articulation in reading to oneself.[3] What though is the sense intended by the word 'law' in verse 2? The word is *tora* and in the Old Testament this has both the technical sense 'law' and also the non-technical and more basic sense, 'instruction'. It is possible that here it can be read in both senses, having probably the narrower sense for the author of the psalm but the wider for the ultimate redactor of the whole Psalter.[4] Once the whole book was arranged in order, it could be clearly seen that meditative reading of it would be of great spiritual value, and that what was originally said of the Law of Moses was therefore true also of this book.

Another possibility is that the author himself intended the wider sense, but also intended an allusion to Joshua 1:8, where Joshua is told by God to meditate in 'the book of the law' day and night so that he may prosper in his leadership of the people of Israel. There are too many coincidences of language between the two verses for their similarity to be accidental. If this is so, then the author of the psalm may in effect be saying that, just as Joshua was to make the Mosaic Law a subject of diligent study, so the Jewish believer should study this further book of divine instruction, the Book of Psalms.

In a sense, by placing it here they were saying that this book should be treated, like the Law, as the revelation of God, and that it should be prayerfully pondered and acted upon. To walk or not to walk in God's ways, therefore, is the big issue which at once faces the reader who opens the Book of Psalms. The psalm does not hold a gun at the reader's head, but it does indicate which is the way of wisdom. It tells us that walking in God's ways in the light of his instruction brings great delight and that it results in a stability and fruitfulness which will endure when the judgment of God comes. This is true, of course, not only of the Law and the Psalms but of the whole word of God as Christians have it today.

It has been well argued that 1 and 2 were intended as a joint Introduction.[5] There is some evidence that they were so regarded quite early in the history of the church. In the second century, as we have seen, Justin Martyr quoted the two without making a division between them, and in the next century Origen knew a Hebrew manuscript in which 1 and 2 were put together as one psalm.[6]

In so many ways these two psalms are well fitted as companions, with each suitable as a kind of commentary on the other. This is not an unique feature in the Psalter, for there are quite a number of psalm pairs of this type. The existence of this phenomenon, therefore, gives further support to the idea that 1 and 2 were intended to be understood together as a general introduction.

In 1 the righteous and the wicked are referred to in very general terms and their attitudes, lifestyle and destiny are delineated. Psalm 2 is quite different in this respect, for it seems to focus on a very specific situation. God has set his king on Zion, his holy hill, and there is a rebellion of nations against him. Even the element of application in the psalm is not addressed to the reader but rather to the rebellious kings:

> Now therefore, O kings, be wise;
>> be warned, O rulers of the earth.
> Serve the LORD with fear,
>> with trembling kiss his feet ... (vv. 10, 11).

The last sentence of the psalm however is quite different, for it makes a general wisdom pronouncement, and in this way is like 1. It ends with the words: 'Happy are all who take refuge in him.'

It is a sound teaching principle to illustrate general principles from particular cases. The psalmist is, however, doing more than this. Psalm 2 is not an illustration of the principles of 1 selected in some arbitrary fashion. The installation of a king of God's own choice ('my king', v. 6) is no mere historical incident but a matter of solemn divine decree and so is central to the purposes of God. Neither is the rebellion of the earth's rulers against him arbitrarily selected, for it shows in a specially marked way their refusal to walk in God's ways.

Wisdom and knowledge are not identical, and the extent of a person's wisdom is not by any means necessarily commensurate with the extent of his or her knowledge. Nevertheless, wisdom is hardly a meaningful concept if it is divorced from knowledge, for it is really knowledge put to right practical uses. The mind needs to be informed if we are to make wise judgments. Both opening psalms show us the importance of the mind. In 1 the wise person meditates on the instruction given by God, setting aside the advice of the wicked, while in 2 the minds of the rebels are put to wicked use in plotting against God.[7]

## Two lifestyles and two destinies

The blessing which opens 1 highlights, through its negative beginning, the difference between the righteous and the wicked, so that the reader becomes aware at once of the importance of choice. Psalm 2, with its series of imperatives followed by a statement of blessing (vv. 10-12) makes the same point but, in the manner of a preacher, insists that a choice be made.

So often in Scripture we see that the wise and unwise ways, the ways of godliness and rebellion, make for stability and instability respectively. The wisdom that Deuteronomy commends, for instance, means faithfulness to the one true God and obedience to his commands. If the nation of Israel adopts this wise course, then its people will enjoy a stable and secure life in the land flowing with milk and honey, but if it does not they will be judged within the land and, ultimately, cast out of it. The Sermon on the Mount ends with a call by Christ for his hearers to build securely on his teaching, and he warns them of the disaster that befalls those who build on sand. In 1 the righteous have the stability of a strong tree, while the wicked are like the chaff that is blown away in the winnowing process. In 2 God has established a place of stability, for he has placed the king in Zion and all the machinations of the rebels cannot dislodge him. In fact, in God's purpose his rule will ultimately extend to the whole world.

As we go through the Psalter, we see that the psalmists faced all kinds of problems and that, when they did so, they often went back to rest on the great certainties, on great unchangeable facts. In these two psalms two such facts are highlighted. In 1 it is the basic fact of an ethical order. Yahweh has established the moral order and pledges himself to bless the righteous and judge the wicked. In 2 the order is governmental. He is the supreme King who governs the nations, who has a purpose in history and who gives a special place to Israel's king. If he is a righteous God and is also in full government of the world, there is the strongest possible basis here for confidence in him and encouragement to walk in his ways.

One interesting feature of 1 is the fact that, although both the present and the future of the righteous and the wicked are in view, on the face of it the emphasis appears to be more on the present for the righteous and the future for the wicked. Happiness, which is either based on or consists of delight in God's law, and prosperity, are the features which introduce and sum up the lot of the righteous, and the final verse indicates the reason for this: 'The LORD watches over the way of the righteous.' All this seems to relate to their present condition. Apart from the terms that describe their character, nothing is said about the present condition of the wicked, except for the words, 'the wicked are not so' (v. 4), which briefly but eloquently indicate that everything said of the righteous is true for them alone and not for the wicked. The main focus however is on their destiny. They are doomed to perish.

In 2 the king is described as God's son and so, by implication, the object of his special care. Like a son, he has his father's ear and is encouraged to petition him. His destiny is worldwide dominion and total victory over the rebellious nations and their rulers. Like the wicked of 1:6, they are destined to perish (2:9-11). Their rebellion is so irrational, so absurd, that God is not only angry with them but they are appropriate objects of his scorn, so different from the inappropriate scorn and scoffing of the sinners in 1:1.

## The Davidic theme and the assurance of divine protection

Three parts of the Old Testament have a strong focus on a particular servant of God. The Pentateuch has a Mosaic focus, the Book of Proverbs, with Ecclesiastes and the Song of Songs, a Solomonic, and the Book of Psalms a Davidic one. Moses is the archetype of the Old Testament prophet, Solomon of the wise man and David of the king. It is notable too that the books of Samuel, Kings and Chronicles also all have something of a Davidic emphasis.

This Davidic emphasis of the Psalter is more clearly recognised today by Old Testament scholarship of most schools than it has been for a long time. This is an encouraging development and we will note its significance at many points in our study of the book's design, from 2 onwards.

In terms at least of its headings, in none of its parts is this Davidic theme more evident than in Book 1. In 2, in what is in effect the introduction both to the whole book and also to Book 1, we find God giving his backing to Zion's king. It recognises that the king has enemies, and so the wicked of 1 now have a particular focus for their rebellion against God. That rebellion will, however, be in vain, and the rebels are exhorted to come to terms with reality and yield obedience to the king.

The reference to the LORD's decree and to the king's sonship are potent reminders of the fundamental promise of God to David recorded in 2 Samuel 7. An important feature of that passage is the assurance that God would not take away the kingship from him as he took it away from Saul. In this passage, the promise of an abiding kingship is a promise to David's son, but it reaches far beyond him to embrace the whole of David's dynasty:

> The LORD declares to you that the LORD will make you a house....Your house and your kingdom shall be made sure forever before me; your throne shall be established for ever (2 Sam. 7:11, 16).

The promise of a lasting dynasty did not carry with it any suggestion of freedom from trouble, and certainly not from enemies. The Psalter constantly shows the king under attack from his foes. Certainly he can rely on God's sure word, but he needs constantly to express his faith by praying to God for protection.

In view of this, it is not surprising to find that 1 ends with an assertion that the LORD watches over the way of the righteous. This suggests special providence, a constant concern by God to secure the blessing of the righteous, and this is particularised in terms of protection at the close of 2, 'Happy are all who take refuge in him' (2:12). As Creach has shown,[8] refuge is a theme of great importance in the Psalter and especially in Books 1 and 2. Here in 2, the basic psalm for the whole kingly theme in the Psalter, we are introduced to it.

## Connections with other parts of the Bible

If 1 and 2 constitute together a double introduction to the Book of Psalms, and if a major purpose of this introduction is to encourage readers to approach it in prayerful meditation as inspired Scripture, we might expect it to have some important links with other parts of the Old Testament. This is what we do in fact discover.

The use of the word *tora* in 1:2 suggests a link with the

Mosaic Law, and this was probably the intention of the author of the psalm, even though the editor of the whole collection saw a further application to other parts of Scripture, including the Psalter itself.

The allusion to Joshua 1 in 1 has already been noted. The command to Joshua to meditate in the law of the Lord emphasised for him that his work was divinely commissioned and had to be done in God's way. In Joshua the reference is a literary and not simply a legal one. This was no oral law, but the law of God as a literary document. We have already noted a link with 2 Samuel 7, the foundation document of the Davidic covenant and should note too that Deuteronomy 17:14-20 gives the Divine constitution for the king in which it is made clear that he is to meditate on the law of God:

> He shall read in it all the days of his life, so that he may learn to fear the LORD his God, diligently observing all the words of this law and these statutes (v. 19).

Perhaps then the close association of the first two psalms is meant to suggest to us that the daily meditation on the word of God which was an important part of the king's divinely-given constitution, should be the daily habit of the people also.

Jeremiah 17:5-8 is a passage which has many links of phrase and idea with 1. It is difficult to determine whether Jeremiah is dependant on the psalm or vice versa. But Holladay, a Jeremiah specialist, considers that in most cases of correspondence between psalms and Jeremiah, the psalms are the prior documents.[9]

We note how clearly 1 comes before us as a wisdom document when we compare it with a passage like Proverbs 2. This whole chapter should be compared with the psalm, but its closing verses (20-22) are especially apposite:

> Therefore walk in the ways of the good,
>     and keep to the paths of the just.

For the upright will abide in the land,
and the innocent will remain in it;
but the wicked will be cut off from the land,
and the treacherous will be rooted out of it.

What about the New Testament? If the Psalter, taken as a whole, has a quite specific message from God, it is rather like an extended sermon. Our Lord's Sermon on the Mount (Matt. 5-7) also begins with benedictions in which the qualities of the blessed life are set forth, and it ends with an encouragement to build on these teachings and a warning of the consequences of failing to do so. The Book of the Revelation, after a couple of introductory verses, declares:

Blessed is the one who reads aloud the words of the prophecy, and blessed are those who hear and who keep what is written in it; for the time is near (Rev. 1:3).

In Revelation's closing verses, there is a warning not to add to or take away any of the words of this book, implying its great importance to the reader (Rev. 22:18, 19).

Without doubt the Book of Psalms, in its totality, is a Wisdom book from which we may learn much about God, his purposes and his ways, provided we commit ourselves to walk in the light of his truth that is here laid bare.

# Chapter 17

## Book 1 – The tribulations and security of David

### The foundational nature of Psalms 1 and 2 for this book

Our study of this book will commence with 3, as we have already treated 1 and 2 as introductory to the whole Book of Psalms. It could certainly be argued that they are particularly appropriate as the introduction to Book 1, and we will see that this is true, without at all downplaying the fact that they are meant to open up for us the entire Psalter.

The foundational nature of these two psalms is evident as we study Book 1, for their themes practically dominate it. We could liken this first book to a series of musical variations on the theme set out in 1 and 2, the theme of God's blessing of the righteous and rejection of the wicked, especially as manifested specifically in Zion's king on the one hand and his enemies on the other. We will consider two pairs of psalms that illustrate this point.

Psalm 15 is a virtual exposition of 1, although we should note that it has a specific application to worship. Acceptance with God means acceptance as a worshipper (cf. Genesis 4). The question goes out:

O Lord, who may abide in your tent?
  Who may dwell on your holy hill? (v. 1)

Bearing in mind the Pentateuchal regulations for worship, we might expect the answer to be that genealogical and physical qualifications are needed. Instead, however, we find ethical qualities prescribed and extolled. The 'holy hill' (v. 1), which is also mentioned in 2:6, is a reminder that Zion is not just the place where the king's throne is, but even more importantly where the temple of God is situated. So to dwell on God's holy

hill is not so much to be a member of the king's court as to be
an acceptable worshipper at the house of God. The ethical
requirements recited here recall 1, because they commence,
'Those who walk blamelessly', thus recalling the use of the
same verb in 1:1.[1]

Psalm 24:3-6 strikes the same kind of note, and once again
commences with a question:

> Who shall ascend the hill of the LORD?
>     And who shall stand in his holy place?

to which the same kind of answer is given:

> Those who have clean hands and pure hearts,
>     who do not lift up their souls to what is false,
>     and do not swear deceitfully ...

If 15 and 24:3-6 virtually expound 1, then 3 and 27 expound 2.

In 3 we meet again the numerous enemies of the king ('ten
thousands of people', v. 6), who, it is clear, are set against God
as well as against the king, and scoff at his conviction that God
will come to his aid (3:1, 2). The king calls on God, as 2:8
encourages him to do, and he finds that God protects him,
becoming a shield around him:

> Deliverance belongs to the LORD;
>     may your blessing be on your people! (v. 8)

reminds us of 2:11: 'Happy are all who take refuge in him.'

In 27 there is no explicit historical setting, but this psalm
shares with 3 a confidence that God will deliver David from the
enemies that assail him. In the first two verses, he says:

> The LORD is my light and my salvation;
>     whom shall I fear?
> The LORD is the stronghold of my life;
>     of whom shall I be afraid?

> When evildoers assail me
>> to devour my flesh –
> my adversaries and foes –
>> they shall stumble and fall.

and that confidence is the basis of the prayers recorded later in the psalm. A number of these are expressed in the form, 'do not ...', which occurs five times in verse 9 and once in verse 12, but this kind of expression betrays no lack of confidence in God but simply asks him to show in practice what the psalmist knows him to be, his divine Protector.

## Troubles of the king

It is said that many who try to read the Bible right through tend to get stuck in Leviticus, as the legislation found in this psalm seems to be remote from life as we know it today.[2] Many who have set out to read the Book of Psalms right through have not managed to get through Book 1 because many of the psalms in this book seem to emerge from such similar situations, those in which the psalmist is beset by enemies and cries out to God to deliver him. In fact, this is such a marked feature of Book 1 that it is impossible even to find half a dozen psalms in it where this is not referred to, either explicitly or by implication.

This should not, however, deter us from diligent study of this book, for it is evident that there is a purpose in it. If we take seriously the Davidic ascription, whether in terms of authorship or in terms of an editorial intent, the lesson is spelled out loudly and clearly: God's general promise that the Lord watches over the way of the righteous (1), and his specific promise to uphold the king (2), are fulfilled, but not without considerable trouble and difficulty.

There is one important difference between 2, the introductory psalm of the king, and 3, and we need to take note of it. The basic promise underlying the Davidic covenant declares of David's dynastic son:

When he commits iniquity, I will punish him with a rod such as mortals use, with blows inflicted by human beings. But I will not take my steadfast love from him, as I took it from Saul, whom I put away from before you (2 Sam. 7:14, 15).

Sometimes the king was suffering for quite specific sins of his own. If we accept the heading of 3, David was experiencing divine chastisement because of his sin, and Absalom was actually reigning in Jerusalem.[3] Of course, Absalom was himself a son of David, so that the covenant promise of God was still inviolate, but David may well have understood this promise to mean that he would not himself be dislodged.

This historical situation explains why 'on Zion, my holy hill' in 2:6 becomes 'from his holy hill' in 3:4. David is not now in Jerusalem but is away from it, but he can still come to God in prayer and trust in him, so that he may confidently lie down to sleep. Perhaps a little surprisingly, there is no confession of sin in this psalm. We should however remember David's words of confession to Nathan, 'I have sinned against the LORD' (2 Sam. 12:13) and his willingness even to be banished from Jerusalem for good (2 Sam. 15:25,26). There can be no real doubt as to his true penitence. Psalms 32 and 38 are also psalms of penitence.

God's concern for the godly is very evident in this book. He has set apart the faithful for himself (4:3). The psalmist's enemies are very much in evidence and are referred to in some way or other in the great majority of its psalms. What is abundantly clear is that God rejects them:

For you are not a God who delights in wickedness;
    evil will not sojourn with you.
The boastful will not stand before your eyes;
    you hate all evildoers,
You destroy those who speak lies;
    the LORD abhors the bloodthirsty and deceitful (5:4-6).

It is, however, particularly the theme of the king under attack and turning to God for refuge and deliverance that quite dominates this book. It seems at times to be almost continuous from 3 (indeed also from 2) onwards.

There are psalms where it is clear that David is not only king *de jure* but also *de facto*, as in 21. The great blessedness of the king, secure in the knowledge of God's support against his enemies and of the certainty of God answering his trustful prayers, is not only portrayed but celebrated in this psalm, and there is much in it to remind us of 2.

It is therefore all the more startling to find a psalm of such kingly assurance succeeded by 22, which is at the farthest remove from it in its emotional tone, at least as far as its first 18 verses are concerned. Here the king has an experience of suffering of a very deep kind. It has a physical dimension, for he writes, for instance, of being poured out like water, with all his bones out of joint (v. 14). It also has a social dimension, for he is surrounded by those who scorn him and mock his trust in God (vv. 6-13) and whom he pictures as being like fierce animals (12, 13, 20, 21). Most terrible of all, however, is the sense that God has himself forsaken him. He cries out to God, apparently in vain:

> My God, my God, why have you forsaken me?
>    Why are you so far from helping me,
>    from the words of my groaning?
> O my God, I cry by day, and you do not answer;
>    and by night, but find no rest (22:1, 2).

But is his agonised cry really in vain?

No, for after a brief impassioned prayer, a major change of tone comes into the psalm, where the sufferer says:

> From the horns of the wild oxen you have rescued me.
> I will tell of your name to my brothers and sisters;
>    in the midst of the congregation I will praise you (22:21, 22).

This note of praise continues to the end of the psalm. This psalm is valued by Christians supremely because the words of verse 1 are found on the lips of Jesus as he hangs upon the cross. Some have seen this psalm to be directly prophetic of him, while others view it as emanating from a particularly deep and dreadful experience of the psalmist himself which foreshadows the even deeper experience of Jesus Christ. David felt himself to be forsaken, but Christ, as the Substitute for sinners, suffered the actual hiding of his Father's face as he bore the penalty of our sins. In the setting of Book 1, this psalm would seem to be yet one more cry to God from a man beset by enemies, but with this profound dimension added to it.

Book 1 is dominated by Davidic psalms, especially if we regard 1 and 2, which do not have this ascription, as introductory to the whole Book of Psalms, as this would mean that they are not really in the strict sense psalms of Book 1. Book 2 also has a large number of Davidic psalms in it, although it is not quite so dominated by them as is Book 1. In both, the psalmist is constantly beset by problems, difficulties and trials, and most often at the hands of others who are determined to make life difficult for him. If we take seriously the Davidic ascriptions, whether in terms of their authorship or in terms of an editorial intent, the lesson is spelled out loudly and clearly: God's general promise that the Lord watches over the way of the righteous (1), and his specific promise to uphold the king (2), are fulfilled, but not without considerable pain and agony, both of mind and body.[4]

### Testimonies of the king

In 2:8 God encourages the king to pray. Time and again in Book 1 David looks to God as his refuge from his enemies and often proclaims with gladness that God has heard him. There is a particularly dramatic example of this in 18. Here the psalmist gives eloquent testimony to the divine deliverance. He pictures himself as a man struggling to extricate himself from the cords of death that were entangling him (vv. 4, 5) or, in another picture, drowning in mighty waters (v. 16). God came to his rescue and that deliverance is most graphically pictured. He says that the very earth reeled and rocked (v. 7), the very heavens were bowed down (v. 9), as God rode on a cherub (v. 10) to rescue his servant.

Actual deliverance is not always mentioned in such psalms, but, where it is not, there is usually an expression of trust that God will in fact come to deliver the king. In 11, for instance, the kind of theology set forth in 1 is the basis of the psalmist's confidence. He is sure that God will visit judgement on his enemies and that he will come to his rescue:

For the LORD is righteous;
he loves righteous deeds;
    the upright shall behold his face (v. 7).

There are times when, although beset by enemies and with no rescue in sight, he is content to commit himself to God and even to sleep despite being surrounded by his foes, as in 3 and 4. As we read 9, it becomes clear that David is thinking here of several different attacks by his enemies. He asserts that they stumbled and fell because God maintained his cause (vv. 3, 4), but he then goes on later to say:

Be gracious to me, O LORD.
    See what I suffer from those who hate me;
    you are the one who lifts me up from the gates of death (v.13).

If 9 and 10 were originally one psalm, as is often thought, the psalmist is now interceding on behalf of the poor (v. 2) and the oppressed orphan (v. 18), confident perhaps because of his own experience that God makes the cause of his people his own.

In fact, much of Book 1 is a series of testimonies to the saving love and power of the God who constantly shows his support for his king, so that the king can in turn assure others that they too, if their cause is righteous, may look to God for salvation from their foes. These testimonies are put into most memorable words in 34 and 40, in both of which others are encouraged to

follow the king's example and put their trust in the Lord. As he
says in 34:2, 3:

> My soul shall make its boast in the LORD;
>    let the humble hear and be glad.
> O magnify the LORD with me,
>    and let us exalt his name together.

## Problems facing the king

This does not mean though that the psalmist is never puzzled
by the ways of God. Delay is a problem to him and in 13:1, 2 he
cries out, 'How long?' four times in succession. In the
providential dealings of God, the right does not always prevail
immediately, as Joseph, languishing in an Egyptian dungeon,
and Jeremiah, suffering many afflictions because of his
faithfulness to God, both discovered. Even in Revelation those
who had been slaughtered for the word of God cry out:

> Sovereign Lord, holy and true, how long will it be before you
> judge and avenge our blood on the inhabitants of the earth? (Rev.
> 6:10).

Noting the words 'holy and true', we recall that the psalmist,
no matter how deep his concern, always came to God with that
concern. Puzzled he may have been, but he did not give up his
belief in Yahweh as a God of justice.

There are times when the king pleads his righteousness, as
he does particularly eloquently in 18:20-24, where he says, for
instance in verse 20:

> The LORD rewarded me according to my righteousness,
>    according to the cleanness of my hands he recompensed me.

This should not be understood as a claim to sinless perfection
but rather to faithfulness to God. In the Books of Kings David
is presented as the standard against which other kings are

judged,[5] although the writer must have known of the sins which the Books of Samuel records. What was true of David was that he never departed from loyalty to God. But that he was aware of his sins is clear in 32 and 38, in both of which he acknowledges them. In 38 he cries to God for mercy and even there he asks God to deal with his enemies. In 32 it is clear that he has found the mercy of God, for he says:

> Happy are those whose transgression is forgiven,
>     whose sin is covered.
> Happy are those to whom the LORD imputes no iniquity,
>     and in whose spirit there is no deceit (32:1, 2).

**The word of God**

If the promise of God to David in 2 is basic to so many of the psalms in Book 1, it is not surprising that there are psalms which celebrate the trustworthiness of all that God has said. In 19, the psalmist asserts that the visible heavens speak eloquently for God but then follows this with a celebration of the perfections of the law of the LORD. Psalms 32 to 34 present God as the great Teacher (32:8), whose word is upright (33:4), again with a comparison with God's creative word (33:6), while in 34, in a passage highly reminiscent of the Book of Proverbs, the psalmist's own word of testimony becomes the means by which others learn spiritual lessons:

> Come, O children, listen to me;
> I will teach you the fear of the LORD (v. 11).

P. D. Miller has pointed out that there is a major focus on the Torah in Book 1.[6] He says that, apart from 119, 'the primary emphases on the Torah are found explicitly and implicitly in the first book.'[7] He instances the entrance liturgies of 15 and 24, where we have already noted the importance of moral qualifications for entry to God's house, and he refers to P. Aufflet's proposal 'that Psalms 15-24 form a particular group of psalms arranged in a ring structure of which Psalms 15 and 24 are the outer ring or inclusion and Psalm 19 is the center.'[8]

Certainly each of the psalms within this group presents the psalmist as a man concerned to do the will of God. Even 20, which might appear to lack this, refers to the offerings and burnt sacrifices the king has offered (v. 3). Psalm 1:2 and many verses in 119 express delight in the Torah of the Lord. Miller points out that the other place in the Psalter where delight is expressed in the Lord's will and so in his Torah is 40:8-9, which comes almost at the close of Book 1.[9] There can be little doubt that he has established his case for an important emphasis on God's Law in this first book of the Psalter.

What then is the overall message of Book 1? It is that God is faithful to his word, that he is, despite all apparent evidence to the contrary, on the side of the righteous (as 1 has established) and that he does fulfil his promise to support his king. At times the king will suffer greatly at the hands of his foes and will even wonder if God has forsaken him altogether, but God vindicates his name and the truth of his word of promise again and again. As David says in 34:19:

> Many are the afflictions of the righteous,
>     but the LORD rescues them from them all.

The Christian is therefore encouraged as he thinks of the ultimate King, Jesus Christ, and of the fulness of the word of God, now given to him or her in a completed Biblical canon.

# Chapter 18

# Book 2 – The tribulations and security of God's people

## Its differences from Book 1

A cursory glance at Book 2 might suggest that it simply continues the general theme of Book 1, majoring on the trials of the righteous and the fact that the Lord delivers from them all. There is, however, much more to it than this.

For one thing, it is not as dominated by Davidic psalms as is Book 1. Only 19 of the 31 psalms in the book are attributed to him. It is true that this is still a larger percentage than in any of the later books, but it falls far behind Book 1 in this respect. There are quite a number of psalms attributed to Levitical authors, and especially a major series, running from 42 to 49 without a break, if we can assume that 43 was originally part of 42.

Not only so, but there is a difference in the use of designations for God. The name Yahweh is by far the dominant one in Book 1, whereas it is Elohim in Book 2. This has led some authors to seek a different place of origin for these psalms, either Book 2 as a whole or at least those of the sons of Korah which find such an important place within it. Michael Goulder has even linked the latter with the shrine at Dan, holding that they were probably brought south after the fall of the northern kingdom and then were adapted for the needs of the Jerusalem temple.

This theory can be well argued, but it faces major difficulties. It seems highly improbable that psalms known to have originated at a shrine regarded in Judah as apostate, would find any favour at the Jerusalem temple. The Arians of the fourth and fifth centuries sang hymns, but it is not easy to imagine these being adapted for worship by Nicene Christians.

Why do we now begin to get psalms by Levitical writers?

Perhaps we may get a clue in the phrase, 'Zion, my holy hill' in 2:6. The implied promise of God here is that he would protect his king, whose royal seat was in Jerusalem. Book 1 shows this happening on many occasions in the life of David. But a protection of Jerusalem for the king's sake also carried with it protection of the temple which itself was situated there, and so it is quite appropriate that this theme should now be taken up. In Chronicles the Davidic dynasty and the temple planned by him and situated in his capital city are both emphasised. Two of the Korahite psalms (46 and 48) in fact celebrate God's protection of Zion, and in the second of these the psalmist says:

> We ponder your steadfast love, O God,
>     in the midst of your temple (48:9).

The Books of Chronicles also make it clear, not only that the Levites made use of Davidic psalms in their leadership of the people's worship, but also that several of them prophesied, meaning, we may assume, that they were themselves inspired persons:

> David and the officers of the army also set apart for the service the sons of Asaph, and of Heman, and of Jeduthun, who should prophesy with lyres, harps and cymbals (1 Chron. 25:1).

Each of the names given here appears in psalm headings.

## The Levitical psalms
As we have seen, Book 1 is virtually all Davidic. There is some evidence in the New Testament that the apostles had a special place as the primary recipients of the revelation of Christ and that what professed to be prophetic utterances were tested by their conformity to apostolic truth.[1] If Book 1 of the Psalter was the first to be compiled, its psalms may have been used as tests of the inspired validity of non-Davidic psalms which were included in later editions. If so, then this would mean that the

whole collection could be regarded as 'Davidic' in the same way that the whole New Testament may be regarded as 'apostolic' despite the presence in it of some books not written by apostles. Something like this could have happened with the psalms, although of course we cannot be sure.

Most of the Levitical psalms occur early in the book. What we might not expect is that it is not only David but these psalmists too who write about enemies and call on God for deliverance from them. This note is much less frequent in these psalms, but it does occur in 42/43, in 44 and in 49. Like the kings, the Levites owed their position to genealogy, and were regarded collectively as divine appointees. So that, as with the kings, their enemies could well be regarded as the enemies of God.

Psalms 42 and 43 were almost certainly one psalm originally. It certainly figures as a psalm of a temple official, for the writer remembers how he led the throng of people in procession to the house of God (42:4), and he prays that God's light and truth might bring him to his holy hill and dwelling (43:3). References to enemies are present but do not dominate the psalm. Rather it is the man's absence from God's house which is the cause of his depression.

Psalm 44 is in a special category, for it is a national lament, and the writer makes no reference whatever to himself. He faces a deep concern; not only has the nation suffered defeat, but he can find no moral cause for this in its conduct. It is a rare example of a psalm of national, innocent suffering. He is not of course suggesting that the nation is sinless, but rather that its leadership has taken it along God's paths.

The psalmist says:

If we had forgotten the name of our God,
    or spread out our hands to a strange god,
would not God discover this?
    For he knows the secrets of the heart.
Because of this we are being killed all day long,
    and accounted as sheep for the slaughter (vv. 20-22).

Kidner's comment is well worth quoting. He says:

> This psalm is perhaps the clearest example of a search for some
> other cause of national disaster than guilt and punishment. It comes
> within sight of an answer at the point of its greatest perplexity:
> 'Nay, *for thy sake* we are slain ...' (22). Momentarily it sees that
> God's people are caught up in a war that is more than local: the
> struggle of 'the kings of the earth ... against the Lord and his
> Anointed' (2:2). The New Testament, with more pieces in position,
> will see the persecuted church foreshadowed here, and diagnose
> not defeat but victory (Rom. 8:36ff.).[2]

It is usually assumed that the fivefold structure of the Psalter
reflects chronological sequence, not of the composition of the
psalms but rather of their collection and ordering. If this is so,
one feature of 44 seems puzzling, for the psalmist says that the
people have been scattered among the nations (v. 11). This might
seem to suggest the experience of the Exile. In relation to this,
Allan Harman says:

> The scattering among the nations could be a reference simply to
> captives taken in battle (cf. the case of Naaman's wife's Israelite
> slave, 2 Kings 5:2). However, captives were often sold off as
> slaves, further increasing the dispersion.[3]

The Korahite group is succeeded immediately by a psalm of
Asaph, representing another tradition of psalmody but still
within the company of Levitical musicians. Prophets like Amos
and Hosea, Isaiah and Micah, and also Jeremiah, often inveigh
against a wrong view of sacrifice.[4] At times of national crisis
the people appear to have brought their sacrifices to the temple
quite excessively,[5] probably with the thought that this might
incline God to defend them from their enemies, so that this was
a kind of religious bribery. It is interesting that the Book of
Psalms itself contains a psalm which is directed against a wrong
theology of sacrifice, and that this was written by a Levite.

No doubt godly Levites were often wearied as they saw

people with no penitential attitude coming to the temple with their offerings. Documents showing the religious outlook of the Babylonians and Assyrians reveal that they thought their gods needed to be fed with sacrifices, and this was clearly the outlook of the misguided Israelites against whom 50 was written (cf. Deut. 32:38).

## The Davidic psalms

Is it significant that the post-Levitical part of Book 2 commences with the most profound of the Davidic penitential psalms? The Levites were concerned with the temple. Certainly they did not officiate at the sacrifices, but they must each have seen a multitude of people coming to the temple with animals to present as sin-offerings. David's sin, however, was one for which no sacrifice was prescribed, for it could by no stretch of imagination be described as a sin of ignorance. In fact he says in this very psalm:

> For you have no delight in sacrifice;
> if I were to give a burnt offering, you would not be pleased.
> The sacrifice acceptable to God is a broken spirit;
> a broken and contrite heart, O God, you will not despise
> (51: 16, 17).

If, as is possible, the Psalter was actually arranged by Levites, the inclusion of this psalm at this point is most significant, for it would suggest a realisation of the limits of the system that was operated in the temple. Verses 18 and 19 contain a call to God to rebuild Jerusalem's walls, followed by the words:

> then you will delight in right sacrifices,
> in burnt offerings and whole burnt offerings;
> then bulls will be offered on your altar.

It has often been suggested that these words were added later editorially, probably during the Exile. If this is so, they would imply that the people were once more accepted by God and not sinning with a collective 'high hand' as they had done by practising idolatry during the reigns of the last three kings of Judah.

We saw that two of the psalms in Book 1 (3 and 18) are linked with particular events in the life of David. This phenomenon occurs also in Book 2 but much more extensively, for this is true of seven of them.[6] It may be that the readers of Book 1 had found it particularly helpful to have reference to David's situation in the two psalms where this is given there, perhaps enabling them to identify with him, so that more of this information was then given in Book 2. Again we cannot be certain of this.

Most of these are concerned with situations where David was in some sort of danger, so that they represent a continuation of the testimony theme of Book 1. The presence of 51 among them, with the use of the language of salvation or deliverance present in it (vv. 12, 14) suggests that here too David faces danger, although in this case it was moral in character. When God has dealt with his sin, he will again testify to him, although in a deeper way this time:

Restore to me the joy of your salvation,
    and sustain in me a willing spirit.
Then I will teach transgressors your ways,
    and sinners will return to you.
Deliver me from bloodshed, O God,
    O God of my salvation,
    and my tongue will sing of your deliverance (51:12-14).

One Davidic psalm is very striking for the purity of David's faith, as this is disclosed within it. This is 62, where he says:

For God alone my soul waits in silence;
    from him comes my salvation.
He alone is my rock and my salvation,
    my fortress; I shall never be shaken' (vv. 1,2; cf. vv. 5-7).

He goes on to exhort his readers also to give God this kind of exclusive trust:

> Trust in him at all times, O people;
>> pour out your heart before him;
>> God is a refuge for us (v. 8).

## The last five psalms in this book

Each of the last five psalms in Book 2 has special interest. Psalm 68 is particularly appropriate in a book which contains both Davidic and Levitical psalms, for it traces the progress of the ark from Mount Sinai to Mount Zion, where David reigned and the Levites officiated in the house of God. It is full of military language.[7] Here the God of the Exodus is seen to be the God of battles, employing thousands of chariots and taking captives (vv. 17, 18), and because of this he is also the God of salvation (vv. 18, 19), whom David had known in this character so often. In this setting we are perhaps being reminded that this is exactly what we should have expected, for this God worked salvation for his people long before the days of David.

Book 1 contained a great psalm of undeserved suffering in 22, quoted by our Lord in the story of the passion as recorded both by Matthew and Mark. There is something similar in Book 2, for 69 too is quoted of Jesus in the New Testament, and it is a psalm of deep suffering. There are however important differences. Psalm 22 contains no confession of sin. Psalm 69 does do so, but only after an affirmation that the psalmist's enemies have no good reason to hate him:

> More in number than the hairs of my head
>> are those who hate me without cause:
> many are those who would destroy me,
>> my enemies who accuse me falsely.
> What I did not steal
>> must I now restore?
> O God, you know my folly;
>> the wrongs I have done are not hidden from you (vv. 4, 5).

It is for God's sake that he suffers as he does (v. 7; cf. 44:22).

Psalm 70 is brief but it is almost identical with 40:13-17, which occupies a similar position towards the close of Book 1. In each there is a plea from David for God to come to his rescue, although this element is also to be found, in Book 1, in its final Psalm 41.

Psalm 71 is an 'orphan' psalm, a rarity in the first two books. It is clear that the author is an old man and that he is reflecting on his life with God. As most commentators indicate, it has plenty of allusions to other psalms. For instance, Kidner notes that verses 12 and 13 echo 22:11; 70:1; 35:26 and 109:29. Each of the psalms alluded to is Davidic, so we see how an elderly believer took great encouragement from God's gracious and strong dealings with David.[8] A lesson from this for Christians today is that both the psalms and the gracious acts of God in the narratives of Scripture may act as means of grace to encourage them.

The psalm which concludes Book 2 (72) is headed 'a Psalm of Solomon'. In this case it may be more with reference to him than composed by him. This is suggested by its contents and also by the fact that it is followed, not preceded, by the words: 'The prayers of David son of Jesse are ended.' These words may have dynastic implications, for they point to genealogical descent, and this was the basis of the Davidic line of kings. It seems as if the promise is here being passed on by David to the next generation, along with the prayer that Solomon's kingdom will excel in righteousness and in extent.[9]

As we have already suggested, Book 2 is the least simple to link with its Pentateuchal counterpart in the Book of Exodus. It certainly contains a great psalm of the Exodus and of Sinai in Psalm 68. Perhaps the psalms of lament followed by praise may be thought to reflect the mood of the people first of all in Egypt under oppressors, and then the change to grateful praise as they were brought out by God.

# Chapter 19

# Book 3 – Why? Why? Why?

## Its general characteristics

These should be noted first of all.

It contains many problem psalms, in which, both at individual and at national levels, the psalmists are wrestling with difficulties of theodicy. The psalm in the earlier books most like those of this book is 44, a psalm of the sons of Korah. In it the author looks back wistfully over the history of his people and recalls how God drove out the nations from the land of Canaan and continued to prosper the armies of Israel in later years. Now however things have become very different. He can identify no spiritual or moral cause for the fact that God allows their enemies to triumph over them. In Book 3 there is quite a concentration of psalms which are somewhat of this kind, although as we shall see, some of them recognise that what has happened is the judgment of God on the people's sins.

Such a concentration of problem psalms would be very appropriate if Book 3 was compiled during the Exile. This was of course a very difficult experience for the people, not simply because it must have seemed in some ways like a repetition of the Egyptian captivity, but also because of the eclipse of the kingship, which had been underwritten by the promises of God. The laments of this book often seem to resemble the Book of Lamentations, itself a product of this difficult experience. Like that book too, it contains affirmations of trust in God's faithfulness,[1] for the psalmists, although puzzled, do not turn away from him but rather face their problems in his presence.

It is also surely significant that all but one of the psalms in this third book are ascribed to Levitical authors, the first eleven of them to Asaph, four others to the sons of Korah and one to Ethan. If this book was compiled during the Exile, the temple was now in ruins. None in Judah would be more disturbed by this than the Levites, because the temple was the focus of their work. No doubt they were deeply downcast by its destruction. It may well be that many of these psalms were actually written, not simply compiled, during this period. This would account for the depressed tone of many of them. The anguish of such men is unmistakable in a passage like the following:

> Your foes have roared within your holy place;
>     they set up their emblems there.
> At the upper entrance they hacked
>     the wooden trellis with axes.
> And then, with hatchets and hammers,
>     they smashed all the carved work.
> They set your sanctuary on fire;
>     they desecrated the dwelling-place of your name,
>     bringing it to the ground (74:4-7).

Another psalm begins:

> O God, the nations have come into your inheritance;
>     they have defiled your holy temple;
>     they have laid Jerusalem in ruins (79:1).

The distinctive function of the Levites as custodians of the temple could no longer be exercised. Was it possible for them, in exile with the rest of the people, to do anything that related to the particular calling God had given them? What would be more natural than for them to spend time in the composition, compilation and arrangement of psalms? Indeed, it may well have been the Levites (the musicians and singers of Israel) who were actually responsible for the eventual shaping of the Book of Psalms as a whole. A psalm like 84, which has many points of similarity with 42/43 and 63 in Book 2, would have special poignancy for exiled Levites. It seems more than likely that this particular psalm was written prior to the Exile, for in it the temple is standing and the psalmist pictures people going up to

Jerusalem on pilgrimage. Read during the Exile, however, it would express and foster that great longing for temple worship which was then beyond satisfaction.

There are also some poignant cries of individual distress here and these too are appropriate. What faced the people as a whole must inevitably have faced many individuals within that nation. Psalm 88 plumbs the very depths of despondency. In fact the writer actually says:

> You have put me in the depths of the Pit,
>   in the regions dark and deep (88:6).

This kind of utterance reminds us of some of the cries that emanated from Job in the midst of his sufferings. Psalm 77 too shows the psalmist going deeper and deeper into despair to a point where he begins to ask anguished questions:

> Will the Lord spurn forever,
>   and never again be favorable?
> Has his steadfast love ceased forever?
>   Are his promises at an end for all time?
> Has God forgotten to be gracious?
>   Has his anger shut up his compassion? (77:7-9)

Here faith seems almost to be in eclipse, although as we shall see, this is not the whole story.

## The importance of Psalm 73

It is increasingly recognised that 73 is of great importance in the structure of the Psalter.[2] It has in fact been well suggested that it virtually sums up the message, not only of the whole Book of Psalms but of the whole Old Testament, and so becomes a kind of Old Testament theology in microcosm.[3] This is certainly true if one takes no special account of the kingly/Messianic theme, which we will see is very important in the Psalter and so should not be overlooked if we are trying to summarise its message.

Certainly the psalmist here faces a major problem. This is the concern that arises if we treat 1 as a statement about the way God deals with the righteous and the wicked within the parameters of this present life. Psalm 73:1 is not dissimilar to the message of 1, when the psalmist says:

Truly God is good to the upright,
to those who are pure in heart.

Immediately after writing this, however, he goes on to say that it is not the righteous but rather the wicked who prosper. In reflecting on this, he reaches something close to scepticism:

All in vain I have kept my heart clean
and washed my hands in innocence.
For all day long I have been plagued,
and am punished every morning (vv. 13, 14).

He goes into the temple however and there he sees things in a different light for it becomes clear to him that the future fate of the wicked and the righteous is to be very different. Then God will put things right.

It is not without significance for the Christian that it was in the place where God was worshipped that this new perspective was given. Job too was given such a new perspective when, at the close of his encounters with the comforters and with Elihu, God disclosed himself to him.

Brueggemann says that the editorial comment after Psalm 72 perhaps reminds us that Solomon's great promise ended in failure, and he then goes on to say:

Psalm 73 is pivotally placed where faith can begin again, after the end of Solomon, after the end of royal effectiveness, after the monarchy and the exile.

A little later he says:

Psalm 73:1 sounds like an echo of Psalm 1. Thus the second half of the Psalter after the end of Solomon, begins as does the first half, with an affirmation of God's faithfulness to the obedient. Psalm 73, however departs drastically from Psalm 1 in its extended argument.[4]

His point is that the psalmist is almost reduced to scepticism before moving on to a stronger, more confident faith.

The psalm ends:

Indeed, those who are far from you will perish;
    you will put an end to those who are false to you.
But for me it is good to be near God;
    I have made the Lord God my refuge,
    to tell of all your works (73:27, 28).

We should notice that the thought of these verses is not really far removed from that of 1. If therefore there was an editorial intention of combating a naive kind of prosperity theology, this must have been due, not to a true reading of 1 but to a misunderstanding of it.

## The Exile and its cause

Was the Exile really an arbitrary act on the part of God? By no means! The use of words like 'anger' or 'wrath' in some of these psalms[5] certainly suggest that there was a moral cause, even if that is not always spelled out. There are in fact some psalms with a deep awareness of sin, and especially a realisation that the authors belong to a nation with a long history of rebellion against God. In many ways these psalms could be used as illustrations of the spiritual principles enunciated in 2 Kings 17, although of course that chapter concerns the northern kingdom rather than Judah.

Psalm 78 is such a psalm. In fact, after the account of Israel's sins in the wilderness, this psalm does concentrate on the northern kingdom. It is not surprising that some writers have suggested that some of the psalms in Book 3 were composed in that kingdom. This is perhaps more likely to be true of 80 than of any other psalm in Book 3, with its reference to the northern tribes of Ephraim and Manasseh (v. 3). Such a psalm could also have been written in Judah, of course, for the people there were aware that all ten tribes were really one nation, although divided for centuries as a result of sin.

The one non-Levitical psalm in this book is 86, which is Davidic, but which, in its content, was perfectly fitted to express the deepest longings of the people in their exilic situation. How moving, read in this historical context, do the words that conclude it become:

> Show me a sign of your favor,
>> so that those who hate me may see it and be put to shame,
>> because you, LORD, have helped me and comforted me (86:17).

With what joy, in such circumstances and with this psalm before them, might the exiles have taken home to themselves the message of Isaiah 40ff, with its opening call to the prophet, 'Comfort, O comfort my people, says your God'! Here once again, then, David's experience of the grace of God would be an encouragement to a people brought to a new penitence.

Confession of sin must be the prelude to divine acts of deliverance and restoration, and 81 spells out this lesson loudly and clearly from the story of the wilderness wanderings. Having said:

> But my people did not listen to my voice;
>> Israel would not submit to me.

God here is represented as going on to say:

> O that my people would listen to me,
>> that Israel would walk in my ways!
> Then I would quickly subdue their enemies,
>> and turn my hand against their foes (81:11, 13, 14).

There are, in fact a number of psalms where there is a plea to God to restore the people. In 79:8, the author asks God not to remember against them the iniquities of their ancestors, and 80 has as a refrain, occurring three times, the words:

Restore us, O God;
    let your face shine, that we may be saved (80:3, 7, 19).

Not only was recognition of sin needed, but also confidence in their God as a God of mercy. In 85, the psalmist recalls God's forgiving mercy to his people in past days, asks him now to restore them to his favour, and shows considerable assurance that God will once again bless his people.

Psalm 77 is a remarkable poem, which might be likened to an eclipse of the sun. In an eclipse, light gradually fades until it seems as if all will be dark and yet it is never quite extinguished, for there is still a corona visible. Then there is further movement and the sun eventually shines in all its glory again. The first half of the psalm, as we have seen, shows the writer getting deeper and deeper into despondency. The psalm does not make clear the exact cause of this, but it is evident that the psalmist can find no relief even by thinking about God and the way he has blessed him in the past. There seems not to be even a corona visible, although we know that the light cannot have entirely gone because, with all his doubting, the psalmist still has light enough to come to cry out to God in his perplexity. It is only when he begins to reflect on God's mercies, not just to himself but to his nation as a whole, that he begins to emerge from his deep despondency. Then, however, his emergence is swift and total.

There were so many things the despondent exiles could learn from God's earlier dealings with his people that could renew their faith and their hope in him. Like the psalmist, it was important for them to ponder the story of God's gracious and powerful acts in their history. Christians too can renew their faith at the cross of Christ.

## Jerusalem's future in God's purpose

For the exiles there was, however, still one major problem. Jerusalem was in ruins and God's holy temple razed to the ground. It would seem that nothing could ever be the same again. It might seem strange then that there should be two psalms in Book 3 (76, 87) celebrating the fact that Zion is the dwelling-place of God. Probably these psalms had been written before the Exile, but it is their place in Book 3 as finally arranged that seems puzzling, if that book was in fact put together before the Exile came to an end. What nostalgia they must have evoked, and how deeply they must have depressed those who read them!

Yet, if the exiles were already beginning to have hope of a return, perhaps through the promises of Isaiah 40-55, they would be a further encouragement. God had a purpose for Jerusalem still. In such a context, each of these psalms must have shone like a beacon of hope. God's love for Zion was not temporary, not evanescent. Here then was the anticipation that it would rise again and once again be crowned with a temple for the worship of their gracious God.

Psalm 87, in fact, goes further than this. It is one of the most remarkable psalms in the entire Psalter. As in Isaiah 19, with its message of grace to Gentile nations, even those who had been the cruellest enemies of Israel and her God, the psalmist sees people from Rahab (Egypt) and Babylon actually enrolled in the number of those born in Zion, and follows this with references to Philistia, Tyre and Ethiopia (87:4). We note the use of the plural ('peoples') when the psalmist writes:

The LORD records, as he registers the peoples,
  'This one was born there' (87:6).

Reading such words, the Christian may surely be excused if he finds himself thinking of 'the Jerusalem above', for it was in writing to largely Gentile churches that Paul said of this city, 'she is our mother' (Gal. 4:26).

It is not inconsistent with this that some of these psalms, for instance, 82 and 83, call on God to judge the whole earth. The Book of Psalms contains a note of universalism in that it recognises the God of Israel to have a saving purpose which goes beyond Israel, but not in the sense that there will be no judgment on sin. God will put all things right eventually, but this will mean for many an experience of his abiding anger, rightly poured out on unrepentant sinners.

## The importance of Psalm 89
Book 3 ends with 89, in which the faithfulness of God to his covenant with David is extolled at considerable length (vv. 1-37), only to be followed by a section in which the psalmist shows great perplexity at what has happened. It seems clear that his perplexity is caused by the Exile and, probably, the taking of young king Jehoiachin to Babylon (2 Kings 24:8-12). Towards its close comes the poignant question: 'Lord, where are your loving-kindnesses which you swore to David in your truth' (v. 49)?

Brueggemann attaches much importance to 89. He says: 'Almost Job-like, the psalmist summons Yahweh to justify the failure of his covenant promises...'[6] Even if 'summons' is felt to be too strong a word, it is evident that the psalmist is here wrestling with a problem of theodicy, and he cries out in puzzled distress:

Lord, where is your steadfast love of old,
    which by your faithfulness you swore to David? (89:49)

Brueggemann sees this as the crisis that the fourth and fifth books of the Psalter sought to meet. He likens the revelation of God's majesty in these two books to the divine disclosure at the close of the Book of Job.[7] We can take his point, and yet also note the significance of the fact that, in the psalm as we have it, those opening 37 verses can still be read. Just as it is possible that the first verse of 73 expresses not only the initial but the final outlook of the psalmist, as a comparison with what that psalm's last verse might suggest, so this long section in 89 may well express a conviction that was never completely eclipsed by the experiences of the Exile. If that is so, verses 38 to 51 express not doubt, still less disillusionment, but rather a deep awareness that God's dealings with his people sometimes have a mystery at their heart. Such a realisation – for the Christian too – is a challenge to keep on believing his covenant promises in the confidence that one day light will come.

And come it did – in Jesus Christ!

# Chapter 20

## Book 4 – The eternal heavenly King

### The end of the Exile

Taking the book as a whole, it would be difficult to find any book of the Old Testament that is a greater encouragement to faith in the true and living God than is this. It must have been a major means of grace from God to those who first read it. We cannot be sure when it was compiled, although there is some evidence that strongly suggests this was quite early.

1 Chronicles 16:7 reads: 'Then on that day David first appointed the singing of praises to the LORD by Asaph and his kindred.' This is the NRSV rendering which follows the Hebrew fairly closely. The NIV renders this somewhat differently: 'That day David first committed to Asaph and his associates this psalm of thanks to the LORD.' J. B. Payne's comment is an apt one:

> In light of the broader context, the NIV's rendering becomes justifiable. David's commission to Asaph (v. 7) does function as the setting of the poem thus introduced (vv. 8-36a); and the response of David's people (v. 36b ...) is at the same time the conclusion of the quoted poetry, proving that it was in existence in 1000 BC.[1]

This psalm in fact consists of 105:1-15, the whole of 96 and 106:1, 47, 48. All this material is from Book 4 of the Book of Psalms, and the last two verses bring Book 4 to its praise conclusion. It seems clear therefore that the Chronicler held them to have been in existence in David's day. It is not without interest that Book 4 includes what is probably the oldest psalm in the Psalter (90) and that many of the psalms in it have a timeless quality.

Of course it is quite possible that other psalms were added to this book at a later date, so that we may still ask when this

collection of psalms, as we have it, came to take its place as
Book 4 in the developing Psalter. It would fit very well into the
situation at the close of the Exile and almost as well into the
early post-exilic period.

If the people were still in exile, but the Levites were aware
that God intended them to be restored to the land, such a book
would be a great encouragement to them to trust God for the
future. Their God was supreme over all the nations, including
the Babylonians and the Persians, and once again Jerusalem
would be a holy city, with a new temple built on it.

If, on the other hand, they had already been restored to the
land, this would spur them on in the actual work of rebuilding,
which was a major task for them after their return. A study of
such books as Ezra and Nehemiah and the prophecies of Haggai
and Zechariah shows that the returned exiles were often in need
of such encouragement.

Creach, among other writers, has explored a possible
relationship between this book of the Psalter and Isaiah, chapters
40-55.[2] If this part of the Book of Isaiah was intended to be an
encouragement to the exiles in the final stages of their time in
Babylon, then some similarity between it and this fourth book
of the Psalter might have been expected. In this respect, although
not necessarily in other ways, the question as to when it was
written is comparatively unimportant, for its function as an
encouragement depends on the time of its reading rather than
that of its writing.

Creach notes, for instance, the similarity between 90:5-6 and
13 and Isaiah 40:6 and 1, between 106:46,47 and Isaiah 54:7
and 105:43 and Isaiah 55:12.[3] Here the combination of comfort
or compassion, gathering (from the nations) and joy and singing
is certainly appropriate language in relation to a return from
exile. We may well imagine the feelings of the people when,
after reading the promise of Isaiah 55:12:

You will go out in joy
    and be led back in peace

they then read 105:43:

> So he brought his people out with joy,
>     his chosen ones with singing.

The God who had once rescued them from Egypt, could surely be trusted to bring them back from Babylon!

## The special importance of Psalm 90

The placing of 90 at the opening of Book 4 is evidence of great spiritual wisdom on the part of the redactor. In so many ways, its position there is particularly appropriate.

First of all, it takes the reader right back in history, for it is 'a Prayer of Moses, the man of God'. If the people were troubled by questions such as those raised towards the close of 89, questions about the Davidic dynasty and its apparent demise, this psalm was a reminder to them that God's purposes for his people did not begin with David, but that the real roots of Israel's position as God's nation are to be found in the Pentateuch. This was just what they needed. The writer of the Books of Chronicles showed the same kind of wisdom when, in a book emphasising Judah and Jerusalem and David, the first word he committed to writing was 'Adam'.

So often in the Old Testament there are reminders of the very manifest acts of God which took place in the birth of the nation out of the trauma of Egyptian bondage, for each generation needed to be reminded of what it owed to him and to recognise how deep and strong were the foundations of its faith. The New Testament equivalent of course is the acts of God in the cross and resurrection of Jesus, and here is the bedrock of New Testament faith. Present perplexities drive us back to Biblical foundations. It is surely significant that Revelation 15:3 tells us about the overcomers:

> They sing the song of Moses, the servant of God, and the song of the Lamb:

'Great and amazing are your deeds,
Lord God the Almighty ...'

This psalm also emphasises, most appropriately, the eternity
of God. The writer says:

For a thousand years in your sight
    are like yesterday when it is past,
    or like a watch in the night (v. 4).

They needed a sense of an ongoing purpose of God. Our
concentration on the things that immediately concern us is understandable, but it is so important to get the longer perspective on
things. All this Isaac Watts expressed so well in a hymn which
is really a paraphrase of part of this psalm:

O God, our help in ages past,
    our hope for years to come,
our shelter from the stormy blast,
    and our eternal home.

This hymn does not, however, include a further important
element in the psalm: its references to the wrath of God and to
the iniquities of the people, followed by the words:

So teach us to count our days
    that we may gain a wise heart (v. 12).

This feature of the psalm would remind the people that the
cause of the Exile was their own sin, and that it was God's
purpose that they should learn from it that wisdom which begins
in the fear of the Lord. It is important too, for us to recall, on
national occasions when the hymn by Isaac Watts is so often
sung, that jingoism is inappropriate and that we should be
grateful to God, not only for protection from aggressors, but
also that God has not dealt with us after our sins.

Psalm 103 is a great hymn of praise which comes later in Book 4, and it has interesting points of comparison with 90 and reinforces for the reader the lessons of that earlier psalm. It too takes the reader back to the days of Moses (v. 7) and reflects on the eternity of God, the frailty of human life and the wonder of his deathless love for those who fear him (vv. 15-18). It acknowledges too the supreme sovereignty of God (v. 19). It is true that it does not stress the sins of the people anything like as much as 90, but it shows deep gratitude for his forgiveness, when the psalmist says:

> as far as the east is from the west,
>> so far he removes our transgressions from us (v. 12).

Psalm 103 is headed 'of David' and so here one Biblical writer endorses for a later generation the truths penned by an even earlier one. As we shall see, the writer to the Hebrews recognised this same principle of the reinforcement of truth over the years by the way he quoted psalms that reflect on earlier events and which themselves relate to the final revelation of God in Jesus, the Son of God.

## The nature of Book 4's message

G. H. Wilson has done much work on the structure of the Psalter[4] and his views on this have become very influential. His view of the function of Book 4 is interesting but problematic. He regards it as the structural heart of the Psalter. Books 1 and 2 focus on the Davidic covenant. In these books the king is often under attack, but he looks to God for protection. Book 3 is, however, largely dominated by psalms of deep anxiety, whose authors are clearly deeply disturbed by events in their own lives or in the life of their nation. Psalm 89, which concludes Book 3, bemoans the demise of the Davidic dynasty. What then is the function of Book 4? It is to direct attention away from the Davidic covenant and monarchy altogether and to place all the emphasis on the sovereignty of the supreme King, Israel's God.

In some ways this seems beyond question. In this book there

is a great emphasis on the supreme kingship of Israel's God and no express reference is made to the Davidic kingship.[5] Does this mean, though, that those who placed Book 4 where it is regarded a hope focused on the monarchy as completely wrong? This view cannot be established beyond doubt, for the functions of the contents of Book 4 can be understood quite differently.

We must ask why so much Davidic material was combined with it by the union of Book 4 with Books 1 to 3, especially the first two? Perhaps, it may be said, because the psalms in these books were hallowed by antiquity and could not simply be abandoned. But of course they were not simply ancient but were the word of God and, presumably, were recognised as such. There are in fact two Davidic psalms (101 and 103) in Book 4 itself, and we should not forget that the primary royal psalm, number 2, is not simply a psalm of the human king but also of the supreme Monarch. Support of the Davidic dynasty was a promised function of the very same sovereign God praised in many of Book 4's psalms, so that such psalms could provide a spiritual context in which hope for a restoration of that dynasty could grow.

What is true, of course, is that the trust of the people was never meant to be in the monarch himself, but only in the God who placed him where he was and promised to support him. To trust in the man himself would be to repeat the sin of those who initially requested 'a king to govern us, like other nations' (1 Sam. 8:5). Other nations looked to their king as their protector, but Yahweh was Israel's great Protector.

Of course Book 5 eventually came to be combined with the other Psalter books, and this last book, as we shall see, certainly strikes a Davidic note and even looks forward, especially in 132, to a Davidic king of the future.

### The divine King and his great purposes

J. L. Mays thinks 90-92 are transitional,[6] and a good case can be made out for this, for it is obvious that there is a new beginning at 93.

This fourth book places much emphasis on the kingship of God himself, which, as we have already noted, is in view also in 2, for there the divine King underwrites the dominion of the earthly king. This book, therefore, is a great faith-building book, and the faith it builds is in God himself. Almost all its psalms point to the greatness and the sovereignty of Israel's God.

Psalm 90 says that this God is the dwelling-place of his people and that he is the great Creator of all things (vv. 1, 2). Psalm 91 exhorts the people to dwell in the shelter, the dwelling-place, of the Most High (vv.1, 9), so that the two opening psalms of this book perfectly complement each other. Psalm 92 extols the greatness of God's deeds.

Psalms 93 and 95-100 are celebrations of the universal scope of the sovereignty of Israel's God. Each of them refers quite explicitly to his kingship, while in 93:1, 96:10, 97:1 and 99:1 the triumphant shout is heard 'The LORD is king', and these psalms are known as 'Yahweh-malak' psalms, for this is what this Hebrew expression means. In this context, the assertions of 94, such as

The LORD will not forsake his people;
    he will not abandon his heritage (v. 14),

and

The LORD has become my stronghold,
    and my God the rock of my refuge.
He will repay them for their iniquity
    and wipe them out for their wickedness;
        the LORD our God will wipe them out (vv. 22, 23),

are seen to be totally justified.

It is interesting to study 102, which comes so soon after these hymns of God's sovereignty and which also reminds us in some ways of 90, the psalm that opened Book 4. It has the unique title: 'A prayer of one afflicted, when faint and pleading before the LORD.' Like 90, it emphasises the eternity of God and the brevity of human life:

'O my God,' I say, 'do not take me away
    at the mid-point of my life,
you whose years endure
    throughout all generations' (v. 24).

Like 90, this psalm sees him as the great Creator of all things. Like the Yahweh-malak psalms it views God as King, and here relates his sovereignty as well as his compassion to Zion's plight:

But you, O LORD, are enthroned forever:
    your name endures to all generations.
You will rise up and have compassion on Zion,
    for it is time to favor it;
    the appointed time has come (vv. 12, 13).

There is much else in the psalm that would be of special relevance to those who looked for or had just experienced the return from exile.

From a literary standpoint, 103 and 104 are highly distinguished even in the Psalter which contains so much wonderful literature. They were probably placed together deliberately by the redactor to show the sovereignty of Israel's God in both redemption and creation, in history and in the visible universe. Both of them begin, 'Bless the LORD, O my soul' and 103 ends in the same way. These words occur also at the close of 104, although they are followed by the words 'Praise the LORD!' In the Septuagint, this final exhortation opens the next psalm instead of closing this one, and this could be correct.

Some of these psalms, and notably the Yahweh-malak ones, reflect the Zion theology in which the holy city becomes the focus of thanksgiving and praise. Hayes, writing of the Zion Psalms, points out that the Zion Theology was not smothered in the ashes of Jerusalem. It was transposed to a new key.... The Zion psalms with their marvellous claims and promises were not discarded but were no doubt sung in anticipation of the new, the true, the ideal Zion to come (cf. Rev. 21).[7]

These psalms would certainly glow with new meaning for the people after the Jerusalem site had been restored to them and the city itself had been rebuilt after the Exile. They might well have encouraged them in the rebuilding in the same way that Nehemiah, Haggai and Zechariah did.

The fourth book actually looks ahead even further than the rebuilding of Zion, for it anticipates in many psalms the eventual triumph of the true faith to such an extent that all nations will come and worship the Lord. If foreign observers had seen the people worshipping in Jerusalem after the return from Babylonian captivity and had heard them sing some of these psalms, they might well have thought these sentiments utterly ridiculous. Here was a small people, not only tiny in relation to many other nations but even in comparison with what it had been in the past, asserting confidently that its God ruled over all and that all nations would come to worship him.

But the Bible is full of this kind of thing. Who would have thought a tiny baby born in Bethlehem would be called 'King of Kings and Lord of Lords'?

## The divine pattern for the King

Psalm 101 is very interesting, particularly in the light of the fact that the concept of a human king, in explicit terms, is completely absent from Book 4. Yet this is a psalm of David. It is an affirmation, made not only in general terms but with many specifics, of his intention to rule righteously. As Kidner says,

The resolve made here to have no truck with evil men does not spring from pharisaic pride but from a king's concern for a clean administration, honest from the top down. How far he was to fall short of this in his own acts and in his appointments is told in 2

Samuel. But it was an inspired pattern, remaining to challenge him and his successors.[8]

It is reminiscent of two earlier psalms. The first of these is 41. This psalm confesses sin but it opens with the words,

Blessed is he who has regard for the weak;
  the Lord delivers him in times of trouble (41:1, NIV).

Was there anybody who had a special responsibility for the weak? Yes, the king. Here David recognises this responsibility and the blessing that goes with its faithful discharge.

Psalm 72 is even more interesting, for, like 101 it focuses on the godly and righteous rule of the king. It is either a longing for such a king or, more probably, a prayer that the king in view would be righteous. Here too we are told, after the manner of 41:1:

For he delivers the needy when they call,
  the poor and those who have no helper.
He has pity on the weak and the needy (72:12, 13).

Structurally, these two psalms from earlier collections are important, for each is the closing psalm in the book in which it is placed. This is not the case with 101, but it comes after a deeply impressive series of psalms celebrating the supreme reign of God. Could it not therefore be a reminder that, in 2, the supreme King supports the anointed earthly king? It may also remind the reader of 1, where it is clear that it is the righteous who know God's blessing, those who have a character like that represented here. It was in large part the folly of kings of David's line in fostering idolatry amongst the people that led to the Exile, and it might be thought that this psalm is placed where it is to show disillusionment with this line of monarchs. Perhaps, but would it not also create a great thirst for the coming of such a monarch, and so be an Old Testament preparation for Christ?

## The final two psalms of Book 4

The closing two psalms taken together, bring Book 4 to a realistic conclusion, just as 90 struck a note of realism at the beginning. Both 105 and 106 are psalms of praise and also reflections on history, but there is an important difference between them. Psalm 105 traces the great faithfulness of God to his people, while 106 traces the great unfaithfulness of the people to their God. This is a salutary reminder to us that historians must, in the very nature of their subject, make a selection from the events of a particular period of history, and that the most optimistic or flattering construction from the past is not always the most accurate.

Yet it is also notable that 106 ends with the faithfulness and gracious deliverance of God, the God who delivers his people from their enemies. This then, for people at the close of the Exile or soon after the return, is a reminder that God has not dealt with them after their sins, but that the restoration to the land is an act of sheer grace.

# Chapter 21

## Book 5 – Pilgrimages, precepts, prophecies and praise

### The date of this book

Theories as to when particular books of the Psalter were put together and when they were linked to others are bound to be somewhat speculative, although the exilic provenance of Book 3 seems probable almost to the point of certainty. Nobody can be sure about Book 5, except that the sequence of the books, in terms of their arrangement, is almost certainly chronological. In some ways it is rather like Book 4, in that both books contain a great deal of material to build faith and to turn the eyes of the people outward to their God, to his greatness and to his grace.

There are some who think that, along with Books 3 and 4, it belongs to the Exile. Certainly, as Wilson notes, 138-144, the Davidic group to be found in this collection contain much to encourage the exiles. He says also that 120-134 constitute 'an almost unbroken song of reliance on YHWH alone.'[1] The long group of those entitled 'A song of Ascents' was employed in the Holy Land in connection with the Feasts, and these could not, of course, have been held during the Exile. There is no reason why they should not have been incorporated in this book ready for their use after the return of the people to the land. After all, compilers of hymnbooks may have completed major sections of their work before their full volume is published.

Strongly in favour of a post-exilic date though, is the fact that this book starts with 107, the first nine verses of which immediately make us think of the returning exiles, and presumably this was an intention of the redactor. Psalm 137 is easier to date than any other psalm, but even though clearly produced during the Exile because of its reference to the Babylonian captivity and in terms which make it certain that it was a present experience for the author, it need not have been incorporated in the collection until after it was over.

Little really depends on the collection's date, but we will assume that here is a book put together soon after the return from Exile and incorporating some psalms which already existed in definite groups. We will also assume that Book 5 originally ended with 145, but will leave to the next chapter the arguments for and against this.

### The importance of Psalm 107

This book has its own terminology, some of the most important of which emerges first of all in 107, its very first psalm. The verbs, *halal* ('praise') and *yadhah* ('give thanks'), are of very frequent occurrence, and interestingly the second of these never appears in 145–150, although the first is very frequent both in 107–145 and in 146–150.

Psalm 107 was well chosen to introduce the collection. It is a psalm that shows great joy in God and it is full of grateful praise to him. He has gathered his people from the nations. A reader who has not been too overawed by the division of the Psalter into books might well have noticed that this is, in fact, an answer to the prayer uttered in 106:47:

> Save us, O Lord our God,
>     and gather us from the nations,
> that we may give thanks to your holy name
>     and glory in your praise.

This is the strongest link there is between the closing psalm of one book and the one that opens its successor.

This opening psalm begins by extolling Yahweh as the God of redemption and calling on those who have experienced this to declare what he has done. This reminds us of the many psalms of testimony in the Davidic collections, particularly the large number of them in Book 1. This call is followed by four pictures, each showing people at the end of their tether, crying to God, who rescues them.[2] The sequence is stylised, with each containing the words:

> Then they cried to the LORD in their trouble,
>> and he delivered them from their distress (vv. 6, 13, 19, 28),

and as each moves to its close there is the exhortation:

> Let them thank the LORD for his steadfast love,
>> for his wonderful works to humankind (vv. 8, 15, 21, 31).

The first picture shows wanderers in the desert and is probably meant to be taken literally, while the remaining three, the prisoners, the sick and the mariners in peril, are probably intended as parables of exile and deliverance. Further descriptions of God's ability to change situations are followed by the exhortation:

> Let those who are wise give heed to these things,
> and consider the steadfast love of the LORD (v. 43).

### The wisdom theme

So then, at the end of the first psalm in this book the reader is reminded that he is meant to learn from it. Further emphasis is given to this for the discerning reader by 108, 109 and 110, which are psalms of David and which contain reminders of the introduction to the whole Psalter in 2.

Psalm 108 extols the faithfulness of God to David, which certainly suggests the covenant promise of God, and shows confidence that God will give the king the whole land of Israel plus the lands which surround it, a reminder perhaps of the promise of dominion over the nations given in 2. The selection of tribal districts and foreign states listed would be particularly meaningful to the returning exiles, for at first they occupied such a small part of the land.

Psalm 109 was obviously written when David was deeply

aware of the antagonism and hatred of his enemies, whose attitude to him is very reminiscent of that of the rebels in 2. He looks to God's 'steadfast love' (v. 21) and trusts him for deliverance from these bitter foes.

As we will see, Psalm 110 has some special features which distinguish it from other psalms of the king, but there is in it an assurance of victory for him, which was promised in 2, the very first psalm of the king.

It is so clear then that the compiler of this book held godly wisdom, the wisdom that rests on God's word, to be very important, that he saw it as a wisdom that takes in the lessons of God's acts in history and lives in their light. This is still more reinforced for the reader by the next two psalms.

Psalm 111 is entirely focused on God, his works, his faithfulness, his covenant, his name, until the last verse, where the psalmist says:

> The fear of the LORD is the beginning of wisdom;
>> all those who practice it have a good understanding.
>> His praise endures forever.

Psalm 112 begins where its predecessor ended, with the fear of the LORD:

> Praise the LORD!
>> Happy are those who fear the LORD,
>> who greatly delight in his commandments (v. 1),

and the psalmist goes on to show the blessed results of such an attitude and how hopeless is the antagonism of the wicked.

So then the reader is reminded again and again in the first five psalms of this book that the psalms have a practical end in view and that is to encourage Old Testament believers in godliness and righteousness. This is thoroughly in line with the overall theme of the Psalter, which is set for us at its very beginning. They have this function still for new covenant believers.

## Psalms of the feasts of the Lord

As we have seen, Book 4 commenced with a psalm of Moses and so it took its readers back to the roots of Israel's history and the foundations of their faith in Yahweh. For new covenant believers there are two main ways in which God reminds us of the roots of our own faith: the Exodus which Jesus accomplished and fulfilled at Jerusalem in his death and resurrection.[3] We are reminded by the reading and preaching of the word of God and we are also reminded by the two great ordinances of baptism and the Lord's Supper which Christ gave to his church. For Israel, reminders came through the word, but also through great annual events, the three pilgrim feasts of Passover, Pentecost and Tabernacles.

Just as appropriate passages from the word of God are read in Christian churches at times when baptism is administered and the Lord's Supper celebrated, so it was for Israel in relation to her annual celebrations. Book 5 contains two great sequences of psalms used in connection with the feasts, and there is little doubt that the combination of word and act would serve to deepen the people's sense of thanksgiving and renewed commitment, at least for those who were spiritually sensitive.

The first of these groups (113-118) is known as the Egyptian Hallel, for it was used at the feast of the Passover, which commemorated God's deliverance of his people from bondage in Egypt. Kidner says:

> Only the second of them (114) speaks directly of the Exodus, but the theme of raising the down-trodden (113) and the note of corporate praise (115), personal thanksgiving (116), world vision (117) and festal procession (118) make it an appropriate series to mark the salvation which began in Egypt and will spread to the nations.[4]

After this group comes 119, the great psalm of the Law. Although the Davidic material in Book 5 is somewhat limited, the reader of the whole Book of Psalms will recall the very strong concentration of Davidic psalms earlier in the Psalter, and may remember that, according to Deuteronomy 17, the Law was to feature in a special way in the life of the king:

> When he has taken the throne of his kingdom, he shall have a copy of this law written for him in the presence of the Levitical priests. It shall remain with him and he shall read in it all the days of his life, so that he may learn to fear the LORD his God, diligently observing all the words of this law and these statutes (Deut. 17:18, 19).

Why though does this psalm occur at this precise point? Is it to remind the people that Sinai was part of that national experience of God which constituted them as the people of God? Is it to remind them that they were redeemed for obedience? Is it to compensate for the fact that none of the pilgrim feasts celebrates Sinai? Is it in fact for all these reasons?

It stands between two great series celebrating feasts that were instituted in the days of Moses and observed during the wilderness period. But in that period too the Law was given at Sinai, and it was fitting that there should be some significant reminder of this. Hence the inclusion of this psalm at this point. After the Exile, the Jews began to give the Law a bigger and bigger place in their outlook and they felt that there should be some annual celebration of the time when it was given to Moses. Accordingly, they linked the feast of Pentecost with this event.

The Ten Commandments, recorded in Exodus 20, are preceded by the words:

> I am the LORD your God, who brought you out of the land of Egypt, out of the house of slavery (Exod. 20:2).

This introduction to the Decalogue could have functioned as an antidote to extreme legalism, for it bears testimony to the fact that the Law was given to a redeemed people who had experienced God's gracious deliverance. The purpose that verse served in Exodus 20 is served by the Egyptian Hallel as the introduction to 119 here.

The Songs of Ascents (120-134), like the Egyptian Hallel, were used at times of pilgrimage. It is uncertain what exactly the title means. There are fifteen of them and, according to the Mishnah, a Levitical choir sang them on the series of fifteen steps which led up to the temple at feast time. This is often questioned, however, and it may be that they were sung by the people as they made their pilgrimage to Jerusalem and its temple just prior to the feasts. No matter from which direction they came, their journey would involve an ascent, the more so as they got nearer to Jerusalem itself.

It is clear that at least some of them were not specially composed for this purpose. There are some psalms of David and even a psalm of Solomon (127). The special appropriateness of some of them is apparent. In 120, the psalmist lives far from Jerusalem and this would certainly mean much to Jews of the Dispersion who were turning their steps towards Jerusalem with great eagerness. Psalm 121 refers to the hills, and they would pass many a hill where pagan shrines had been located and would remember that the only real source of help is the living God. Psalm 122 rejoices in the prospect of meeting with others in the house of the Lord, and so on. Solomon's psalm makes important reference to the house and the city as built by God, appropriate from a man who was himself a great builder. In the final psalm in the group (134) there is an exhortation to those who minister in the Lord's house, so it would be very fitting as a psalm to be sung on arrival there.

Howard, in commenting that 'most readily admit that the final form of the Psalter incorporated fixed sequences of originally liturgical material', says, 'the parade example being the psalms of ascent.'[5] No matter what we may say about other psalm groupings, there can be no doubt from the title that these psalms were intended to be viewed as an ordered sequence.

After the Psalms of Ascents come two psalms which continue the note of praise sounded in the last ascent psalm. It is not clear how these were used in relation to the Songs of Ascents. The term 'Great Hallel' was sometimes used of the whole sequence from 120 to 136, sometimes it was confined to 135 and 136, and sometimes it was used of 136 alone. Both of these psalms would be highly appropriate for use at the feasts, for both make reference to the deliverance from Egypt and God's gift of the land of Canaan to his people.

A glance at a good reference Bible will show that 135 is remarkable for the number of quotations and allusions to other psalms it contains. All this material is brought together in a psalm of praise, which would be so apt when used in the temple at one of the Great Feasts, for it would call to mind many other occasions when the people had joined together in glad songs in praise of their God. Like 134, it starts with an exhortation to those who officiate in the house of God to praise the Lord, and towards its close addresses such an exhortation to the house of Aaron (the priests) and the house of Levi.

Psalm 136 is the only psalm in the whole Psalter which has a repeated refrain in its every verse. It is a far-reaching celebration of the love and covenant faithfulness of Yahweh to his people, for 'steadfast love' is the love which honours and works within the covenant.

## The Davidic psalms and the Messianic King
There are fourteen Davidic psalms in this book, and they occur in three groups. First of all, there are three (108,109,110) which come near the start of the book. We have already taken a look at these. Then there are four (122, 124, 131, 133) which have their place in the sequence of Psalms of Ascents, and finally there is a sequence of eight, running from 138 to 145.

The four Davidic Psalms of Ascents are somewhat varied. The most distinctive feature of the Davidic psalms in the first three books of the Psalter is the constant presence of enemies, and David's frequent plea to the Lord to deal with them or else his thanksgiving that he has already dealt with them. This is true of only one of these four (124), but of course David's devotional life must have been a rich one, and so we are not surprised to find some variety of theme here.

The eight psalms in the final Davidic sequence are fairly representative of him, for all of them make reference to trouble or to enemies, although the final one (145) simply by implication, in verses 18 to 20. Perhaps one of the reasons for putting them here is to emphasise again the importance of David for the Psalter.

A notable feature of Book 5 is the way it looks towards the future for a great Davidic king. In 110, he is said to be priest as well as king. This is a Davidic psalm,[6] and in it the king addresses somebody he calls, 'lord', and the New Testament, which quotes from and alludes to it with some frequency, consistently applies it to Christ, so regarding it as Messianic.

Psalm 132 is one of the Psalms of Ascents. There is no clear quotation of it in the New Testament, but it is highly significant for the Davidic and Messianic themes in the Book of Psalms. It opens with a prayer, in which the writer says:

> O LORD, remember David
> and all the hardships he endured (v. 1, NIV).

He refers to two oaths. The first of these is the oath of David that he would not rest until he found a dwelling-place for the Lord, followed by a poetical account of the finding of the ark and its transportation. Then comes another plea,

> For the sake of David your servant,
> do not reject your anointed one (v. 10, NIV).

It is clear that this anointed one is not himself David. Is he a reigning king? Perhaps when the psalm was written this was the meaning, but we have to ask what it would mean if in fact the collection is post-exilic (or even exilic), with this psalm therefore brought into the collection at a time when there was no Davidic king reigning over the people. We are probably given a clue in the reference to the oath of God that established the covenant (vv. 11-13), its assertion that God has made Zion his resting place for ever, and especially the words of verses 17, 18:

> There I will cause a horn to sprout up for David;
>> I have prepared a lamp for my anointed one.
> His enemies I will clothe with disgrace,
>> but on him, his crown will gleam.

The fact that these verses relate to the future should not be missed. Whether it was intended to be a promise of a lasting dynasty or not, the point is that, in the historical context of the post-exilic period, with no Davidic king actually reigning, it must have come to have clear Messianic significance, as so many of the royal psalms did.[7] Here we see that the Jewish reader of this final book was reminded of the great promises and acts of God in the past and encouraged to hope in the ultimate fulfilment of his promises in the future. It may well be that the reader of the Psalter, going through it consecutively perhaps for a second time, is meant to understand the Davidic theme in Messianic terms, to re-interpret many of the Davidic psalms, and to apply them to God's great King of the future. It is not surprising then that the New Testament relates a goodly number of them to Messiah Jesus.

## The significance of Psalm 145
A final comment should be made on 145. Wilson considered that Book 5 originally ended with it, and he makes out a good case for this. It is not to denigrate the majestic fivefold conclusion to the whole Psalter to say that 145 would not have been out of place as a conclusion to the whole. It is worth noting too, as Warren Wiersbe points out,[8] that the five psalms that precede it are all prayers. The proper response to answered prayer is heartfelt praise. It might almost be a study text for the Old Testament doctrine of God, so full is its presentation of

what the Old Testament teaches about him.[9] In verse 5, David says:

> On the glorious splendor of your majesty,
>     and on your wondrous works, I will meditate.

How appropriate this would have been if this had been the terminating psalm of the collection at one time, especially so if 1 had by then been placed at the beginning, for that psalm also commended godly meditation. Wilson says that 145 embraces many of the themes so far from Psalm 1,[10] and an examination of it will show this to be true.

## The climax of the whole Book of Psalms (Psalms 146-150)

The final psalms furnish not simply a conclusion to the Psalter, but a climax. The last six are all praise psalms, and they are purely this. There is no note of lament or complaint in them. It is true that there are occasional references to enemies or affliction, but never as subjects for prayer but rather for praise that God has answered and dealt with these situations.

There are of course psalms of praise elsewhere in the Psalter. The first four books all end with an ascription of praise (41:13; 71:18-20 or 17-20; 89:52; 106:48 or 47,48),[11] and these were probably specially written for this purpose. Was the final psalm, or even the final group of five,[12] written especially to conclude the Psalter? Either is possible although, of course, real proof is probably impossible. What we can say, however, is that the concentration on praise at the end of each book and the special stress on it at the end of the whole collection strongly suggests that a main purpose of the Psalter is praise.

Most scholars take 150 as the final praise conclusion both to Book 5 and to the Psalter as a whole. Wilson, however, has argued against this. He makes out a good case for regarding 145 as the original conclusion to Book 5, with the five that follow it as a later addition.[13] Psalm 145:21, the last verse of that psalm, would be a most fitting conclusion, uniting as it does the personal and the universal notes of praise:

My mouth shall speak the praise of the LORD,
and all flesh will bless his holy name for ever and for ever
(145:21).


He points out that this is similar to the other closing
doxologies. It is also interesting that this and the six which
preceded it are all psalms of David, which is not true of those
that follow it. It would not be inappropriate for a Psalter which
contained so many Davidic psalms to come to its climax with a
final Davidic collection. Wilson also points out that the final
Hallel (146-150) draws impetus from 145:21.

In this verse David looks beyond his own praise to the praise
of 'all flesh'. How significant then that in the final group of
psalms, the only one that strikes an individual note is 146, and
even that only in its first two verses! All the others are
completely communal. It is fitting that those whose hearts are
full of praise should not simply utter that praise in isolation but
should come together to extol their Lord and King. The Book
of the Revelation reveals the final and eternal praise uttered by
the saints of God and, wherever this is shown to us, it is
communal, and, in chapters 4 and 5, within a cosmic setting.

Sometimes a composer, having written a movement of a great
symphony and given a final recapitulation of its great themes,
will follow this with a coda related to, and yet in some ways
different from, what has gone before, and providing a climax
beyond the normal climax. If Wilson is right, the editors of the
Psalter have done something like this at the close of the Book.
No praise can be too great or too extensive for such a God!

There is an interesting contrast between 107 and 145, which
we are taking to be the intended opening and closing psalms of
Book 5. Zenger points out that 'whereas Psalm 107 concretizes
its message of the saving goodness of YHWH in a theology of
Israel (the gathering of Israel together from the nations and the
return to "the city"), Psalm 145 expressly extends the vision of
the rescuing God to all creatures ("all flesh").'[14]

Each psalm in this final group begins and ends with the

words, 'Praise the LORD!' The fact that there are five of them may well be significant, suggesting perhaps a comparison with the five books of the Pentateuch. If this is so, then it reinforces the comparison already suggested by the existence in the Psalter of five distinct books.

Psalm 1, as we have seen, refers to meditation on the Law, and we have already suggested that the term *tora*, for the author of the psalm, may have been intended to refer to the Pentateuchal Law, but that the editor (s) of the whole Psalter were suggesting a further reference, to other Scriptures and particularly to the Psalter itself. If this is correct, the fivefoldness of his final paean of praise, with a further implied Pentateuchal comparison, may have been intended to remind the readers of this meditative purpose for the book.

We have already seen that some students of the psalms, for example Franz Delitzsch, have noted the way in which the whole collection is linked by a series of catchwords or phrases.

In this final sequence there are certainly ideas which enable the reader to see how the theme of one psalm may be intimately linked with that of its predecessor and also its successor. This is true even of 145, for in 145:20 David says:

> The LORD watches over all who love him,
>   but all the wicked he will destroy (NIV),[15]

and in 146:9 the psalmist says:

> The LORD watches over the alien
>   and sustains the fatherless and the widow,
>   but he frustrates the ways of the wicked (NIV).

We note also the references to Zion in 146:10 and 147:13, to the heavens and the earth in 147:4, 15-18 and 148:13, the place of God's faithful ones in his purposes in 148:14 and 149:9, and the place of music and dancing in the praises of the people in 149:3 and the whole of 150.

These all provide links that make these psalms not simply distinct hymns of praise but a symphony of praise in five movements. This symphony of praise loses nothing in its use by New Testament Christians. Rather, deeper understanding of its appropriateness is seen in those who recognise, serve and worship Christ as Creator, Redeemer and Judge.

# Chapter 22

# The message of the book as a whole

If this book was eventually organised to convey a message from God, what is that message? What would it be for the Jews who first read it as a whole, for the Jews of our Lord's day and for Jesus himself, and what is its message for Christians today? Essentially it will be one message, although with somewhat different significance for those living at different periods.

We will seek to express this message in a series of statements.

## 1. The way of wisdom is godliness
For the ancient Greeks, understanding begins with the knowledge of oneself, and the most distinctive features of modern Western philosophy are often traced to Descartes and the fact that he inferred his own existence from the contents of his mind.

The people of the Old Testament, however, were encouraged to begin with God, for the fear of the Lord is the beginning of wisdom (Job 28:28; Ps. 111:10; Prov. 15:33, cf. 1:7). So the Book of Psalms commences with a wisdom psalm in which the righteousness that is grounded in God is extolled, and this note recurs frequently in later psalms.

The modern world needs to hear this message, for although knowledge has greatly increased so that we talk now of an information explosion, experience of modern society shows us that departure from God has so often shown itself in failure to cope wisely with the issues of life and death.

## 2. This involves delight in and meditation on God's word
The writer of the first psalm encouraged this, and the same delight is shown also in 19 and 119.

The 'law' is, firstly, the Torah, the foundational five books of Moses, but we have seen good reason to believe that the

Book of Psalms is to be viewed as new Torah, in the wider sense of 'instruction'.

In fact, of course, instruction from God expanded more and more down the centuries until finally came 'the word of Christ', the final disclosure of God in the Person and Work of Jesus Christ. Just as the psalmist commended meditation on the Law of the Lord, so Paul, in Colossians 3:16, urged his readers:

> Let the word of Christ dwell in you richly; teach and admonish one another in all wisdom.

So, in the setting of church worship, we seek godly wisdom for ourselves and encourage others to seek it, in the word of God, which includes the whole Book of Psalms.

## 3. God promises blessing for the righteous and threatens judgment for the wicked

The clear distinction between the two, established in 1, is carried on through the book and is never blurred. What is the happiness of 1:1 and the prosperity of 1:3? We may say that it is pictured in the stability, fruitfulness and evergreen nature of the tree and in the insubstantial nature of the chaff, but how does this work out in practice? Without much doubt, we need the Psalter as a whole as a kind of exegesis of this happiness and that prosperity on the one hand and its reverse ('the wicked are not so', 1:4) on the other.

It is important therefore that we allow God to teach us the meaning of his own word. No passage or verse of Scripture is intended to be understood out of connection with the rest of the Bible. The New Testament writers brought material from all parts of the Old Testament to bear on the great task of expounding the meaning of Christ. To base everything on one passage or one Biblical theme or word-picture would be to risk a distorted view of him. After all, nearly all heresies quote Scripture, but in a dangerously selective way as, for example, in modern-day prosperity theology.

## 4. God has established a king and pledges to support him

Neither godliness nor ungodliness is viewed in a purely individual fashion in the Psalter. Psalm 2 points to the Davidic king and records God's decree establishing and promising to support him. 'The advice of the wicked' (1:1), with its assumption that insights and plans are shared, for good or ill, in 2:1-3 takes the form of a plot against God's anointed king. Wisdom is to be found in submitting to and taking refuge in him, that is, in obedience and trust.

Here then a distinctive plan of God comes into focus. God's own authority is undergirding that of the Davidic monarch. To rebel against him is to rebel against God himself.

## 5. God's support for the king does not mean he will be without suffering

The very promise of support in 2:7,8 comes in the context of a rebellion, so that life for the king will not be easy, and this can be seen time after time, especially in Book 1. Indeed he may feel utterly forsaken by God (22:1ff), and such cries as 'Why?' and 'When?' are often heard in the Davidic psalms. Not only so, but when the Exile came, the very dynasty itself seemed to have come to an end (89:38-51). Some of this suffering will, of course, be because of his own sins (as in 51), but often it was in pursuance of his God-given calling.

We are reminded of Job and of Jeremiah, whose sufferings were part of their God-given vocation, and of the afflictions of Paul and others for the sake of the gospel of Christ (2 Cor. 11: 21-33). Some preaching gives the impression that to become a Christian is to have all our problems banished, but this does not fit the real facts at all. A study of the Psalter can be an exercise in godly realism.

## 6. The blessing and the judgment need to be viewed eschatologically

The overall thrust of 1 is eschatological in relation to the wicked. If this is true for the wicked, then we may be intended to view the prospects of the righteous primarily in eschatological terms too. If, as has been suggested, the message of the Psalter can be seen in its essence in 73, then this too encourages the view from the end. This enables us to accept that the afflictions of the righteous and the prosperity of the wicked are not by any means evidence of God's unfaithfulness, but rather, a reminder to us to judge nothing before the end.

Even in Revelation 6:9-11, those who had been slain because of God's word and their testimony ask, 'how long?' and are told to wait a little longer, but with the clear implication that after this God would put all things right.

### 7. God has established foundations on which his people may rest in times of perplexity

He has established a created and a moral order, he has shown his grace and faithfulness in redeeming Israel from Egypt, and he has promised David a lasting dynasty. When questions arise even about one of these, the believer goes back to others. So problems about the dynasty sometimes drove the psalmists back to the time of Moses and the Exodus for the strengthening and, perhaps at times, the rebuilding of their faith.

Christians too experience problems and ask questions about some of these foundation truths, and they should go back to rest on the great facts of the cross and the resurrection of Christ.

### 8. True godliness is driven to God, not away from him, by affliction and perplexity

Although psalmists often faced real suffering and discouragement, they always brought these things to God. They therefore faced all life's difficulties in fellowship with him.

In the time of his greatest agony, the Lord Jesus, using the words of a psalm, asked, 'Why have you forsaken me?', but prefaced this question, as does the psalm, with a statement of a relationship conviction when he said, 'My God'. Here ultimate godliness embraced ultimate suffering, with no loss of hold on God even when there was no sense of being held by him.

Here too is faith's ultimate expression, quite unsupported by feelings. We see this, at least in lesser forms, in the Book of Psalms.

## 9. Life for the believer should be punctuated by and will reach its consummation in praise

Even those sections of the Psalter which seem to be dominated by laments are punctuated by psalms of praise, for these occur in all five books. After great experiences of loss and affliction, Job declared, in worship: 'The LORD gave and the LORD has taken away; blessed be the name of the LORD' (Job 1:21). Later these afflictions became virtually his whole world until he gained a new perspective when God had revealed himself to him in power. Christian readers, embracing the will of God and then passing through valleys of affliction and trial, no doubt identify with the psalmists in the psalms of laments. They too can gain a new perspective when they read the psalms of praise.

These psalms become more frequent as the Book of Psalms moves towards its close, with far more of them in Books 4 and 5 than in Books 1 to 3. Viewing this feature in the overall context of the book, we learn that difficult experiences should not mute our praise, for each experience has been entered into, not in solitude but with God, and, whether our circumstances or even our emotions have changed, we can give him praise for grace given to face life as it really is. This is not a recipe for a 'Praise the Lord anyway!' attitude, but for a profound orientation towards God no matter what life may bring.

The final psalm, 150, is perhaps the purest expression of sheer praise that even the Old Testament contains. In it, the one function of a human being is to worship and adore Yahweh. Brueggemann is surely right when he says:

> Only those who willingly begin in Psalm 1 can honestly and gladly end in Psalm 150.... Praise as glad exuberant yielding and self-abasement ... takes place only when one comes to terms

emotionally, psychologically, dramatically and theologically with the demanding sovereign reality of God. Affirmation of this God becomes the reason, warrant, ground and substance of praise.[1]

Allen too says we have to depart from the safe world of Psalm 1 and move through the psalms of pain. He says:

> The way from torah obedience to self-abandoning doxology is by way of *candor about suffering* and *gratitude about hope* (his italics).[2]

The reasons the psalmist, and the ancient Jewish or modern Christian believer reading the book, can praise the Lord in such a full-throated and unqualified way, emerge in the course of reading the Book of Psalms through. The reader finds the assertions of the first psalm tested by experience, the experience of the psalmists, during the course of the book, and has seen them to be true, not in a superficial but in a deep sense. Can it be that in the modern Christian church we too easily sing Psalm 150 and psalms and hymns of that general type, and do it sometimes in a spirit of escapism, and not after proving God in the midst of the harsh realities of life? This can produce a triumphalism that may be a half-way house from Biblical Christianity to prosperity theology, and that is certainly foreign not only to the Psalter but to the whole Bible.

## 10. God's purpose moves forward to its great climax in Christ

If we are to see the kingly psalms as intended, in the context of the book as a whole, to point forward to the coming Messiah, this enables us to view the great purpose of the book in the context of the whole Bible. As J. P. Brennan puts it:

> The Psalter comes to be seen as a magnificent dramatic struggle between the two ways – that of Yahweh, his anointed king, and the company of the just, and that of the wicked, the sinners the evil-doers.[3]

Walter Kaiser Jr. has argued that the great theme of the Old Testament is promise.[4] If the Book of Psalms is a microcosm of the Old Testament, then he certainly has a strong case, for it has an orientation towards the future on the basis of God's word of promise.

So then, the Book of Psalms reassures the reader of the faithfulness of God, specifically in reference to his promise to David in 2 Samuel 7. Here is a whole book so arranged that it virtually serves as an exposition of that one Old Testament passage. Despite all that happened to David himself, despite all his successors faced, and despite the trauma of the Exile itself, God was still on the throne and the promises to David would be fulfilled in a King of the future, who would reign and also function as priest eternally. The New Testament tells us who this is.

# D. Its Glorious Fulfilment

# Chapter 23

# New Testament interpretation of the psalms

The Book of Psalms is of course a Jewish book. It is written in Hebrew, its setting is the worship system of the people of Israel, its devotional flavour that of Old Testament piety. What claim does it have to be considered Christian?

Christians treat it as Scripture because Jesus did so and because the New Testament writers followed him in this. Much of it is understood Christologically in the New Testament, for the Psalter is quoted more frequently there than any other Old Testament book with the possible exception of Isaiah.[1] This is not, of course, surprising, as it is the Old Testament's longest book. It is specifically mentioned in Luke 24:44, where, revealing himself to his disciples as risen from the dead, Jesus says, 'Everything written about me in the law of Moses, the prophets and the psalms must be fulfilled.' This instance of special mention could however be due simply to the fact that the Book of Psalms is the largest component of the third section of the Old Testament canon. From its earliest days, the Christian Church has seen Christ in the psalms.[2]

Are the psalms actually quoted the only ones we may apply to him? Much of their application to Christ is by way of typology, in which the experiences of the psalmist foreshadow what happened to him in some way or other. Without doubt typology has become overdone in some quarters from time to time, and it is clear that it must accept some discipline lest it run riot. When it is employed in the New Testament, this gives it the same authority as the Old Testament passages it interprets, so that the New Testament use of the Old Testament is the obvious filter through which we may put such interpretations.

It may be, however, that we can go a little further. It seems reasonable to apply other psalms to Jesus, at least in general terms, if they reflect the same kind of experiences we can see in those that are quoted, notably the unjustified antipathy of enemies and the support given to him by God. Those who stood firmly for the true God and who suffered as a consequence were showing, at least to some degree, the same spiritual qualities which were to be exemplified perfectly in Jesus himself, so that, in this respect, they were anticipating him. For Davidic psalms this is particularly appropriate because of David's kingly role, for Christ is the supreme King.

Various theological disciplines must come into operation here. Exegesis seeks to show the original meaning of these passages, Hermeneutics how they may be applied to Christ. Old Testament Theology relates them to other 'Messianic' passages and New Testament Theology shows how their great themes are taken up in the New Testament. Then Systematic Theology may employ them in showing the Biblical roots of Christian Theology, Apologetics will defend the Christian understanding of them and Practical Theology will seek to establish the appropriate practical response to them for Christians. In this way, both our understanding of Christian truth and our practical life as Christians in the world will be influenced by this great Old Testament book.

When a New Testament writer quotes from the Old Testament, including the psalms, he will most often employ the main Greek version, the Septuagint, either verbatim or with modifications. This version was used in the synagogues of the Dispersion and so was well known to Jews outside Palestine. The Book of Psalms was probably one of the latest Old Testament books to be translated in this version, and is generally quite close to the Massoretic text, the basis of the main Hebrew manuscripts we have. There are however some differences.

In a very few cases, it is possible that the Septuagint has preserved the original wording more accurately than the Massoretic text. This may be the case in 102: 23-28, part of which is quoted in Hebrews 1:10-12, where the writer uses the Septuagint. This part of the psalm is about the creation of the world and the writer to the Hebrews takes it that it applies to Jesus as Creator. In the Septuagint this section of the psalm, including the word, 'Lord', can be viewed as addressed by God to the person who speaks in the psalm, and in much of the psalm this person is clearly passing through a deep valley of suffering, as in 22 and 69. If those two psalms can be applied to Christ, and they are so applied in the New Testament, there seems no good reason why this cannot be also.

To explore the New Testament understanding of the psalms as fully as the subject deserves would take us considerably beyond the limits of this volume, but a number of points need to be made.

Matthew 4:5-7, with its parallel in Luke 4:9-12, is of special importance, for it presents an example of deliberate misinterpretation of a psalm. Here the devil quotes 91:11, 12:

'He will command his angels concerning you,'
   and 'On their hands they will lift you up,
so that you will not dash your foot against a stone.'

Satan uses this as an inducement to Jesus to cast himself down from the temple. In his reply, Jesus made no reference to the psalm, probably indicating that to him it had no application whatever to what Satan was tempting him to do. When we examine it, it is very clear that its true application is to a person who trusts and loves God, and so not to one who responds to Satan's temptations. Not only so, but, like every psalm, it comes within the context of godly obedience laid down for the whole Book of Psalms in 1. How could obedience to Satan ever be justified from Scripture, which consistently calls us to delight ourselves in God's word and to yield our obedience to God!

Jesus and the New Testament writers often saw a principle of abiding validity in the psalms. So, for instance, 78:2:

I will open my mouth in a parable;
   I will utter dark sayings from of old,

is quoted in Matthew 13:35 to give Old Testament support to
the value of teaching by comparisons and parables. Psalm 44:22
is applied to Christians in Romans 8:36, for, like Israel when
the psalm was written, they faced death for God all day long
and were considered as sheep to be slaughtered. Because God
does not change, the writer to the Hebrews employs 95 in
Hebrews 3 and 4. This is because the readers of the epistle need
to learn that they too, like Israel in the wilderness as seen in
that psalm, could through rebellion be denied God's beneficent
gift of rest.

Ethically also there are important points of continuity
between the godly authors of the psalms and New Testament
believers. This also is due to the fact that the God of the Old
Testament and of the New is one God, completely consistent in
character and therefore unchanging in his character requirements
of his people.

Paul must have spent much time with the Book of Psalms.
His assertion, 'I delight in God's law in my inmost self' (Rom.
7:22), reminds us of verses where the psalmist writes of the
great joy he has in the word and will of God. For instance, in
1:2 he says of the righteous, 'but their delight is in the law of
the LORD.' In 40:8, the writer says,

> I delight to do your will, O my God;
>   your law is within my heart.

This delight comes across to us a great deal in 119, not only in
verses which use the language of pleasure or delight, but in the
whole atmosphere of the psalm. Ephesians 4:26, 'Be angry but
do not sin,' quotes from 4:4. In Romans 3:12-18 Paul gives a
long catena of passages to provide Old Testament evidence of
human sin, and the majority of these are drawn from the psalms.
In Romans 4:6-8 he finds an Old Testament experience of
justification by grace through faith in David's words in 32:1, 2:

Blessed are those whose iniquities are forgiven,
and whose sins are covered;
Blessed is the one against whom the LORD will not reckon sin.

It is true, of course, that God's purpose moves on and his dealings with his people do not always take the same form. The very existence of two testaments in one Bible shows us this. Nevertheless, as the use of 95 in Hebrews which we have already noted shows us, God's unvarying and consistent character underlies the whole story.

There is an interesting example of this in Romans 10:18. Here Paul quotes the words of 19:4:

Their voice has gone out to all the earth,
and their words to the ends of the world,

and applies them to the proclamation of the gospel. In the psalm the words clearly relate to the way the created universe speaks of God, but of course they are also quite apt if used of the gospel. A few verses further on, however, the psalmist writes about a further example of God speaking, this time in the Law. How appropriate then that Paul should go further still and suggest in this way that the same God speaks in creation, in law and in gospel, so that the listener or reader may believe and obey![3] In this way he has summed up the three chief ways in which God has disclosed himself to human beings, generally in his universe and then more particularly in the Old Testament and in Christ.

It is not surprising to find that the language of the psalms appears to have influenced that of worship in the New Testament, whether this be in the prophetic utterances of praise in Luke 1 and 2 or in the praises of the heavenly courts in the Apocalypse. It is not that there are many clearly identifiable quotations, but that the poetic style and the whole atmosphere remind us of the psalms of praise. What lover of the psalms can read Luke 1:50: 'his mercy is for those who fear him from generation to generation', without being reminded of 103:17, or Revelation 7:15, 16:

> and the one who is seated on the throne will shelter them.
> They will hunger no more, and thirst no more;
>     the sun will not strike them,
>     nor any scorching heat,

without recalling 121:5, 6? The use of the psalms in this way is eminently appropriate, for the God of the psalmists and the God of Christ is the same God.

Looked at from the standpoint of the psalms, Christ may be seen as the perfect Worshipper. Like David, he is a man, but his dedication to God is complete and perfect, for he, even more than David, was a man after God's own heart. This means that David's assertion in 40:8, that he loves to do God's will because his law is within his heart, is even more appropriately applied to Christ and to his perfect offering, in life and in death, as it is in Hebrews 10:5-10. In 31, the psalmist is facing physical weakness and the arrogance of his enemies, and he uses language which another sufferer, Jeremiah, was to employ[4] and which Jesus himself takes as an expression of his trust in God. This is found in verse 5: 'into your hands I commend my spirit' (Luke 23:46).

If however we are guided by New Testament Christology, Jesus Christ is not simply the supreme Worshipper, but also the perfect Object of worship, because, unlike David, he is also God. As he himself said, in reference to 110:1, the Messiah is not just David's Son but also David's Lord (Mark 12:35-37). There is therefore no incongruity in finding that it is to him that praise is directed in some passages of the Apocalypse in language that is highly psalmic in style and vocabulary (Rev. 5:12-14).[5]

A psalm was sometimes viewed as forming part of a pattern of passages and events which all showed God's consistency and yet which revealed too that his purpose had moved forward in Christ to its great consummation. This is a particular feature of the Epistle to the Hebrews and the way the writer does this is full of interest.

In Hebrews 2:5-11, for instance, we find the writer applying to Christ the words of 8 about the created dignity of human beings and their rule over the animal creation. The psalm itself of course rests on Genesis 1, and its language is strongly reminiscent of it. Through these three passages we see God's purpose for humankind from its start in Genesis to its consummation in Jesus. The psalm therefore occupies a very important place, standing theologically between Genesis and Hebrews.

In Hebrews 7 the writer is seeking to show that Jesus is a true priest despite the fact that he was of the tribe of Judah and not of the priestly tribe of Levi. This would have been an important issue for people with a Jewish background. He uses the figure of Melchizedek to do this. He comments on his historical appearance and Abraham's recognition of him as an authentic priest in Genesis 14, and then applies 110, which refers to a kingly figure as 'a priest for ever according to the order of Melchizedek', to Christ. Once again, theologically, a psalm stands between Genesis and Christ. This feature of the epistle gives us a particularly strong sense of the theological unity of Scripture.

Incidentally, the extent to which this epistle makes use of the psalms is very striking. Kistemaker points out that 14 out of the epistle's 35 Old Testament quotations are from the psalms and he argues that four psalms (8:4-6; 95:7-11; 110:4; 40:6-8) and their interpretation in terms of Christ carry the main weight of the epistle's argument.[6]

In Acts 2:25-32 and 13:35-37, both Peter and Paul point out that 16 contains language where it is said that a particular man's flesh will not experience corruption, and they argue for the fulfilment of this in Christ. This psalm is applied by them to the resurrection of Jesus. We note also that both 22 and 69 are used in the passion narratives and applied to his sufferings and death.

Maybe the implication here too is that the psalmist wrote what, in the fullest sense, was fulfilled only in Jesus.[7]

This does not necessarily mean, of course, that none of these psalms was in any respect based on the psalmist's own experience. Understandably, the men of the New Testament concentrated on the Christological interpretation and the fact that his experience went beyond anything that happened to David, its writer, so that the words of a psalm found total fulfilment only in Christ. It is noticeable that, although in 69 the psalmist refers to those who hate him without reason, he also confesses personal sin. In the nature of the case, this element must be applicable to him and not to Jesus (69:4, 5).[8] The major theme of a psalm, such as suffering caused by the undeserved hatred of his enemies in the case of 22 and 69 and support by God in the case of 16, can be seen to be true both of the psalmist and of Christ, but every detail cannot be applied to both. A study of New Testament typology makes it abundantly clear that Christ, the Antitype, always went beyond the type. Types are essentially partial and not full comparisons, and a little thought will reveal that human types especially must be imperfect, because only One was morally perfect.

In a number of New Testament passages, Christ is thought of as being in intimate union with his people, perhaps as Vine and branches or as the body's Head and members. It is not surprising then to find a psalm quotation like 2:9, 'You shall break them with a rod of iron,' given an application to them (Rev. 2:27) as well as to him (Rev. 12:5; 19:15).[9]

It should be mentioned that although the majority of the quotations from the psalms in the New Testament are applied in some way to Christ, there are some exceptions. It is no surprise to find that many of these are in Romans 2 and 3, where Paul is writing about the fact that both Jews and Gentiles are sinners under condemnation and therefore in need of the salvation which only Christ can provide. In Romans 2:6, the words 'he will repay according to each one's deeds' appear to be from 62:12. In Romans 3:10-18 Paul accumulates a long catena of passages, most of them from the psalms, which reveal the universality of sin.

The minds of the New Testament writers were steeped in the language of the psalms. This is certainly not surprising, for they were used so regularly and systematically in the synagogues where these writers had been reared. In Paul's Areopagus sermon in Acts 17, he is preaching to pagans who knew nothing of the Old Testament preparation for Christ, and so he never quotes it, but his language is nevertheless full of psalm phraseology and ideas.[10]

No serious reader of the New Testament can doubt that its writers, and the preachers whose sermons are recorded in it, regarded the Book of Psalms as a Christian book with a many-sided application to Jesus Christ. We now turn to consider the main themes of this Christological application.

# Chapter 24

## The person of Christ

We have already become aware that the testimony of the psalms to the Christ who was to come is extremely varied, and a study of the various aspects of his person and work which are linked to psalms in the New Testament confirms this.

The Chalcedonian Definition of AD 451 is the classic statement of the convictions of the Christian church about the person of its Lord. It affirms 'that our Lord Jesus Christ is one and the same Son, the same perfect in Godhead and the same perfect in manhood, truly God and truly man.' Its authors made this affirmation because they believed this to be the teaching of the New Testament. It is not the purpose of the present volume to explore the New Testament grounds for this doctrine, which has been done many times with great effectiveness elsewhere, but rather to see how the New Testament writers used the Book of Psalms to illustrate their convictions about Jesus.

### a. His humanity

The human story of Jesus begins of course with his conception and birth. Matthew and Luke record these events. Although neither explicitly quotes the psalms in immediate connection with them, Matthew refers to Jesus as the son of David in the introductory verse of his Gospel and Luke records the words of the angel Gabriel to Mary, 'The Lord God will give to him the throne of his ancestor David' (Luke 1:32). These verses would remind the readers of the Old Testament promises and of the testimony of the Davidic psalms to the coming Messiah.

It is not surprising then to find that the language of the psalms has deeply affected the way praise to God is expressed by Mary in the Magnificat (Luke 1:46-55) and by Zechariah in the Benedictus (Luke 1:67-79).[1] These two great songs focus on

God's favour to his people and on the fulfilment of his ancient promises, promises as old as the days of Abraham and so often celebrated in the psalms. It is clear then that the coming of the Messiah and the purpose of God in sending him were closely bound up in their minds with great themes expressed in the Psalter. So often in societies which experience oppression by aliens or by dictators and where there is longing for freedom, hope is kept alive in the songs of the people. How much more would we expect this to be true in a society which had already experienced the liberating power of God in the Exodus and many subsequent events, and so where hope and worship could be united!

A great many of the New Testament psalm quotations applied to Christ are about his sufferings, and these obviously testify to the reality of his manhood. The very plenitude of them is evidence that he was believed to have lived a human life that involved pain, both physical and mental. We will consider them in some detail in the next chapter.

The reaction of Jesus to the use made of 91:11, 12 by Satan during his wilderness temptations, recorded in Matthew 4 and Luke 4, is illuminating for the light it casts on his awareness of his humanity. In the psalm an unspecified godly man is assured of protection by God through the agency of angels if he trusts himself into his hands. Satan used the psalm to tempt Jesus to cast himself down from the temple. Our Lord's reaction was to quote another Old Testament passage, this time from Deuteronomy 6:16: 'Do not put the Lord your God to the test.' In their original context these words are addressed to Israel. His use of them shows that Jesus considered them to be applicable to him, certainly as man and also perhaps as truly representing Israel in his conflict with Satan. He was not to act on the basis of a Scripture quotation, spuriously interpreted by Satan, but rather on the basis of another, taken at its clear face value. The misuse of Scripture, especially in attempted justification of acts outside the will of God, is a serious matter.

In Hebrews 2:5-18, the writer shows, largely by quoting and

interpreting Old Testament Scripture, the solidarity of Christ with those he came to save. His purpose in this, as the close of the chapter shows, was to demonstrate the appropriateness for them of his office of high priest, for priests, as representatives of the people, needed to be one with them.

First of all, and quite fundamentally, he quotes from 8:4-6:

> What are human beings that you are mindful of them,
> or mortals that you care for them?
> You have made them for a little while lower than the angels;
> you have crowned them with glory and honour,
> subjecting all things under their feet.

Here the psalmist is obviously influenced in his thought and language by Genesis 1, and in the light of this great chapter is meditating on the high status of humanity revealed in the position God has given human beings, including lordship over the animal kingdom. After asserting that this is not true at the present time (presumably because of the Fall, although this is not spelled out), he then relates the quotation to Christ. What was no longer true of humanity as a whole was true of Jesus. It has been well said that the real question is not whether Jesus was truly human but whether we are! So then here is the true Man, fulfilling all that God originally intended man to be, and doing so through his willing acceptance of death.

Hebrews 10:5-7 quotes from 40:6-8 in the Septuagint version:

> Sacrifices and offerings you have not desired,
> but a body you have prepared for me;
> in burnt offerings and sin offerings
> you have taken no pleasure.
> Then I said, 'See, God, I have come to do your will, O God'
> (in the scroll of the book it is written of me).

Here is a case where there is some difference between the Septuagint Greek, 'a body you have prepared for me', and the Massoretic Hebrew, 'you have given me an open ear'. This may seem to be a major difference, but in fact, in terms of their significance, it is not really so. Both use physical language of the man who speaks in the psalm, and both indicate the importance of practical obedience. These are the main points and are equally clear in both readings. The context in the epistle shows the writer to be convinced that in surrendering his body to be crucified, Jesus was offering willing obedience to his Father. Once again, the true manhood of Jesus is clear. We too show our real humanity, humanity in terms of God's intention, when we walk the pathway of obedience.

## b. His deity

The divine status of Jesus is indicated in all kinds of ways in the New Testament and we can see that the psalms were understood to testify to his deity. Not only so, but this testimony often occurs at important points in the Gospel records of his life and ministry.

It has often been observed that the voice of God, speaking at his baptism, spoke in familiar language, the language of the Old Testament, and that in particular the words, 'You are my Son,' come from 2:7.[2] This verse was important also to the writer to the Hebrews, for he quotes from it twice. The first time it is part of a series of Old Testament passages pointing to the greatness of Jesus (Heb. 1:5) and the author employs it to show that, in contrast to the angels, Sonship for Jesus meant a special relationship to God. An examination of the context in Hebrews 1 also shows that the writer thought of the Sonship of Jesus as his possession of a quite special status. The chief point of the whole passage is to show the greatness of Jesus and especially his vast superiority to angels. The writer's use of this psalm passage in Hebrews 5:5 is in line with this, if, as seems probable, he is there saying that it was his status as Son that was the reason in God's mind for his appointment as high priest.[3]

Psalm 110 features at a most significant point in the ministry of Jesus. It was the Day of Questions, a day during Holy Week when Jesus spent much time teaching in the temple. A number of questions were raised by parties and individuals that day. Each was answered by him with great wisdom, but clearly the question he raised at the end was of special importance. It was not a response to the queries of others but came on his own initiative, and therefore he must have viewed it as vitally important. He asked:

> How can the scribes say that the Messiah is the son of David? David himself, by the Holy Spirit, declared, 'The LORD said to my Lord, Sit at my right hand until I put your enemies under your feet.' David himself calls him Lord; so how can he be his son? (Mark 12:35-37).

Here he was setting his own understanding of the Messiah, and so of his own self-understanding, over against the teaching given by the religious leaders of the people. They certainly taught the greatness of the Messiah, but as a special man who would be sent by God for a special purpose, not as God incarnate. Jesus could hardly be rejecting the title, 'son of David', altogether when he had accepted it from Bartimaeus (Mark 10:47, 48) and from the Passover pilgrims (Matt. 21:9) so recently. The Jews were used to the strongly-worded posing of alternatives in this way to make an important point in a memorable fashion.[4] He was indicating that simply to call him the son of David did not go anything like far enough, and he did this from David's own writings.

What does the comment of Jesus mean? In this passage from Mark and in its parallels in Matthew 22:44 and Luke 20:42,43, the Greek term *kurios* occurs three times. This noun is used in the Septuagint to translate both *Adonai* (lord) and the great name *Yahweh* (LORD), and the Septuagint translators employed it in their rendering of 110:1. Jesus could hardly have made his high conception of the Messiah clearer, and his demonstration of it from this psalm is very important, especially so perhaps because he did this at the close of his public ministry. He was not just David's Son but his Lord.

So then his special status was highlighted, both at the beginning of his ministry, where he was designated Son of God by the voice of God from heaven, and at its close, when he underlined his divine Lordship, and in both cases with reference to the psalms. Some modern literary theorists point out the importance of the beginning and ending of a book or of an important section of a book as indicating matters viewed by the writer as important.

This question and answer on the Day of Questions, taking place as it did only shortly before his death and resurrection, must have meant a great deal to the New Testament writers, for 110 is quoted or alluded to more often than any other Old Testament passage in the New Testament. Peter quoted the first verse of it at the close of the very first Christian sermon (Acts 2:34, 35), and the many references to Jesus being at the right hand of God seem to show its influence (e.g. Mark 16:19; Rom. 8:34). The writer to the Hebrews makes very full use of it, not only citing verse 1 at the end of an interpreted catena of Old Testament passages as the clinching evidence for the greatness of Jesus (Heb. 1:13), but spending a whole chapter (chapter 7) in expounding its fourth verse:

> The Lord has sworn and will not change his mind.
> 'You are a priest forever, according to the order of Melchizedek.'

Finally, we note that Jesus is not only rightly called 'Son' and 'Lord', but even 'God' on the authority of a psalm. For understandable reasons, the actual term 'God' is used of him somewhat rarely in the New Testament. Jesus was the Coming One of Old Testament prophecy and, because passages where this one is referred to as prophet or as priest or as king have largely in view his possession of some particular divinely-given office rather than his status as God, it was appropriate that the actual term 'God' should be used in most cases to designate the One who had sent him, that is God the Father.

This makes exceptions all the more significant, and an important one is to be found in a psalm. Psalm 45:6,7 is quoted in Hebrews 1:8, 9, as follows:

But of the Son he says,
'Your throne, O God, is forever and ever,
and the righteous scepter is the scepter of your kingdom.
You have loved righteousness and hated wickedness;
therefore God, your God, has anointed you
with the oil of gladness beyond your companions.'

This translation has been disputed and two other renderings have been made of the passage in which 'Your throne, O God' is replaced either by 'Your throne is the throne of God', which makes little difference to the sense, or else by 'God is your throne', which makes a very great difference. Murray J. Harris, after a full discussion of the various renderings in the psalm itself, concludes:

> The traditional rendering, 'Your throne, O God, is for ever and ever', is not simply readily defensible but remains the most satisfactory solution to the exegetical problems posed by the verse.[5]

So then, exalted titles pointing to his possession of the highest status are used of Jesus in the New Testament and very important evidence for their appropriateness comes from the Book of Psalms. All this has important implications for us in terms of our acceptance of Christ's authority and our whole-hearted worship of him.

# Chapter 25

## Christ's sufferings and vindication

An examination of the New Testament and its kerygma, its message, shows that the centre of that message was the cross and resurrection of Jesus, or to put it in other terms, his sufferings and vindication. The Gospel writers show their view of the importance of these climactic events in the life of our Lord by giving them a good deal of space. This was also the burden of the apostolic preaching, and the elements of this message can be seen in many of the New Testament epistles. It is not true to the witness of the New Testament to treat the Christian faith simply as a philosophy of life or a new ethic; it is the message that God offers forgiveness and new life through some very specific events, the cross and resurrection of Jesus.

Suffering and vindication have a huge role in the psalms, particularly in those attributed by their headings to David. It is not surprising then to find them applied to the sufferings and vindication of the one who was addressed as Son of David, even though, as his understanding of 110 showed, this was not a full enough designation of him.

If we take the ascription of many psalms to David in their headings seriously, there is in them a great deal of reference to his sufferings. Sometimes the trouble is not specified, but with great frequency he is seen as the object of the hatred, plotting and general malignity of his foes. In fact his sufferings are caused far more by his enemies than by any other factor. Often he cries out to God for vindication and at times he writes in an imprecatory tone.

Often psalms of this kind are quoted in the New Testament, sometimes by Jesus himself and sometimes by others. In 41:9 the psalmist writes about the treachery of someone close to him, when he says:

Even my bosom friend in whom I trusted,
who ate of my bread, has lifted the heel against me.

In John 13:18, as the context makes clear, Jesus applied this to Judas Iscariot. Also the causeless hatred that his enemies directed against him is backed by a quotation either from 35:19 or 69:4, or perhaps from both, in the words of John 15:25: 'They hated me without a cause.'

Without doubt, 22 had a special place both for Jesus and for the New Testament writers as Old Testament witness to his sufferings, but also to his vindication. This very moving psalm changes dramatically in the middle. The first twenty-one verses are a description by the sufferer himself of his spiritual, social and physical sufferings and they refer also to his cries for help. He is surrounded by bitter enemies who pour out their loathing against him and inflict both indignities and physical suffering on him. In this respect it is somewhat like other psalms of affliction, although none of these is as intense. What makes this psalm so distinctive, however, is the fact that it opens with an anguished cry asking why God has forsaken him.[1]

This cry is found on the lips of Jesus in the Matthean and Marcan narratives of the crucifixion (Matt. 27:46; Mark 15:34). Seven sayings from his lips as he hung on the cross are recorded in the Gospels. Three of these are recorded in Luke, three in John. Only two of the evangelists, Matthew and Mark, record the same saying and they give us nothing else from his lips in his dying agony. This awful cry stands in all its starkness on the pages of these two Gospels in their record of a scene which contains many reminders of the context in the psalm, and it has great power to challenge the minds and consciences of those who read these Gospels. In his own crucifixion record (John 19:24), John refers to a later verse of the same psalm:

they divide my clothes among themselves,
and for my clothing they cast lots (22:18).

At the end of the first twenty-one verses of this psalm there is a most dramatic change of tone, and the psalmist begins to pour out his thanksgiving to God for hearing and vindicating him. The use of this psalm in the Epistle to the Hebrews is interesting, for the one express quotation of it given there (Heb. 2:13) is from this section of the psalm, in fact from its very beginning in verse 22.

The writer of this epistle also shows clear evidence of acquaintance with other psalms associated with the events of Passion Week, not only 110 to which reference has already been made, but also 118:6, 7, which is quoted in Hebrews 13:6:

> The Lord is my helper;
> I will not be afraid.
> What can anyone do to me?

We will probably be correct to assume that the epistle's writer knew of the application of the early part of 22 to Christ's sufferings and death, although this cannot be established with certainty. If it is in fact the case, his use of verse 22 here must mean that he had reflected on the evidence for Christ's vindication that the psalm contains.

It is probably in the light of this that we should understand Hebrews 5:7-10, where the reality of Christ's sufferings is poignantly presented. Verse 7 reads:

> In the days of his flesh, Jesus offered up prayers and supplications, with loud cries and tears, to the one who was able to save him from death, and he was heard because of his reverent submission.

Many of the psalms present the strong crying and tears of the psalmist, his desire to be saved from his enemies and from death itself, and his cry for God to vindicate him. How many of these psalms were thought by the New Testament writers to have been fulfilled in Jesus? We have no means of knowing, but clearly several were and, outstandingly, 22. This psalm, as we have seen, presents not only his cry but the answer to it. His situation becomes one of imminent peril of death in verses 20 and 21, where the sword, the dog[2] and the lion are all pictures of great and pressing danger. It is quickly after this that the vindication comes.

There is, however, an obvious problem for us here. Jesus was not delivered from death but rather experienced it in a particularly horrific and horrifying way. The writer of the epistle knew this very well, of course, for the whole epistle shows how deeply he had reflected on the sufferings of Christ. Even so, there is a very important sense in which he *was* so delivered, but delivered out of it rather than from experiencing it. This is probably what the writer of the epistle had in mind and the way that he understood the total psalm as fulfilled in the experience of Jesus. His interest in the psalms and their interpretation is so great, and his understanding of them so profound, that something that would stimulate deep thought in the reader would be very much in character. Puzzling passages in Scripture may often give us very helpful new light if we seek divine illumination as to their meaning and significance.

The Bible is full of surprises and in both testaments we see God at work so often in ways that confound human thinking. As we have seen already, the Book of Psalms as a whole seems to be telling its readers the message that human history is to have a wonderful denouement, but not until the godly have faced all manner of trials and tribulations. These trials and tribulations were experienced in the greatest intensity by Jesus himself.

There are a number of other quotations from psalms which combine references to suffering with either the prayer for or the conviction of ultimate vindication by God. So, in John 2:17, Jesus quotes 69:9, 'Zeal for your house will consume me', while Peter, speaking in Acts 1:20 of the defection and destiny of Judas Iscariot, says:

For it is written in the book of Psalms.
'Let his homestead become desolate,
and let there be no one to live in it';

and

'Let another take his position of overseer.'

These quotations are from 69:25 and 109:8, both psalms which describe deep suffering.

The triumphal entry of Jesus into Jerusalem was heralded by the people, including children, who lauded him in the language of Psalm 118. In Mark 12:10, Jesus is recorded as quoting verses 22 and 23 of this psalm:

The stone that the builders rejected
   has become the corner-stone.
This is the LORD's doing,
   and it is amazing in our eyes.

This was the last of the psalms in the Great Hallel (113–118), a group of psalms always sung at the Passover Feast, which was, of course, just about to take place when Jesus entered Jerusalem for the last time. This psalm's focus is on the temple, and in it the temple's building becomes a kind of allegory of the history of the people. The capstone or testing stone or top-stone has to be put on to complete the building. This stone furnishes a test of the design or else of the execution of the design by the workmen, for if it does not fit something has gone wrong. Who then are the builders in the psalm? It is not clear, but in the Gospel story they are clearly the religious leaders who were contemporary with our Lord. They had missed their way and rejected the final Stone, but God would reverse this and make him the cornerstone, which would show how well the edifice of God's purpose had been built. It is obvious that Jesus was speaking of himself. Peter also applies these words to Jesus in Acts 4:11, and gives the healing of a lame man as evidence of the vindication of his ministry.

John's Gospel indicates that there is evidence in the psalms that the sufferings of Jesus would not extend beyond limits set for them by God. Psalm 34 refers to the protection of a righteous man by God and the words of verse 20 are quoted by John in his passion narrative in application to Jesus, 'None of his bones shall be broken' (John 19:36).

How then was Jesus vindicated by God? In a number of ways, but finally and conclusively by way of his resurrection, and other psalms are applied to this in the New Testament. It is always interesting to find the same passage employed by two different people and this applies to 16:8-11, which is said both by Peter (in Acts 2:25-28) and by Paul (in Acts 13:35) to be fulfilled in Jesus. At the close of his first sermon, Peter takes 110:1 to refer to the exaltation of Jesus to the right hand of God, when he says (Acts 2:34-36):

For David did not ascend into the heavens but he himself said,
'The Lord says to my Lord,
Sit at my right hand,
    until I make your enemies your footstool.'
Therefore let the entire house of Israel know with certainty that God has made him both Lord and Messiah, this Jesus whom you crucified.

The New Testament writers saw clearly that the vindication of Jesus has profound consequences. One important result of it, and indeed evidence for it, was the coming of the Holy Spirit on the disciples at Pentecost. The Day of Pentecost is linked, not only by Peter in Acts 2 but also by Paul in Ephesians 4:8, with the exaltation of Jesus. In the latter passage Paul quotes 68:18, doing so in a form which keeps contact with the main sense of the original but which takes account of the special significance of Pentecost. In the psalm the verse reads:

You ascended the high mount,
    leading captives in your train
    and receiving gifts from people.

In a very interesting way, as we will see, this links up well with the rejected stone passage from 118, quoted and applied to Jesus by himself and by Peter, for example in Mark 12:10 and 1 Peter. 2:7. It is not easy at first to see how the different parts of 68 belong together, but the key to this is the military language of which it is full. It follows the story of the God of Sinai and his dealings with his people from the Sinai desert[3] into the Promised Land and to the establishment of a sanctuary on another mountain, which, of course, although not named such, was a very clear reference to the temple on Mount Zion.

There is no rejection of a temple stone here but rather, by a dramatic piece of apostrophe, other mountains are pictured as envying Zion, perhaps a graphic way of suggesting the antagonism of human enemies. It was though at this exalted place that the Lord took captives and received gifts (probably tribute) from others. All this is applied to Christ, although now in terms of gifts dispensed rather than received, for the most important difference in the words as quoted by Paul is the change to 'he gave gifts to his people' instead of 'and receiving gifts from people'. Kidner has well said: 'This summarizes rather than contradicts the psalm, whose next concern is with the blessings God dispenses (19ff, 35).'[4] Another possibility is that Paul had in mind that the Holy Spirit was first given by the Father to Christ before he himself dispensed him, along with his gifts, to his people.

Christ's high priestly work for his people, as we have seen, is a very important theme in Hebrews, and has its Old Testament justification in 110. This is spelled out in some detail in Hebrews 7. In this epistle, just as Melchizedek was both priest and king, so is Jesus. This means that he can offer an acceptable sacrifice (himself) and then sit at God's right hand to rule as King.

The crowds had praised Jesus as King on his entry to Jerusalem by their use of 118, and his eventual rule over all the nations is seen in Revelation 12:5 and 19:15 to be a fulfilment of 2:9: 'You shall break them with a rod of iron.'

In 18, David rejoices in God's powerful aid to him in his

conflicts and the victory given to him so that nations were subdued under him, and this is applied to Christ's universal rule through the gospel in Romans 15:9, where 18:49 is quoted:

> Therefore I will confess you among the Gentiles,
>     and sing praises to your name

This is followed in Romans 15:11 by the call of 117:1:

> Praise the Lord, all you Gentiles,
>     and let all the peoples praise him.

How full is the testimony of the Book of Psalms to our Lord Jesus Christ!

# Practical conclusion:
## How should we use the psalms?

Many of the finest Christian hymns, such as the best of those written by Charles Wesley, are a good blend of doctrine and experience and so satisfy both the mind and heart of a Christian believer who uses them in corporate worship or in private devotion.

### Their importance for Christian understanding
In the pages of Holy Scripture God reveals himself to his people, and the Old Testament lays an important basis for all that the New Testament was later to reveal of him. The revelation of God in the psalms is many-sided, because in them we see him relating to people of various kinds and in all kinds of circumstances, and it is in the context of such relationships that much of the revelation is given.

The psalms take up all his dealings with people, both the godly and the ungodly. The very first psalm makes this distinction and it is clear that God relates to the godly in blessing but to the ungodly in judgment, so revealing different aspects of his own character. There are many psalms where the worshippers are clearly at the house of God and engaged there in his praise, but there are also psalms where they are far away and long to take the pilgrimage road to Jerusalem. There are psalms which look back at history or look out at the present or contemplate a future marked by the fulfilment of promises and threats of the God who never breaks his word.

It embraces virtually all the doctrinal themes of the Old Testament. Here we find many great matters treated, often more than one in the same psalm. Here God is both creator and lawgiver (19). He deals with both Israel and the nations (98). He enters into covenant with his people (132) and accepts their offerings and sacrifices (20:3). He delivers them from their enemies as their Saviour (106:21) and, even though he was the Most High God, they were able also to use of him the much more intimate term 'Redeemer', with its suggestions of kinship (78:35). They came to him in the warmth of prayer and the awesomeness of worship; they saw him as the One who had given them their king and who was himself the supreme King (2).

One of the characteristics of the postmodern outlook is the lack of a 'metanarrative'. This term is used of a great over-arching story which embraces all the little stories that represent the lives of men and women, both the great and the small. The nineteenth century was a century of conflicting metanarratives.

There was the metanarrative of Hegelianism, the story of how human thought developed over the centuries by the pattern of thesis, antithesis and synthesis, all moving towards the final goal of perfect understanding of truth. There was the somewhat similar metanarrative of evolutionary philosophy, in which the metanarrative was related to the survival of the fittest in the realm of ideas. There was the metanarrative of Marxism, in which the major story was one of class struggle leading to the production of the perfect Communist society.

There is no story like the meta-narrative of the Bible, the great overarching drama of God's great redemptive purpose, embracing all the little stories of the Bible, in so many of which the redemptive theme is present in microcosm, stories in which there are many blessings and yet many hurts for God's people, which finds its heart in the sufferings, death and resurrection of Jesus of Nazareth, and which moves on to its great consummation when he comes again. The Book of Psalms, with all its variety, will deepen our awareness of that great story and how the lives of the psalmists, and so our lives, are embraced in it. We need to read it with this in mind.

**Their importance for Christian experience**
Tremper Longman has well said, 'the Psalter represents theology in its most vibrant form ... theology written in intimate

relationship with God and in close touch with life.'[1] In the psalms we see godly people placidly contemplating, agitatedly questioning, rapturously worshipping, thankful for revelation given, eager for more, anticipating the fulfilment of promises or seeking to avoid the execution of warnings.

This is a major reason for the love Christians have for the psalms, and why it seems so appropriate when some printed New Testaments have this book bound at the end. In comparison with other parts of the Old Testament, these poems touch Christian believers at a deep spiritual level, that of personal and sometimes rapturous, at other times agonizing, experience.

Modern and postmodern people should find much to interest them in the psalms, because of the current preoccupation with experience. Just as Ecclesiastes may ring a bell for people today because it shows a search for meaning and may be a means in God's purpose to lead them to discover purpose in Christ, and Job, because it focuses on the ever-contemporary concern with suffering, so the psalms reveal the many-sidedness of godly experience. So the psalms have been found relevant to the lives of Christians everywhere and in every age. Cultures change, but life's basic experiences are common to us all.

As the Word of God, though, the psalms not only reflect godly experience, they create it. Rowland Prothero's book, *The Psalms in Human Life*,[2] is full of stories of the way the psalms have touched people, and the way God's Spirit has used them creatively for their blessing. How greatly, for example, both Augustine and Luther valued the penitential psalms because of the way the Holy Spirit used them to convince them of their personal sin as a necessary step on the road to faith in Christ!

## Their importance for worship

Sometimes today worship and theology are sharply distinguished, even in the pulpit ministry of some churches, usually to the downgrading of theology. In fact, worship without a theological basis is empty and it may move in the direction of pure mysticism, drifting further and further away from authentic

Biblical Christianity. Christian worship today is often lively, at times exciting, but it is also often thin on theological content. We need to worship God in accordance with the great truths he has revealed about himself. It is after saying, 'Let the word of Christ dwell in you richly; teach and admonish one another in all wisdom,' that Paul urges his readers, 'with gratitude in your hearts sing psalms, hymns, and spiritual songs to God' (Col. 3:16).

In Protestant churches, but especially in those of the Presbyterian and Reformed traditions, the concept of the 'regulative principle' has been seen to be important in its application to worship. This is the principle that all worship is to be God-directed, that he is to be worshipped only in accordance with his revelation of himself. A study of 50 emphasises the importance of this, for it is clear there that some in Israel had Baalized ideas of God in their minds, actually imagining that he needed, for his own sustenance, the flesh and blood of the sacrifices they were offering him in their worship. It is sobering to realise that this was happening within the community of God's people.

This principle has often been applied to the Book of Psalms, because of the fact that within Scripture it is almost the only God-given source of sung worship material.[3] For instance, it was not until 1781, when paraphrases of other parts of Scripture began to be used, that anything else was sung in Presbyterian worship in Scotland. This outlook is not so widely held today, and many consider that other worship material that is in complete accord with Biblical truth is permissible, but there are still churches that use only the psalms, and every hymn book or Christian song book contains some metrical versions of psalms. In every age and culture the Book of Psalms is a great source of material for worship.[4]

Listen to the prayer in which a godly minister leads his people to the throne of grace and you may well recognise some of the phraseology of the psalms. Open a hymnbook and study its language for Biblical phraseology and content and you will discover the profound influence of the psalms on Christian praise. This influence is not confined to hymns that are virtual psalm paraphrases, in the way, for instance that the great 'Praise, my soul, the King of heaven' paraphrases 103, but in phrases which are woven into hymns which, in their complete form are certainly not psalm paraphrases. A hymn by F W Faber contains the verse:

> There is plentiful redemption
>   in the blood that has been shed;
> there is joy for all the members
>   in the sorrows of the Head.

The phrase 'plentiful redemption' comes from 130:7 (AV). Joseph Addison wrote the words:

> The spacious firmament on high,
> with all the blue ethereal sky,
> and spangled heavens, a shining frame,
> their great Original proclaim.
> The unwearied sun, from day to day,
> does his Creator's power display,
> and publishes to every land
> the work of an almighty hand.

Is it possible to doubt that the inspiration of this was 19, even though the remaining verses depart from the psalm completely?

## Their importance for preaching

Preaching too needs theology, or else it may become empty rhetoric or mere emotionalism, and sermons may become little more than philosophical speculation or vaguely religious ethical pragmatism. It is doubtful if any academic subject is of more importance for the preacher than Biblical Theology, to which, of course, a theology of the psalms belongs, for he needs to have a grasp of the great truths of Scripture if he is to preach them. Biblical Theology gives depth to preaching and teaches congregations to think Biblically, as Edmund Clowney shows in his book, *Preaching and Biblical Theology*.[5]

To understand the psalms Biblically is, of course, ultimately to understand them in terms of Christ. A series of sermons based on selected psalms may show how strong is the Old Testament basis for what the New Testament says about him, and the hearts of the hearers will be warmed as they see him in this great Biblical book.

Those who are new to preaching sometimes fight shy of the expository type, because of the demands it makes on the preacher, and they hesitate to launch a series of messages on one Bible book, especially if that book is a substantial one. A series on the psalms could be a good introduction to expository preaching for young preachers, and the advantage is that even though there are threads of significance running through the book and linking psalms together, each psalm is also a distinct entity, and may be treated as such. There is such variety there that a rich diet of Biblical truth may thus be given to the people of God.

## Their importance for personal devotion

Doctrine in the psalms comes to us in a devotional context, and this gives them great value for personal devotion. The Book of Psalms is the chief devotional book of the Old Testament and has had an immense influence on Christian spirituality, as a perusal of any great devotional classic from the past will quickly reveal. Holladay[6] gives plenty of examples of this. All Scripture is given by divine inspiration and is therefore spiritually edifying, but there are some books and passages which do not seem promising at first sight, although further thought and prayer to God for light leads to greater realisation of their devotional value. The Book of Psalms, however, needs little adaptation, for all that is required is to 'translate' it into the form taken by the experience of salvation in the New Testament and, of course, today. Some of our hymns do this. 'The Lord's my Shepherd' keeps close to the actual text of Psalm 23, but 'The King of love my Shepherd is', with expressions like 'Thy cross before to guide me' interprets it in the light of the New Testament. Many modern Christian songs are based on the psalms, sometimes very closely.

The psalms deal with perennial issues. After all, praising God and concern about experiences of affliction are not exclusive to the people of the Old Testament. Christian believers want some vehicle for praising God and they desire to express their pain, puzzlement, even their anger, as well as their joy and thanksgiving, their trust and their love. Miller comments on the big time and culture gap between the Bible and ourselves, and says this is better bridged in the Book of Psalms than anywhere else.[7] This is undoubtedly true, for God calls all his people of every age and place to talk with him and to bring him their worship.

## A book for prayer, praise and reflection

The Book of Psalms may be looked at from three points of view, and these in fact reflect stages in the historical development of the book.

At the first stage, many of them arose out of the individual experience of the psalmists. Sometimes that experience was difficult and the writer came to God to have his wounds bound up and sometimes to enquire, 'Why?' At other times it was very positive and he wanted to come with thanksgiving. So such psalms may be viewed as separate entities, but together they furnished a book of prayers which others might appropriate for their own use.

Then it became a book for worship. The material was gathered together over some period of time, and earlier collections were incorporated in later ones until the book as we have it today stood complete. It was employed, presumably at the earlier as well as at the last stage, for corporate worship in the house of God. Its use in the New Testament makes us aware that it can still be employed today, and Christian worship has often been renewed out of the contents of this book.

Then came the third and final stage. With its psalmic introduction (1, or 1 and 2), it became a book for godly reflection, a testimony to the faithfulness of God experienced in the psalms and believed in for the future, and especially a book for rebuilding faith when that has been shattered by difficult experiences. Thinking of it purely as a totality and in terms of its final arrangement, it presents a kind of search which finds its goal, a divinely-intended one, at its close, very much like the books of Job and Ecclesiastes.

It is widely recognised that much of the world's greatest literature is in the form of tragedy. If we possessed only Books 1 to 3 and not the complete volume, the Book of Psalms would be in many ways like a tragedy. In fact this would be true for the whole Bible if everything had come to its end at the Exile. God however intended a 'happy ending', but not in the unconvincing or contrived manner in which some novels contradict the life-experience of many of us, but rather because life's deepest agonies have been experienced in all their power to grieve, and in the process have had their sting drawn. It is that which makes the cross a victory and the resurrection inevitable.

The Book of Psalms was also, of course, like the Law, a book for obedience. Brueggemann says of 1, 'Standing at the beginning of the Psalter, this Psalm intends that all the Psalms should be read through the prism of torah obedience.'[8] He goes on to say:

> As an entry point into the Psalter, this poem asserts that the Psalter is intended for and intends to evoke and authorise a community of trusting, joyous obedience. The songs which follow in the Psalter, so Psalm 1 proposes, are for a disciplined community of piety which takes the saving tradition seriously, believes that God's command stands at the centre of life, and affirms that the honoring of commands is a matter of joy and wellbeing.

This is its canonical purpose.

Now it is important for us to see that there is no sense in which the first or second stage is left behind at the third, but that each stage is an enrichment and not an alteration of what has already taken place.[9] For instance, each of the Psalms of Ascents is of value to us in so far as we can identify with the outlook of the writer, then it takes its place in a sequence of psalms used for worship by pilgrims, and finally becomes part of a book with an overall message.

So the Psalter which began in personal experience may still enrich such experience. It may give words to experience that has already taken place or it may itself, as God's word, be creative in the realm of experience. So the Christian may read the opening verses of 40, where the psalmist says:

> I waited patiently for the LORD;
>> he inclined to me and heard my cry.
> He drew me from the desolate pit,
>> out of the miry bog,
> and set my feet upon a rock,
>> making my steps secure.
> He put a new song in my mouth,
>> a song of praise to our God.
> Many will see and fear,
>> and put their trust in the LORD (vv. 1-3).

He or she will be thankful that the psalmist has put into words something of his own experience of God's gracious intervention in his life. On the other hand, somebody without Christian assurance may be challenged by such a reading to seek a like confidence in God.

The material gathered together in the book became a vehicle for the praises of Israel and so was not only 'a mirror of life' with God but also 'a manual of devotion' to God and of corporate devotion at that. It is still that and Christian worship is often renewed from this source.

A healthy Christian life and a healthy Christian church needs this unique combination of three essential elements, a 'threefold cord not easily broken', so that Christian experience is real and is constantly enriched; Christian worship is real and heart-felt and has a corporate as well as an individual dimension; and the Word of God never becomes a book simply for the study but always also for the personal and practical daily life of the Christian and the joyful and yet realistic worship of the church that Christ has redeemed with his precious blood.

# NOTES

## Introduction

1. For a thorough critique of Deconstruction, see K.J. Vanhoozer, *Is there a meaning in this text? The Bible, the reader and the morality of literary knowledge*, Leicester: Apollos, 1998. The value of this book lies in the fact that Vanhoozer not only criticises Deconstruction sensitively (agreeing that it has something to teach Christians) but presents a most helpful positive approach to the doctrine of Biblical authority.

2. In the collection of his writings on the subject entitled *The Inspiration and Authority of the Bible,* London, Marshall, Morgan and Scott, 1951 (original date 1932).

3. J.I. Packer says that 'the concept of biblical inspiration is essentially identical with that of prophetic inspiration', and, while recognizing that diverse psychological processes must have been involved in the production of different Biblical genre under the inspiration of the Spirit, he affirms that 'the theological reality of inspiration is the same in each case' (in his chapter 'The adequacy of human language' in Geisler, N.L. (ed.), *Inerrancy,* Grand Rapids: Zondervan, 1979: 197, 198.

4. Kraus, 1986, 13. Derrida, the originator of Deconstruction, would find serious fault with Kraus here because he believes such following of the text to be impossible, as the intention of the writer can never be fully known. Vanhoozer, in the book mentioned above, deals effectively with this objection.

5. See Chapter 13.

6. The question the psalmist asks is a perfectly legitimate one, for the Bible is essentially an honest book in which real questions are faced. Considered simply in itself, it suggests that true faith is consistent with perplexity.

7. 1990: 152f.

8. In 'The Semantics of Biblical Literature' in Carson, D.A. and Woodbridge, J.D. (eds.), *Hermeneutics, Authority and Canon* (Leicester: IVP, 1986), 94, he asks, 'What kind of authority is shared by the Psalms, the Song of Moses (Ex 15), and Mary's Magnificat (Luke 1:46-55)? We may say that God is here using human Expressives to communicate something of the human response when confronted with the majesty and character of God. As C.S. Lewis rightly observed, the response speaks eloquently (in a qualitatively precise manner) about the person who evoked it. These Expressives thus constitute normative responses in which the reader is invited to share and participate. We too must respond to injustice with

laments and prayers for justice. We too must respond to God's mercy and love with sincere praise. We too must have imaginations captive to the vision of the kingdom of God. Not only our minds but also our emotional responses are brought under scriptural authority.' J.I. Packer makes much the same point, in N.L. Geisler (ed.), *Inerrancy*, Grand Rapids: Zondervan, 1979, p. 198, when he refers to 'the poems, whose giant-size delineations of adoration and devotion set worshippers in every age a standard for what their own praise and prayer should be'.

9. 1958: 17.

10. We can find instances of the same kind of thing in the epistles of Paul, e.g. in his use of *katoptriómenoi* ('reflecting' or 'beholding') in 2 Cor. 3:18.

11. 1990: 153.

12. 1990: 74.

13. 1990: 180.

14. 1998: 34.

15. 1990: 140. He says, 'A theology of the Psalter would be a most confused affair; at best it could be constructed as a framework into which the whole collective witness of the psalms could be fitted' (1990: 152).

16. See especially Chapter 15.

17. For *tora* ('law', v. 2) means 'instruction' and may be applied more widely than to the Mosaic Law.

18. Whybray (1997) is doubtful about the whole thesis of a reflective intent for the Book of Psalms, although he does not deny that it has reflective value.

19. This idea is so central to Brueggemann's thought that it comes into most of his publications on the psalms. See the bibliography.

20. The influential philosophical system of G.W.F. Hegel (1770-1831), who maintained that truth always progresses dialectically as a thesis and its antithesis collide, producing a reconciling synthesis.

21. There is an interesting comparison with the Book of Job, which is explored, although at perhaps a somewhat elementary level, in G.C. Morgan, *The Answers of Jesus to Job,* London: Marshall, Morgan and Scott, 1950.

22. R.P. Carroll in his chapter, 'Is Humour among the Prophets?' in Radday and Brenner (1990:176) points out that Elijah gives a mocking parody of religious beliefs, echoing the psalms of lament (e.g. *cf.* 1 Ki. 18:26: 29 with Pss. 44:23-26; 89:46-51).

23. Dumbrell says 'The Book of Psalms is a compendium of biblical theology, and issues touching every aspect of Old Testament thought and life are taken up within it' (1989: 211).

24. 1993: 115.

25. Murphy compares 1 and 2 with Hosea 14:9 which he calls 'a wisdom tag': 'Let the one who is wise understand ... Straight are the paths of the Lord, in them the just walk...' (1993: 9,20). He might also have mentioned

the interesting link with Hosea 14:8 where there is a reference to a green pine tree and its fruitfulness, and also other tree images earlier in the chapter, all of which remind us of 1.

26. 'Laughing at the Bible: Jonah as Parody' in Radday and Brenner (eds), *On Humour and the Comic in the Hebrew Bible*, Sheffield: Almond, 1990: 208.

27. 1991: 27.

28. The series entitled *New Studies in Biblical Theology* currently being published jointly by IVP and Eerdmans is testimony to this conviction.

## Chapter 1: The history of its study

1. *St. Athanasius on the Incarnation: the treatise de Incarnatione Verbi Dei*, ET, London: Mowbray, 1953.

2. Kraus 1986: 108

3. Dahood 1970.

4. Craigie 1983.

5. Gerstenberger, E. S., *Psalms, Part 1, with an Introduction to Cultic Poetry*, Grand Rapids: Eerdmans, 1988.

6. 1986: 232. See D. Sylva (1993).

7. 1981: 21.

8. 1981: 253.

9. 1981: 256.

10. See especially Allen (1987), Brueggemann (1991), Creach (1996), Holladay (1993), Mays (1987, 1994), Seybold (1990), Sheppard (1980), Wilson (1984, 1985, 1986, 1992) and the symposium edited by McCann (1993). For some criticisms of this approach, see Whybray (1997).

11. See Goulder, M. D., 'The Fourth Book of the Psalter,' in *JTS* 26, 1975: 269-89; *The Psalms of the Sons of Korah* (JSOT Suppl. 20), Sheffield: JSOT, 1982; *The Prayers of David (Psalms 51-72): Studies in the Psalter II*. (JSOT Suppl. 102), Sheffield: JSOT, 1990; also Brennan, J. P., 'Psalms 1-8: Some Hidden Harmonies,' *Biblical Theology Bulletin* 10, 1980: 25-29, Nasuti, H. P., *Tradition History and the Psalms of Asaph*. SBL Dissertation Series 88. Atlanta: Scholars, 1988 and Rendsburg, G. A., *Linguistic Evidence for the Northern Origin of Selected Psalms*. SBL Monograph Series. Atlanta: Scholars, 1990.

12. 1982, ix

13. e.g. Willis, J. (1979), Psalm 1 – An Entity. *ZAW* 9: 381-401; Berry, D. K., *The Psalms and Their Readers: Interpretive Strategies for Psalm 18*. (JSOT Suppl. 153). Sheffield: JSOT, 1993; McCann, J. C., 'Psalm 73: A Microcosm of Old Testament Theology,' in K. Hoglund, et al. (eds.), *The Listening Heart*. (JSOT Suppl. 58), Sheffield: JSOT, 1987: 247-257 and Soll, W., *Psalm 119: Matrix, Form and Setting*. Washington DC: The

Catholic Biblical Association of America, 1991.

14. These have included Broyles, C. C. (1989), Creach, J. F. D. (1996), Eaton, J. H. (1986), F. Lindström, *Suffering and Sin: Interpretations of Illness in the Individual Complaint Psalms.* Stockholm: Almqvist and Wiksell International, 1994; Zenger, Erich (1996)

15. There have been a number of studies of the prophetic type of psalm, for instance in W. H. Bellinger, Jr. (1984). R. J. Tournay too takes this up in his 1991 volume. A useful study of the Torah-Psalms is Mays, J. L. (1987). See also an earlier study: Murphy, R. E., 'A Consideration of the Classification "Wisdom Psalms",' in *V.T Suppl.* 9, 1962. Leiden: Brill: 156-67.

16. This is the argument he develops through his whole book (1996).

17. 1997.

18. P. E. Satterthwaite, R. S. Hess, G. J. Wenham (eds.), *The Lord's Anointed: Interpretation of Old Testament Messianic Texts*, Carlisle: Paternoster, 1995.

## Chapter 2: Its diverse authorship

1. There is really no consensus of opinion as to the dating of psalms with superscriptions. Tournay (1991: 18,19), giving a conspectus of views, stresses that the whole matter is very conjectural. This is certainly true if the authorship references are regarded as totally unreliable, but are we really warranted in saying this?

2. The Greek translation (usually identified as LXX), which was widely used in the Greek-speaking Jewish synagogues in New Testament times. There is some difference of opinion among scholars as to the dating of the LXX translation of the Book of Psalms, but in a recent study Schaper (*Eschatology in the Greek Psalter*, Tübingen: Mohr, 1995: 45) argues for a date not later than the late 2nd. Cent. BC.

3. Heb. *ledavid.*

4. 1988: 39.

5. Although as recent a writer as Seybold can say that no single psalm can with any probability be ascribed to David because too many linguistic, cultural and theological difficulties stand in the way (1990: 37,38).

6. Ps. 18 is the one most commonly treated as Davidic. Holladay (1993: 23, 24) argues for 2, 18 and 110 as originating in David's day.

7. NRSV translates 'the favorite of the Strong one of Israel.' For discussion of the translation, with support for the NIV rendering see R. F. Youngblood, '1, 2 Samuel' in F E Gaebelein (ed.), *Expositor's Bible Commentary*, Vol. 3, Grand Rapids: Zondervan, 1992: 1082.

8. Those who do not accept that David wrote many or any psalms nevertheless recognise his unique place in the Old Testament psalmic tradition. Tournay says: 'The father of Israelite psalmody according to tradition, David

has a role as initiator in as much as he is a prophet at the head of the Levitical singers who too are inspired by the same Spirit' (1991: 44).

9. 1990: 35.

10. 1979: 552.

11. 1993: 23.

12. 1987: 122ff. Allen points to the presence of 19 in a royal group, shows it has important links with 18, and says: 'The accumulation of parallels leads to a clear conclusion: the purpose of setting the two psalms side by side was to relate David's experience to the individual pious believer who sought models for personal living in the "Torah" of the Psalms' (1987: 125).

13. Books like *The Screwtape Letters* and *The Great Divorce* by C. S. Lewis are examples of this.

14. 1973: I, 16-18, 32-46.

15. Longman accepts the authorship titles but says we must be cautious about pronouncing them canonical (1988: 38-40). He has more difficulties with the historical titles and says it is best to regard them as non-biblical but as reflecting reliable early tradition (1988: 40-42).

16. See especially Mark 12:35-37; Acts 2:29ff; 34ff; 13:35-37.

17. Together with its Matthean parallel (Matt. 22:41-46).

18. An interesting phenomenon of the historical psalms, such as 78, 105 and 106, is that in them the history terminates quite early. Seybold, noting that we do not get echoes of the Persian and Greek periods with their problems, says that no satisfactory reason for this fact can be given (1990: 175, 176). Surely the answer could lie in an early date for such psalms!

19. 1973:36.

20. cf. Gen. 1-3.

21. cf. Gen. 3-5.

22. cf. the many prayers of Moses for the people as recorded in the Pentateuch.

23. 1 Kings 6:37-7:12.

## Chapter 3: The variety of its forms

1. The division of the Book of Psalms into 5 books will be considered in Chapter 15.

2. This is uncertain in relation to 36, as difference in the translation of v. 1 in the NRSV and NIV indicates.

3. Nathan's prophecy recorded in 2 Samuel 7.

4. See especially Bellinger (1984) and Tournay (1991). Tournay says that recent commentaries have neglected this prophetic dimension of the Book of Psalms, although it was evidently recognised in the New Testament (Acts 2:25ff; 4:25). He does however go on to say: 'Commentators ... agree in emphasizing the countless contacts in style and motifs between the prophetic writings and the psalms' (Tournay 1991: 28).

5. 1991: vii.

6. 1 Chron. 25:1

7. This term is often employed to cover passages in which there is frank self-disclosure by the prophet. They are Jer. 11:18-20; 12:1-4; 15:10, 15-18; 17:14-18; 18:19-23; 20:7-11, 14-18.

8. The promise of God to David recorded in 2 Sam. 7:4-17 is the evident basis of both.

9. Some of the language in this psalm looks like a summary of parts of Gen. 1.

10. From v. 10 to the end there appear to be strong echoes of Exod. 15, especially vv. 11-13.

11. e.g. Exod. 3:15; 18:11; Num. 21:21ff; 33; Deut. 32:26; Pss. 115:3, 36, 8-11; Jer. 10:13.

12. In other words the life setting *(Sitz im Leben)* of each psalm.

13. e.g. I Engnell *Studies in Divine Kingship*, Uppsala: Almqvist and Wiksells, 1943

14. Ollenburger, B. C., *Zion, the City of the Great King: a Theological Symbol of the Jerusalem Cult,* Sheffield, JSOT Suppl. Series 41, 1986, pp. 23-33, discusses Mowinckel's theory, cautiously accepts it in general terms, but then says: 'There is insufficient evidence, it seems to me, to reconstruct this festival in detail, to ascribe a dominant role within it to the earthly king, or to assign a whole range of Psalms to specific movements within the festival' (33), but he does link 47 and 93-99 with it.

15. Dumbrell warns us, 'Caution must be exercised where liturgical material of the Psalter is used to postulate an emphasis (such as a theology of kingship) which differs from or is nowhere else attested in, the rest of the OT.' *The Faith of Israel: its expression in the books of the Old Testament,* Leicester: IVP, 1989: 208.

16. R. de Vaux, *Ancient Israel,* New York: McGraw-Hill, 1961, p.114.

17. 1980: 26, n. 39.

18. 1986: 67, n.8.

19. 1989: 20.

20. 1970: 218.

21. 1981: 11.

22. 1991: 24.

23. Tournay's analysis has somewhat influenced the title of the present volume.

24. 1996: 15.

### Chapter 4: The characteristics of its poetry

1. All the consonants are mild-sounding ones in v. 1 and much of v. 2.

2. See T Longman III, 'A Critique of two Recent Metrical Systems' in *Biblica 63* (1982):230-254.

3. e.g.   'I will bless the LORD at all times;
          his praise shall continually be in my mouth' (34:1).
4. e.g.   'The young lions suffer want and hunger,
          but those who seek the LORD lack no good thing' (34:10).
There is a great deal of this kind of poetry in the Book of Proverbs, especially in contrasting descriptions of the righteous and the wicked.
5. e.g.   'This poor soul cried, and was heard by the LORD,
          and was saved from every trouble' (34:6).
6. 1988: 100.
7. *Psalm Structures: A Study of psalms with Refrains*, Sheffield: JSOT, 1990: 213. The same phenomenon may sometimes be discerned in Pauline thought where, for instance, in 2 Cor. 3:18, the same Greek word may be translated 'behold' or 'reflect', and the two senses taken together yield a particularly helpful thought.
8. 1990: 148.
9. Here the cords are clearly figurative, taken probably from a hunter's snares. V. 16 is also almost certainly figurative so that this raises questions about vv. 4 and 5. In 22, the animals are clearly figurative, especially in v.10, so it is highly likely that all the other wild animals here are figurative too.
10. 1990: 60, 61
11. e.g. in 1:3, we may draw lessons from the planting, power to refresh, fruit-bearing, and evergreen nature of the tree, for these are referred to, but hardly from its branches or bark or its ability to shelter people!
12. 1987.
13. 1987: 95.
14. 1987: 95.
15. 1987: 95, 96.

## Chapter 5: The God of the Psalms

1. 1973: 5. He says it is 'comparable to the preferences and aversions found in our own circles, where one group tends to speak of "God" and another of "the Lord", or one generation uses "Thou" in worship and another "You".'
2. As Kraus puts it, at Ugarit, 'in a continuing, unchangeable sense the position of honor as king of the gods is accorded only to El' (1986: 28, 29). In practice, however, other deities, particularly the 'junior' god Baal, were frequently more prominent in Semitic religion.
3. The way it is used by Christ in John 10:34-36 strongly favours the first of these interpretations.
4. Whether it was the name or its meaning which was revealed to Moses is fully discussed in R. W. L. Moberly, *The Old Testament of the Old Testament: Patriarchal narratives and Mosaic Yahwism,* Minneapolis: Fortress Press, 1992. He argues for the former.
5. See especially 22:22: 'I will declare your name to my brothers', and

119:55, 'In the night I will remember your name, O Lord.' His name is majestic in all the earth (8:1, 9).

6. As does Adonai ('Lord') which, although fairly frequent, is less so than either Elohim or Yahweh.

7. Fuller discussion of the names and titles treated here plus others may be found in Kraus (1986: 17-31).

8. As Harman, writing on this psalm, points out, 'While other "gods" are referred to, their existence is denied in verse 5. The psalmist puns on the Hebrew word for God (*'elohim*), saying that the heathen gods are only worthless idols or nobodies (*'elilim*)' (1998:322).

9. We should note though that Paul recognised that there is a supernatural realm of evil even though that realm is not peopled by gods (1 Cor. 10:18-21; cf. Deut. 32:15-18).

10. cf. 89:10.

11. e.g. in John 12:30-33; Col. 2:14,15: Heb. 2:14, 15; Rev. 20:7-10.

12. In one place Leviathan is a great creature of the sea, perhaps a whale, so called because inspiring fear in the traveller because of its size and power (104:26).

13. Deut. 4 gives particularly full teaching as to the nature and ways of Israel's God and in the course of it Moses says: 'Since you saw no form when the Lord spoke to you at Horeb out of the fire, take care and watch yourselves closely, so that you do not act corruptly by making an idol for yourselves' (vv. 15, 16).

14. See especially Hosea's comment on the story of Jacob at Peniel (Gen. 32:22-32) in Hos. 12: 3-5.

15. See Tournay (1991:86) for fuller information.

16. 1992: 2, 3.

17. e.g. in 91:4.

18. 1993: 80.

19. Many of these are used elsewhere in the OT but are less frequent in the NT, where 'Father', used so much by Jesus, takes over as by far the most frequent 'picture' of God, with 'King', especially as suggested by the phrase 'kingdom of God', coming second. We should not forget however that 'God', when used in the NT, has the whole OT revelation of him, including all the verbal images, as its background.

20. Of course, to distinguish between the literal and the figurative is not always easy when the language used is as concrete as Hebrew, but all languages have terms which started life in the physical realm, became metaphors and then through frequent use cease to be thought of as figurative, as in such a phrase as *'standing* for election to Parliament'.

21. cf. the biting sarcasm of Isa. 41:21-24.

22. e.g. 10:1; 22:1; 35:22-25; cf. Rev. 6:9, 10.

23. Ps. 145 is a good example of this.

24. Sometimes distinguished as his majesty-holiness and his moral holiness respectively.

25. The high-priestly prayer of Jesus shows that Jesus had this understanding of God when he calls him 'Holy Father' (John 17:11).

26. It is an impassioned refrain in 107.

27. e.g. in 19:9; 25:10; 36:5; 89:1-8 and 96:13.

28. e.g. see how in 31:5, 18 the psalmist expresses his trust in the God of truth and asks that the lying lips of his enemies should be silenced.

29. e.g. the words of Job in Job 16:6-17.

30. e.g. Jer. 15:15-18.

## Chapter 6: God Creates His People

1. 1990: 137.

2. In 93, a psalm of great divine stability, the mighty waves seem like a threat to that order but their waves beat on the shore in vain, because God is mightier than they.

3. It is interesting to see that 144:3,4, using similar language, complements this thought with the reflection that man is in fact transient, like a breath or a passing shadow.

4. The writer quotes a section of the psalm and then makes several comments on various elements of it, much in the way he later handles 110 in chapter 7.

5. Kidner says, 'Since the outcome of this praise is the enemy's defeat, as in the Heb., the LXX wording is probably a paraphrase to show what the psalm means by its unusual metaphor of an audible bulwark. *Cf.* 2 Ch. 20:22; Ne. 8:10' (1973: 67 n.1).

6. The structure of Calvin's *Institutes of the Christian Religion* shows his understanding of this.

7. Heb. *ki.*

8. 1991: 26.

9. Tournay, 1991: 27.

10. See Chapters 19-21.

## Chapter 7: God Rules His people

1. Harman also regards the Divine Kingship as of central importance in the psalms (1998: 38-42).

2. 1994: 7.

3. 1997: 73.

4. cf. also Is. 52:7.

5. It is most doubtful if Mowinckel has really made out his case, although Westermann (1981: 146) appears to accept his thesis at this point.

6. See 2 Kings 24:8-16.

7. 1981: 146, 147.

8. 1981: 151.

9. Heb. *mabbul* is used only here and in Genesis, where it refers to Noah's Flood.

10. Elohim here, if intended in a singular sense, means 'God', but if as a true plural, it will mean 'heavenly beings' or angels. The latter is the way the LXX took it and this was followed when it was quoted in Heb. 2:7-9.

11. This psalm also influenced the language of passages like 1 Cor. 15:25-28 and Eph. 1:22.

12. 1986: 110-114. He says: 'It is necessary to show that such foreign religious terminology as calling the king the "son of God" has been brought under the theology of the divine choice and thus has been demythologized' (1986: 110).

13. 1986: 135-197.

14. The Hebrew is ambiguous. A survey of English translations will show that translators have not always taken the same line on this.

15. The word in 58:1 which is translated 'gods' in the NRSV AND 'rulers' in the NIV, has several possible meanings. If the people addressed are 'gods', this is clearly figurative and based on their sharing God's function of judgment, for it is clear from the context that, in literal terms, they are human; cf. 82:1 and John 10:34, 35.

16. This is why the Books of Kings treat him as the model for other kings; see 1 Kings 11:4-6; 15:11, et al.

17. cf. the reassuring words of Isa. 52:13, with which the Fourth Servant Song, with its picture of deep suffering, commences; also John 1:5, 'The light [i.e. Christ the Light] shines in the darkness, and the darkness did not overcome it.'

18. W. J. Dumbrell says we can hold the view of the King as 'the regular dispenser of blessing for Israel as its corporate head (see Pss. 22, 28, 61, 63, 71, 89, 144).... It is clear that he is regarded as a divine appointee assured of divine protection and blessings' (Ps. 2:6; 18:50; 21:3; 78:70; 89:18) (1989: 213).

19. R. E. Prothero, *The Psalms in Human Life*, London, Nelson, 1903: 119.

20. As Hayes says (1976: 97): 'The beliefs and convictions about the king were the grounds upon which Jewish messianism was built.'

21. 1988: 67, 68.

22. Dumbrell says: 'The thought of several of the psalms, however, goes well beyond historical kingship and is clearly messianic. In such psalms the king's role as an adopted son, his spectacular victories, his priestly prerogatives, and other messianic motifs, are extravagantly presented (e.g. Pss. 2, 45, 72, 89, 110, 132). These avowedly messianic psalms explain the extreme interest in historical kingship which the Psalms betray, providing a

religious understanding of the king as an ideal figure, which ran quite contrary to historical experience' (1989: 213).

23. R. de Vaux, *Ancient Israel; Its Life and Institutions*, London: Darton, Longman and Todd, ET, 1973:110.

24. He says, with reference to 2: 'One cannot escape asking the question why such a psalm was preserved (and this would apply to the other royal psalms as well) because Israel ceased to be a kingdom with the destruction of Jerusalem in 587. The best answer is that the psalm came to be interpreted in a messianic, eschatological sense: in the end time, the messiah, as new David, would restore the kingdom to Israel' (1993: 18, 19).

25. 1983: 81.

## Chapter 8: God Speaks to His People

1. Harman, pointing out that this psalm has certain similarities to Canaanite poetry, says: 'It could be a polemical psalm directed against the heathen notions of the Canaanites and in particular a denial of the place of Baal in the world of nature' (1998:137).

2. The NIV text of v. 3 reads: 'There is no speech or language where their voice is not heard', but the margin renders it, 'they have no speech, there are no words; no sound is heard from them' (*cf.* 'There is no speech, nor are there words; their voice is not heard', NRSV) and this is the more natural translation. It also fits the context well, providing a paradox. The word goes out from the heavens, even though it is without audible language.

3. Tournay points out how rare *tora* is in the psalms. In addition to 1, 19 and 119, it is found only in 37:31; 40:9; 78:1, 5, 10; 89:31 and 94:12 (1991: 27, 28).

4. Murphy, writing of Psalm 1, says: 'Although it is torah, not the following psalms, that is the explicit subject (Ps. 1:2), the rest of the psalms mediate the teaching of the Law, which is taken up again explicitly in Psalms 19:8-12 and 119' (1993: 18). Kraus does not agree, saying that under no circumstances should *tora* be translated as 'law' (1986: 34, 35). Perhaps with NT Pharisaism in mind, he seems to have difficulty conceiving of a law that could be written about with such enthusiasm, but why not, if it was God's good word? cf. Rom. 7:12, 22.

5. He says: 'The *tora* of which the psalmist speaks is here, as in Deuteronomy, a summary term encompassing "statutes, commandments," etc.; it is the sum total of the obligations YHWH requires of Israel and as an instrument of government for a people' (1991: 35, 36).

6. 1991: 121, 122.

7. Ps. 1:1 shows the reverse side of this, for following bad advice and walking in the bad way comes to its climax when somebody sits 'in the seat of scoffers', for the seat was the teacher's position.

8. 1990: 35.

## Chapter 9: God Meets with His People

1. e.g. in Anglican worship.

2. Typically in Presbyterian worship.

3. Hayes says: 'One should, in a fashion, read the book of Leviticus, with its rituals for sacrifice, and the Psalms, with its prayers, in parallel columns. Psalm and sacrifice, ritual and spoken word, go together' (1976: 57). We could in fact read together Leviticus for the regulations, Chronicles for the history and the Psalms for the poetic content of the worship.

4. 1981: 118. Longman says that in the psalms: 'God is not praised for abstract qualities, but rather for the way in which he has entered into the individual and corporate lives of his people,' and again, 'The single most important reason for praise given by the psalmist is certainly that the Lord has delivered Israel out of distress' (1988: 25,26).

5. *Israel's Praise: Doxology versus Idolatry and Ideology*, Philadelphia: Fortress, 1988: 2, 3.

6. 1981: 135.

7. 1993: 113.

8. 1993: 14

9. 1992: 10.

10. Hayes points out that although circumcision, weddings and burial services were observed in OT days, they were secular and were not performed in a place of worship. But he also says there were many cultic activities in which the individual was involved, such as offering firstfruits and tithes (Deut. 26:1) and engaging in petition and thanksgiving in relation to disease (Lev.13-15) (1976: 13-16).

11. cf. e.g. Micah 6:6-8.

12. 1976: 56.

13. There has been much interest in these psalms and Kraus summarizes the views of many scholars when he says: 'the cultic traditions of Jerusalem ... stem for the most part from pre-Israelite times. Ancient Canaanite and Syrian motifs and concepts came to be applied to Zion, Jerusalem, the city of God. This occurred in part in the Jebusite period, and in part in Israelite times' (1986: 83). This is debatable, but our main concern, is, of course, with the theology of these psalms and not with the history of the ideas contained in them.

14. Seybold says: 'Probably at these services God's answer would have been given in the form of oracles of salvation, delivered by the prophets (*cf.* Ps. 60:6-8; 1990: 115).' We cannot, of course, be certain of this.

15. Gerstenberger is unusual in connecting these psalms, not with the cult, but with healing ceremonies within the family circle. He thinks of this as a kind of group-therapy, relating it to the sociology of the extended family. See his book, *Psalms*, Part 1, with an introduction to Cultic Poetry, Grand

Rapids: Eerdmans, 1988: 5-22, and, more fully, 'Der "bittende Mensch" ' in *Wissenschaftliche Monographien zum Alten und Neuen Testament* (Neukirchen; Neukirchener, 1980), 134-160. Miller says of Gerstenberger: 'His work is at least a challenge to others to assess theologically the sociological reality of the significance of the human existence of small groups (e.g. families, circles of friends, groups with common interest or needs) as the context of meaningful existence' (1986: 7).

16. *Hymns and Psalms*, Methodist Publishing House, 1984, Preface.

## Chapter 10: God Distinguishes His People

1. It may seem rather late to be discussing who the people of God are, as we have been dealing with God's relationship with them in all kinds of ways already. There have been good reasons however for delaying the matter, but we do now need to recognise that there were distinctions within Israel between the godly and the ungodly.

2. Preceded by the compilers of Book 1 which probably existed long before the whole Book of Psalms was compiled.

3. We have already seen that there is good reason for relating the two parts of a couplet in this way.

4. 1958: 27-30.

5. 1996: 71.

6. 1996: 47-50.

7. 1996: 50.

8. Keel, O., *The Symbolism of the Biblical World: Ancient Near Eastern Iconography and the Book of Psalms.* London: SPCK, 1972.

9. Harman writes helpfully on them, especially on 137. He points out that 'two passages from the prophets (Hos. 13:16; Isa. 13:16) provide the background for the curse in this imprecatory psalm.... In particular Isaiah 13:16 had already prophesied the downfall of Babylon.' See his whole discussion (1998: 59-62).

## Chapter 11: God Protects His People

1. 1988: 57

2. Heb. *chesed.*

3. See Lev. 25.

4. e.g. in Rom. 3:24,25.

5. Kidner says: 'At whatever level David understood his affirmation of 22a ... the whole verse is pregnant with a meaning which comes to birth in the gospel, and which is hardly viable in any form that falls short of this. The Christian can echo the jubilant spirit of the psalm with added gratitude, knowing the unimagined cost of 22a and the unbounded scope of 22b' (1973: 141, 142).

6. Mason points out that the figure is both pastoral and political and that Hammurabi was referred to as the shepherd of his people (1993: 143).

7. e.g. in Jer. 23, Ezek. 34, Zech. 10.

8. Mason says that 46 shows how the warrior tradition of Yahweh of hosts was taken over by the royal Zion theology (1993: 163).

9. Kraus gives it pride of place in his discussion of the God of Israel. He refers to its use in 24:7-10 and views it as 'the solemn, cultically legitimate name of the God who was present in the sanctuary of Jerusalem and honored there' (1986: 17). If this is correct, 68 may be the clue to it, for it views Yahweh as the divine Warrior, whose victories over his people's enemies culminate in his entrance to the sanctuary. The psalm concludes with v. 35: 'Awesome is God in his sanctuary, the God of Israel; he gives power and strength to his people. Blessed be God!' Jerusalem was taken from the Jebusites in warfare, so that Israel's God as Lord of hosts would be protecting what he had enabled his human hosts to secure.

10. On the other hand, Anderson suggests it could refer to the asylum provided by the horns of the altar, and this is certainly possible (1972: 155).

11. 1996.

12. He is particularly interested in the root *hsh*.

13. He notes that its association with the temple is probably the reason why it is never used in reference to false reliance on other gods or on human power (1996: 30).

## Chapter 12: God Judges and Blesses His People

1. 1993: 131.

2. The chief Hebrew word for judgment.

3. 1993: 130. He refers also to 10:16-18; 26:1; 35:24; 43:1 (1993: 130). The NIV and some other English versions have somewhat obscured the presence of this word in the Hebrew text by their translation, often preferring verbs like 'vindicate' or 'defend' to 'judge' in such cases.

4. cf. Mason (1993: 136).

5. Not quite invariably, see 33:12; 89:15.

6. W. L. Holladay refers both to Jer. 12:1b-2 and 17:5-8 and says that if, as he is convinced, these passages are genuinely from the prophet, then the psalm is prior. The Architecture of Jeremiah 1–20, London: Associated University Presses, 1976: 153.

7. cf. also 21:6; 89:15, etc.

8. Even in such a psalm as 51, sinful as he is, he has been brought to deep penitence.

## Chapter 13: God Refines His People

1. Heb. *hsh* and *bth*.
    2. 1990: 144-146.
    3. J. Barr, *The Semantics of Biblical Language*, Oxford, OUP, 1961.
    4. Brueggemann makes use of this distinction in several of his books. See especially his 1984 volume.
    5. Brueggemann himself recognises this. He says, 'I suggest a convergence of a contemporary pastoral agenda, together with a more historical exegetical interest' (1980: 4).
    6. 1990: 137, 138.
    7. He expounds his view in 'A Shape for O.T. Theology', in B. C. Ollenburger, E. A. Martens and G. F. Hasel (eds.), *The Flowering of Old Testament Theology: A Reader in 20th Century O.T. Theology*, Winona Lake: Eisenbrauns, 1992: 406-426.
    8. He first wrote on the Lament Psalms in 1954. His major work on this theme is 'Praise and Lament in the Psalms', which did not appear in its final form until 1977 ( Eng. trans. 1981), but which included much of the thinking and research which had gone into his articles over the years. Westermann claimed to be continuing the work of Gunkel, for he reckoned the whole movement set in motion by Mowinckel to be a kind of over-specialized by-path in psalm research largely neglectful of the individual psalms.
    9. 1986.
    10. *Psalms, Part 1, with an Introduction to Cultic Poetry*, Grand Rapids: Eerdmans, 1988
    11. 1989.
    12. 1984, 1986.
    13. Craven (1992:27,28)
    14. 1993: 56.
    15. 1986: 69, n.25.
    16. 1989: 14.
    17. See the discussion in Seybold (1990: 164, 165), who particularly emphasizes how inexhaustible 22 is in this respect.
    18. 1976: 79.
    19. For an Old Testament Theology which lays great emphasis on this element, see S. Terrien, *The Elusive Presence: Toward a new Biblical Theology*, San Francisco: Harper, 1978.
    20. There is wide agreement that these include 30, 32, 40, 42, 66, 92, 116, 118 and 138.
    21. 1990: 117.
    22. Westermann gives the following as examples of this: 3, 6, 10, 13, 22, 28, 31, 54 and 56 (1981: 79).
    23. 1981: 79.
    24. 1981:1.

25. Longman refers to this theory (1988: 29).

26. 1981: 114.

## Chapter 14: God Fulfils His Purpose for His People

1. Childs says: 'However one explains it, the final form of the Psalter is highly eschatological in nature. It looks toward the future and passionately yearns for its arrival.... As a result, the Psalter in its canonical form, far from being different in kind from the prophetic message, joins with the prophets in announcing God's saving Kingship' (1979: 518).

2. See Section C.

3. See Chapter 5.

4. We cannot be sure how universal the conspiracy is thought to be.

5. As Kidner says: 'In its enigmatic, staccato phrases this remarkable psalm speaks of Zion as the destined metropolis of Jew and Gentile alike. Nothing is explained with any fullness, yet by the end there remains no doubt of the coming conversion of old enemies and their full incorporation in the city of God' (1975: 314).

6. cf. Eccles. 9:7-10.

7. Johnson, P, 'Left in Hell': Psalm 16, Sheol and the Holy One, in (eds.), P. E. Satterthwaite, R. S. Hess and G. J. Wenham, *The Lord's Anointed: Interpretation of Old Testament Messianic Texts.* Carlisle: Paternoster, 1995: 218.

8. See the whole discussion in P. Johnson, 213-222

9. 1986: 174.

10. 1973: 74.

11. Are we really quite sure that it cannot have the resurrection significance it has in Dan. 12:2?

12. Schaper shows that the translators of the LXX even read the resurrection of the dead into the words of Ps. 1:5, as does the Targum on the verse, but without warrant in the Hebrew text (*Eschatology in the Greek Psalter,* Tübingen: Mohr, 1995: 47).

13. 1995: 72, 73.

14. 1973: 50.

15. See Chapters 21 and 22.

16. Although not necessarily beyond the scope of a prayer for him.

17. The terms of this last prayer (or statement, for the Hebrew can be read either way, see NIV) means that we are not at liberty to translate the Hebrew *eres* 'earth' as 'land', which would certainly be possible in some contexts but not in this one.

## Chapter 15: The Significance of its Structure

1. See e.g. J. K. Kunz, 'King Triumphant: a Rhetorical Study of Psalms 20 and 21, *Hebrew Annual Review* 10, 1986: 157-176; J. L. Mays (1987: 3-12).
2. Pss. 14 and 53 are the most obvious exceptions.
3. 1973: 68, 69.
4. W. Zimmerli identified 20 such pairs in a brief but valuable study not intended to be comprehensive and in which some were not contiguous: 'Zeillingspalmen', in J. Schreiner (ed.), *Wort, Lied, und Gottesspruch: Beiträge zu Psalmen under Propheten,* Würzburg: Echler, 1972: 105-113.
5. See Chapter 5.
6. M. Dahood (1970: I, xxxi) refers to this and also gives the wording of the Midrash quoted above. See also D. Barthélemy and J. T. Milik, *Qumran Cave I* (Discoveries in the Judaean Desert, I; Oxford: OUP, 1955): 133.
7. For further information, see Holladay (1993: Chap. 7).
8. 1982: 1.
9. In McCann (ed.), (1993, 22).
10. McCann (ed) (1993: 43).
11. Wilson makes trenchant criticisms of some of the views of John Walton, M. D. Goulder and Anton Arens in McCann (ed.) (1993: 42-48).
12. K. Vanhoozer has robustly defended this view. See our Introduction, n. 1.
13. We will consider this in chapter 16.
14. Noted, e.g. by Mitchell (1997: 301).
15. 1986.
16. 1985: 209-214. Eaton, who has argued for the royal classification of a great many psalms, gives good reasons for treating this psalm as royal (1986: 45, 46).
17. Wilson (1985: 214-219).
18. In J. C. McCann (ed.) (1993: 78). In the light of the New Testament fulfilment of the covenant of David in Christ, 'failure' should be 'apparent failure'.
19. R. E. Murphy, in McCann (ed.) (1993: 21-28). He makes the point that we should be cautious about seeing this kind of thing as significant (p. 24).
20. 1992, 133, 134.
21. 1997: 75.
22. April 1992, 134.
23. In McCann (ed.) (1993: 81).
24. 1985: 213.
25. In McCann (ed.) (1993: 75).
26. In McCann (ed.), (1993: 23).

27. 1990, 150.
28. Heb. *hsh*
29. 1990: 146, 147.
30. 1996.
31. G. T. Sheppard points out that the term 'refuge' occurs 30 times in 3-89 and that all but two are in Davidic psalms. It is found only once in the Torah, in Deut. 32:37 (1992:150), which has influenced the Psalms much through its Rock imagery, although at that point it is applied to false gods.
32. 1987: 14,16. He also says that 33 is placed with a Davidic group in order to accentuate the truth of 32:10-11 and the Asaphite 50 is placed, not with other Asaphite Psalms which come in 73-83 but between 42-49 (Korahite) and 51-71 (Davidic) because it stands as a theological bridge between them (1987: 16).
33. 1993: 14.
34. 1979: 524-525.
35. 1997: 83, 84.
36. 1997: 84.
37. 1997: 186.

## Chapter 16: The Introductory Psalms *(Psalms 1 and 2)*

1. McCann, ed.(1993: 83-92).
2. The two psalms are one in the LXX.
3. cf. perhaps Jos. 1:8: 'This book of the law shall not depart out of your mouth; you shall meditate on it day and night.'
4. After all, the narrower sense is included within the wider.
5. See e.g. P. D. Miller in McCann (1993), 83-92 , and contrast R. E. Murphy, 'Reflections on Contextual Interpretation of the Psalms' in the same volume: 22, 23.
6. The Western text of Acts 13:33 reads 'the first psalm', in its quotation of what other MSS call 'the second psalm', which seems to reflect knowledge of that tradition.
7. 'Meditate' in 1:2 and 'plot' in 2:1 translate the same Heb. word.
8. 1996.
9. 1993:41-45.

## Chapter 17: Book 1 – The tribulations and security of David

1. See also 24:3-6.
2. Of course, a study of the Epistle to the Hebrews soon shows the relevance of Leviticus for a Christian's understanding of the work of Christ.
3. See 2 Sam. 15-18.
4. Miller notes the Royal theme in Book 1 in 18, 20, 21 and that 20:7 echoes 2:1.

5. e.g. see 1 Kings 11:4-6; 2 Kings 22:2.
6. in J.C. McCann (1993: 86, 87).
7. op. cit. 86.
8. ibid.
9. ibid.

## Chapter 18: Book 2 – The tribulations and security of God's people

1. 1 Cor. 14:37, 38.
2. 1973: 168.
3. 1998: 184.
4. See Amos 5:21-24; Hos. 6:6; Isa.1:10-15; Mic. 6:6-8; Jer. 7:21-26.
5. This is particularly clear in the Isaiah and Micah passages referred to in the previous note.
6. Pss. 51, 52, 54, 57, 59, 60 and 63.
7. cf. 68:1 and Num. 10:35.
8. This is not dissimilar to the way in which earlier prophets are quoted in Zechariah, in the 'old age' of the Old Testament.
9. It is not of course impossible that it is by Solomon and that it is a prayer, not for a particular king, but rather for each king that would occupy the throne, so that he is asking God to make the ideal a reality in the reign of each of his Davidic successors. The concluding verse might then find its explanation in the fact that Solomon is praying for them what he recalls David will have prayed for him.

## Chapter 19: Book 3 – Why? Why? Why?

1. e.g. cf. Lam. 3:22-27 and Ps. 89:1-5
2. See e.g. W. Brueggemann, (1991: 63-92); W. Brueggemann and P. D. Miller, 'Psalm 73 as a Canonical Marker', *JSOT*, 72 (1996), pp. 45-56. It is symptomatic of the great change that has come in psalm scholarship during the 20th century that, while it was once held that hardly any of the psalms relate to the Davidic line of kings, Brueggemann and Miller here contend for this kind of background for a psalm not even headed 'of David'!
3. See J. C. McCann, 'Psalm 73:A Microcosm of Old Testament Theology' in K. G. Hoglund et al. (eds.), *The Listening Heart: Essays in Wisdom and the Psalms* (JSOT Suppl. 58), Sheffield: JSOT Press, 1987: 247-257.
4. In Mays (ed.) (1993: 39, 40).
5. e.g. in 77:9, 80:4, 88:7, 16.
6. April 1992: 140.
7. ibid.

## Chapter 20: Book 4 – The eternal heavenly King

1. J. B. Payne, 'I Chronicles', F. Gaebelein (ed.) Expositor's Bible Commentary Vol. 4, Grand Rapids: Zondervan, 1988: 390. Payne's whole comment is worth reading.

2. See J. Creach, 'The Shape of Book Four of the Psalter and the Shape of Second Isaiah', *JSOT* 80, 1998: 63-76.

3. Creach, as in note 2 above, p. 74. He has found language similarities between the two blocks of material. He thinks it probable that the Isaianic chapters are the earlier and that the shape of Book 4 was modelled on them.

4. See especially his 1985 volume.

5. But note the comments on 101 later in this chapter.

6. In Mays (ed.) (1993: 17).

7. 1976: 56.

8. 1975: 357, 358.

## Chapter 21: Book 5 – Pilgrimages, Precepts, Prophecies and Praise

1. 1985: 224.

2. cf. Mark 4:35-5:43, which also contains four stories of people being delivered from humanly impossible situations, and, in these cases, by Jesus. It is particularly interesting to note that there are similarities between the two groups, for each has a story of mariners in danger, each a story of bondage, and each a healing. Only the stories of the wanderers in the desert in the psalm and the woman with the issue of blood in Mark have no real parallel in the other group.

3. Luke alone of the evangelists tells us the subject of the conversation between Jesus and Moses and Elijah at the Transfiguration. He says, 'They spoke about his departure [literally "Exodus"] which he was about to bring to fulfilment at Jerusalem' (Luke 9:31 NIV).

4. 1975: 401.

5. in McCann (ed.) (1993: 65).

6. Both in terms of its heading and in terms of Christ's comments on it in Mark 12:36,37.

7. See especially K. Heim, 'The Perfect King of Psalm 72: An Intertextual Enquiry', in (eds.) P. E. Satterthwaite, R. S. Hess, G. J. Wenham, *The Lord's Anointed: Interpretation of Old Testament Messianic Texts,* Carlisle: Paternoster, 1995: 223-248. He concentrates on 72 but also makes general comments on the royal psalms. See also the quotations from De Vaux and Murphy given on p. 99 above.

8. W. B. Wiersbe, *Meet Yourself in the Psalms*, Wheaton: Victor Books, 1984: 12.

9. It might be compared with Deut. 4, which also has a remarkably full presentation of Old Testament truth about him.

10. 1985: 226

11. There is some difference of opinion as to the length of the praise conclusions to Books 2 and 4 and all major commentaries debate the issue. It is of minimal significance for our theme.

12. Ps. 145, of course, is ascribed to David, whereas the other 5 contain no ascription.

13. 1985: 226, 227. This is also the view of E. Zenger, 'The Composition and Theology of the Fifth Book of Psalms, Psalms 107-145', *JSOT* 80 (1998), pp. 77-102 and P. D. Miller, 'The End of the Psalter: A Response to Erich Zenger', *JSOT* 80, 1998: 103-110.

14. Zenger, 'Composition and Theology': 89.

15. Note here a possible reminder of 1:6.

## Chapter 22: The Message of the Book as a whole

1. 1991: 69.

2. 1987: 72.

3. 'Psalms 1-8: Some Hidden Harmonies', *Biblical Theology Bulletin* 10, p. 29.

4. *Towards an O.T. Theology,* Grand Rapids, Zondervan, 1978. It is the main theme of his whole book.

## Chapter 23: New Testament interpretation of the psalms

1. There is little difference between them and the question of number turns upon whether some passages are to be reckoned quotations or allusions, for there is a fine borderline between the two.

2. M. Hengel, *Studies in Early Christology,* Edinburgh, T and T Clark, 1995: 244, quotes Tertullian in *De carne Christi,* 20:3f, as saying that David 'sings to us about Christ, and through him Christ sings about himself.'

3. Earlier in the same chapter, in vv. 6-9, Paul also uses words originally written about the Law in quoting Deut. 30:12-14 and applying them to the gospel.

4. E.g. in Jer. 6:25; 20:10; 46:5; 49:5.

5. For the application of the psalms to Jesus both as God and man, see Longman (1988: 68-73), where he says, 'There are two general grounds for seeing the Psalter as a book which anticipates the coming of Jesus Christ. He is God and he is the son of David' (70); also E. P. Clowney, 'The Singing Savior' in *Moody Monthly* 79, 1978: 40-43.

6. 1961: 101, 130, 131. G. B. Caird, 'The Exegetical Method of the Epistle to the Hebrews', *Canadian Journal of Theology* 5 (1959), 47, argues for 8, 95, 110 and Jer. 31 as the four OT bases of the epistle's argument. See also L. D. Hurst in *The Epistle to the Hebrews: its background of thought,* Cambridge, CUP, 1990: 132.

7. It is David in the superscription of each of the three.
8. See the discussion in W. C. Kaiser, Jr. 'The Promise to David in Psalm 16 and its Application in Acts 2:25-33 and 13:32-37', in *JETS* 23:3 (Sept 1980): 219-229.
9. But see the comments of Murphy (1993: 26-31) concerning this.
10. E.g., we might compare v. 24 with 136:5-9, v. 25 with 145:15,16, v. 29 with 115:4, v. 31 with 9:8, 96:13 and 98:9, and 31 with 16:10.17:31. Also compare the ideas of Acts 17:24 with 50:1b, v. 25 with 50:9, v. 30 with 50:21, and v. 31 with 50:4-6. It is not that the language is always close enough to demonstrate that it is allusive, but rather that the mind of the preacher is full of theological truth that can be found in the psalms.

## Chapter 24: The Person of Christ

1. This feature is quite extensive and will become evident by the study of any good reference Bible. Note, for instance, Luke 1:54 and Ps. 98:3, and Luke 1:69 and Ps. 132:17.
2. This is widely although not universally agreed.
3. The term 'Son of God' (or 'Son') elsewhere in Hebrews often appears in contexts where it appears to be a very great title. See e.g. Heb. 1:2, 6:6, 7:3; 10:29. Its place as a leading term in Heb. 1:1-2:4 alongside 'God' and 'Lord' applied to Jesus establishes its greatness from the very start of the epistle. We might compare Paul's use in his epistles, which is sparing and which so often occurs in passages of elevated style, such as Rom. 8:28-39, where it occurs twice.
4. Cf. Luke 14:26 and Matt. 10:37 for a somewhat similar case.
5. 'The Translation of *Elohim* in Psalm 45:7-8' in *TB* 35 (1984), 87. See the full discussion on pp. 66-89. Harris also discusses 'The Translation and Significance of *Ho Theos* in Hebrews' 1:8-9, in TB 35, 1984: 130-162, vindicating the traditional translation from the passage's context in the epistle. To comment further here would require a lengthy technical discussion and so interested readers should consult these articles.

## Chapter 25: Christ's sufferings and vindication

1. There are other psalms where this kind of question is asked, e.g. 44:23, 24 and especially 74:1. In both these psalms however it is the community, not an individual as here, which poses the question. We know from the New Testament witness to Jesus that there is such a thing as completely innocent suffering at the individual level, his own suffering, but this could not be true of a whole community.
2. Apart from puppies, dogs were not kept as pets in Israel and hungry packs of them roaming at large could be very dangerous.

3. 68:1 actually quotes Nu. 10:35.

4. 1973: 242, n.2.

## Practical Conclusion: How should we use the psalms?

1. 1988: 53.

2. London: Murray, 1913.

3. There are of course some passages of praise elsewhere in Scripture, e.g. in passages in the prophets, such as Isa. 6:3; 12:1-6; 26:1,2, in Luke, chs. 1 and 2 and in the Book of the Revelation.

4. Davidson (1990: 120) complains that the great issues of faith are not included in our worship today, unlike the psalms, where of course they are faced. He says that he is 'deeply suspicious of an approach to faith and worship which seems to deal only with answers and certainties, and not with questions and perplexities.'

5. London: Tyndale Press, 1962.

6. 1993.

7. 1986: 22.

8. 1991: 64.

9. G. H. Wilson says: 'In its "final form" the Psalter is a book to be *read* rather than to be *performed*; to be *meditated over* rather than to be *recited from*' (1985: 207). We do not really have to choose, for there is no reason why the Book should not have been viewed as having more than one function.

# Select Bibliography

Allen, L. C. (1983), *Psalms 101-150* (Word Biblical Commentary 21), Milton Keynes: Word

Allen, L. C. (1987), *Word Biblical Themes: Psalms*, Waco: Word Inc.

Anderson, A. A. (1972), *The Book of Psalms*. New Century Bible (2 Vols.), London: Marshall, Morgan and Scott

Bellinger, W. H., Jr. (1984), *Psalmody and Prophecy* (JSOT Suppl. 27), Sheffield, JSOT

Broyles, C. C. (1989), *The Conflict of Faith and Experience in the Psalms: A Form-Critical and Theological Study* (SOT Suppl. 52), Sheffield: JSOT

Brueggemann, W. (1980), 'Psalms and the Life of Faith: A Suggested Typology of Function', in *JSOT* 17, pp. 3-32.

Brueggemann, W. (1984), *The Message of the Psalms: A Theological Commentary*, Minneapolis: Augsburg

Brueggemann, W. (1986), 'The Costly Loss of Lament', in *JSOT* 36, pp. 57-71.

Brueggemann, W. (1991), 'Bounded by Obedience and Praise: The Psalms as Canon', in *JSOT* 50, pp. 63-92.

Childs, B. S. (1979), *Introduction to the Old Testament as Scripture,* Philadelphia: Fortress, pp. 504-525.

Clines, D. (1967), 'Psalm Research since 1955: 1. The Psalms and the Cult', *TB* 1967 (18), pp.103-126.

Clines, D. (1969) 'Psalm Research since 1955. 2. The Literary Genres', *TB* 1969 (20), pp. 105-125.

Clines, D. (1987), 'The Parallelism of Greater Precision', in E R Follis (ed.), *Directions in Biblical Hebrew Poetry.* Sheffield: JSOT, pp. 77-100.

Craigie, P. C. (1983), *Psalms 1-50* (Word Biblical Commentary 19), Milton Keynes: Word

Craven, T. (1992), *The Book of Psalms,* Collegeville, Minnesota: Liturgical

Creach, J. F. D. (1996), *Yahweh as Refuge and the Editing of the Hebrew Psalter (* JSOT Suppl. 217), Sheffield: JSOT

Croft S. J. L. (1987), *The Identity of the Individual in the Psalms* (JSOT Suppl. 44), Sheffield: JSOT

Dahood, M. (1970), *Psalms* (Anchor Bible), New York: Doubleday

Davidson, R. (1990), *Wisdom and Worship,* London: SCM

Eaton, J. H. (1986), *Kingship and the Psalms,* 2nd edn., Sheffield: JSOT

Eaton, J. H. (1995), *Psalms of the Way and the Kingdom : A Conference with the Commentators* (JSOT Suppl, 199), Sheffield: JSOT

Gunkel, H. (1967), *The Psalms: A Form-Critical Introduction,* ET, Philadelphia: Fortress

Harman, A. (1998), *Commentary on the Psalms* (Mentor Commentary), Fearn: Christian Focus Publications

Hayes, J. H. (1976), *Understanding the Psalms,* Valley Forge: Judson

Holladay, W. L. (1993), *The Psalms through Three Thousand Years,* Minneapolis: Fortress

Kidner, F. D. (1973, 1975), *The Book of Psalms* (2 Vols.), London: IVP

Kistemaker, S. (1961), *The Psalm Citations in the Epistle to the Hebrews,* Amsterdam: Van Soest

Kraus, H-J. (1986), *Theology of the Psalms,* ET, Minneapolis: Augsburg

Lewis, C. S. (1958), *Reflections on the Psalms,* London: Geoffrey Bles

Longman, T. III (1988), *How to Read the Psalms,* Leicester: IVP

McCann, J. C. (1992), 'The Psalms as Instruction', in *Interpretation* 46, pp.117-128.

McCann, J. C. (ed.) (1993), *The Shape and Shaping of the Psalter* (JSOT Suppl. 159), Sheffield: JSOT

Mason, R. (1993), *Old Testament Pictures of God,* Oxford: Regent's Park College

Mays, J. L. (1987), 'The Place of the Torah-Psalms in the Psalter', *JBL* 106, pp. 3-12.

Mays, J. L. (1994), *The Lord Reigns: A Theological Handbook to the Psalms,* Westminster: Knox

Miller, P. D. (1986), *Interpreting the Psalms,* Philadelphia: Fortress

Mitchell, D. C. (1997), *The Message of the Psalter: An Eschatological Programme in the Book of Psalms* (JSOT Suppl. 252), Sheffield: JSOT

Mowinckel, S. (1962), *The Psalms in Israel's Worship.* ET ( 2 vols.), Oxford: OUP

Murphy, R. E. (1993), *The Psalms are Yours,* N York: Paulist

Seybold, K. (1990), *Introducing the Psalms,* Edinburgh: T and T Clark

Sheppard, G. T. (1980), 'Wisdom as a Hermeneutical Construct: A Study in the Sapentializing of the Old Testament', *BZAW* 151. Berlin: de Gruyter, pp.136-144.

Sheppard, G. T. (1990), 'Theology and the Book of Psalms' in *Interpretation* 46:2, pp. 143-155.

Soll, W. (1991), *Psalm 119: Matrix, Form and Setting,* Washington DC: The Catholic Biblical Association of America

Sylva, D. (1993), *Psalms and the Transformation of Stress: Poetic-Communal Interpretation and the Family,* Louvain: Peeters Press

Tate, M. E. (1990) *Psalms 51-100* (Word Bible Commentaries 20), Waco: Word

Tournay, R. J. (1991), *Seeing and Hearing God in the Psalms: The Prophetic Liturgy of the Second Temple in Jerusalem,* ET, Sheffield: JSOT

Westermann, C. (1981), *Praise and Lament in the Psalms,* ET, Edinburgh: T and T Clark

White, R. E. O. (1984), *A Christian Handbook to the Psalms,* Exeter: Paternoster

Whybray, R. N. (1997), *Reading the Psalms as a Book* (JOTS Suppl. 222), Sheffield, JSOT

Wilson, G. H. (1984), Evidence of Editorial Divisions in the Hebrew Psalter, *VT* 34, pp. 337-352.

Wilson, G. H. (1985), *The Editing of the Hebrew Psalter,* Chico: Scholars

Wilson, G. H. (1992), 'The Shape of the Book of Psalms', *Interpretation* 46, pp. 129-42.

Wilson, G. H. (1986), The use of Royal Psalms at the 'Seams' of the Hebrew Psalter, *JSOT* 35, pp. 85-94

Zenger, E. (1996) *A God of Vengeance? Understanding the Psalms of Divine Wrath,* ET,. Louisville: Westminster John Knox

# Subject Index

# Persons' Index

Other titles by
Geoffrey W. Grogan,
available from
Christian Focus Publications

# The Christ of the Bible

**This book is a theological study**

In the main, the odd-numbered chapters are theological. The first five of these set out the biblical evidence for our understanding of Jesus, while chapters 11 and 13 reflect on this theologically at a somewhat deeper level.

**It is an apologetic study**

This is the function of the even-numbered chapters. They deal with the main difficulties that have been and still are raised by those who are interested in Jesus but are not yet committed to him. It is to be hoped that they will also be of help to the committed. Each of these chapters follows the theological chapter most closely related to it.

The book will be useful to ministers and theological students. It has however been written in such a way that many Christians without theological training may be able to benefit from it, plus other readers who have not yet come to personal faith in Christ but are interested enough to read a serious book about him.

304 pages             ISBN 1 857 92 266 2              demy

In this wide-ranging and well-written study, Geoffrey Grogan provides a clear, scholarly and reliable account of the identity of Jesus of Nazareth. The fruit of prolonged thought about the New Testament's teaching, *The Christ of the Bible* is marked on every page by clarity of exposition and reliability of judgment. Here we have a careful and thoughtful sifting of evidence and a steady pursuit of conclusions which are in harmony with it.

While familiar with trends in New Testament studies during the past two centuries, and grateful for the work of fellow scholars, Geoffrey Grogan has listened first and foremost to the witness of the apostles. He concludes that there is only one answer to the ancient question which Jesus himself asked them, 'Who do you say that I am?'

The result is this sturdy volume. Theological students, Christian ministers and leaders will find it invaluable, but any serious reader to whom Jesus of Nazareth remains an elusive figure will also come to the conclusion that this is a book well worth reading.

Sinclair B. Ferguson
Westminster Theological Seminary
Philadelphia, Pennsylvania, USA


This is an apologetic and theological study aimed at preachers, theological students, thinking Christians and interested agnostics. It succeeds in its aims admirably.

Donald Macleod
Free Church College
Edinburgh, Scotland


This beautifully-written book is a feast of scriptural analysis and argument about our Lord Jesus Christ. With profound learning but with lightness of touch, Geoffrey Grogan discusses all the main lines of the presentation of Jesus in the Bible, and then skilfully relates these to the questions that trouble people today about him. So the book is an attractive combination of Christology and apology – explaining Jesus in a way that answers modern doubts and puzzles, cleverly arranged in alternating chapters. Hearts will be warmed and heads cleared by this book – and doubt and unbelief will be turned into confidence and faith.

Steve Motyer
London Bible College

# Wrestling With The Big Issues

In this much appreciated book, Geoffrey Grogan examines the principles and methods used by Paul to assess and solve the doctrinal and practical problems that appeared in the early Christian Church. Most of these problems have reappeared throughout church history, and can be found today in evangelical churches. Geoffrey Grogan is convinced that the answers to many of today's difficulties are to be found in applying to current situations the Spirit-inspired instructions of the apostle.

Howard Marshall says about *Wrestling With The Big Issues*: 'This book is remarkable for being written by a New Testament scholar in such a simple and relevant way that any reader will be able to understand what is being said and see how Paul's letters still speak to Christians today.'

Sinclair Ferguson comments that 'Geoffrey Grogan brings to his teaching, preaching and writing a life-time of study. He combines careful exposition with practical care.'

And Clive Calver says that 'Geoffrey Grogan possesses the uncanny knack of setting truth on fire: here the personality of the apostle shines through its pages; the life of a man who Christ used to transform the history of his church.'

ISBN 1 85792 051 1                                        256 Pages

In the Focus on the Bible commentary series, Geoffrey has also contributed the commentaries on Mark and 2 Corinthians.

Dr. Geoffrey Grogan is Principal Emeritus of Glasgow Bible College. His theological studies were undertaken there and at the London Bible College. He served the College as a full-time lecturer for fourteen years before going south in 1965 to teach at LBC. In 1969 he returned to Glasgow as principal. He has served on four missionary councils, on the Strathclyde Education Committee and the Management Committee for the Cambridge University Diploma in Religious Studies. He has written books on the *Trinity*, the *Person of Christ, Paul,* and commentaries on *Isaiah, Mark and 2 Corinthians*.